Concrete Mama

Prison Profiles from Walla Walla

Concrete Mama
Prison Profiles from Walla Walla

Photographs by Ethan Hoffman

Text by John McCoy

Foreword by Tom Wicker

University of Missouri Press

Columbia & London

1981

Photographs copyright © 1981 by Ethan Hoffman
Text Copyright © 1981 by The Curators of the University of Missouri
University of Missouri Press, Columbia, Missouri 65211
Library of Congress Catalog Card Number 81-4482
Printed and bound in Japan
Second Printing 1982

Library of Congress Cataloging in Publication Data

Hoffman, Ethan.
     Concrete Mama.

     1. Prisoners—Washington (State)—Case studies.
2. Washington State Penitentiary—Case studies.
I. McCoy, John, 1947–   II. Title.
HV9475.W22W374   365′.979748   81-4482
ISBN 0-8262-0340-X   AACR2

Acknowledgments

There are many people who have lent their help and encouragement to the production of this book. In particular, we would like to thank our spouses, Karen Chesledon and Rebecca Collette, for their unfailing support and continued willingness to be our first readers and editors.

We also owe thanks to Marty Huie and Bill Fry, who allowed us frequent and long use of their photo darkrooms; to Declan Haun, who gave us adivce and support; to Jim McCoy, the writer's father, who freely sacrificed his time to type drafts of the manuscript; to Roxanne Park, whose considered and diligent editing of first drafts shaped the final manuscript; to Eric Gabrielsen, the education director of the Washington State Penitentiary, who kept us going with his humor and advice; to Douglas Vinzant, the warden who gave us permission for the prison project; and to James Spalding, the warden who allowed us to carry the project out.

We want to thank the staff of the University of Missouri Press for their outstanding editorial assistance.

Last, we owe special thanks to the inmates and staff of the Washington State Penitentiary. Without their cooperation, this book would never have been completed.

J. M./E. H.

Seattle/Washington, D.C.

11 May 1981

Foreword By Tom Wicker

Nearly two centuries ago, Americans invented prisons because of a humanitarian impulse. They maintain them today out of fear and the urge to punish.

The national inmate population certainly didn't grow by 5 percent to 329,122 in 1980, or by 61 percent in the decade of the 1970s, because anything in the history of prisons suggested that those incarcerated would be purged of criminality by the experience.

Take a poll of policemen, prosecutors, judges, and prison administrators, and you will be able to count on your fingers those who believe that prison is *good* for those who go there. You might well find a majority who concede that prisons are *bad* for people, even for some criminals.

Yet both state and federal governments continue to use what they euphemistically call "correctional institutions," even to increase their reliance upon them. In mid-1981, federal, state, and local prison-expansion plans totaled 162,466 new spaces for incarcerated persons, even though the United States already imprisoned more people per capita—244.3 per 100,000 population—than any industrialized nation except the Soviet Union and South Africa.

The reason for this dependence upon prisons clearly isn't success. For one thing, these steel-and-concrete fortresses are enormously costly. In 1981, for example, estimates for adding four thousand cells to New York's cage capacity ranged generally from $50,000 to $100,000 apiece, with one vaulting to $213,000 per cell. That's *really* throwing money at problems.

Every person kept in one of those cells for a year will cost the taxpayers about twenty thousand dollars a year—not for "rehabilitation" or other good effects—but for custody, security, and administration (which claims 22 percent of the "corrections" budget in New York).

The return on this investment (which, of course, is smaller in some less populous, less urban states) is miniscule. Measured by the number of inmates returning to do more time for new crimes, prisons are egregious failures. Recidivism rates vary from state to state and so does the method of measurement (few states, for example, know if one of their ex-inmates subsequently serves time in another state), but it's safe to say that more than half of all those convicted and imprisoned once will be convicted and imprisoned again—and again. Add those who *don't* get caught for a second or third or fourth or any number of other crimes, and the failure rate would soar.

The original idea was that prisons would be "penitentiaries" where criminals in solitary reflection would come to renounce their lawless ways, but why it's never worked as planned seems clear. By the very nature of incarceration, inmates are likely to become *more* angered and embittered and antisocial than they were in the first place. Putting men and women in cages and depriving them of amenity may be deserved punishment, but it can hardly make them think better of themselves or their captors.

Two other aspects of the modern American fortress-prison seem almost to guarantee its failure as a "correctional institution." One is that most mix relatively young and perhaps redeemable offenders with hardened and aggressive criminals, with the predictable result that the former are led, taught, exploited, and coerced by the latter; thus, prisons become "universities of crime."

The other built-in flaw is that within the prison the law that sends offenders to their cages *cannot be maintained*—and the

larger the prison, the more certain that rule. Guards (called "corrections officers") are few and mostly ill-paid, ill-trained (if at all), undereducated, and under intense pressure—not least from fear for their own physical safety. Their charges are almost always alienated misfits and often the most violently antisocial persons.

As a result, prisons are cauldrons of murder, assault, homosexual rape, extortion, and general brutality; drug traffic and addiction flourish, as do all the minor rackets, with the corruption often engulfing guards and administrators. Given such an atmosphere, it is not surprising that more hardened, violence–prone criminals come *out* of prison, by reliable estimates, than go in.

The *deterrence* of crime, often cited as a justification for imprisonment, may be effective with educated, middle-class persons. For most of them, prison offers not only an unacceptable stigma of criminality; it also suggests all sorts of terrors, including physical violation. The criminality deterred in their cases, however, is most likely to be of the white-collar variety, which is admittedly serious but not terrifying.

As for the kind of offenses that rightly frighten so many Americans—murder, violent street crime, rape, robbery, burglaries, and the like—little or no evidence suggests that prison has a deterrent effect. Such crimes usually are committed in the heat of passion or in the (usually justified) confidence that apprehension and conviction are unlikely. At best, prison only prevents, for a stated period, some people from committing such crimes on the outside; many, instead, commit them on the inside.

The Washington State Penitentiary at Walla Walla, where John McCoy and Ethan Hoffman spent four months "inside the walls" in 1977–1978, seems to represent neither the worst nor, certainly, the best of American prisons, although some will be shocked at McCoy's account and Hoffman's photographs of how inhumane and lawless such a place really is.

And Walla Walla is typical in countless ways. It is old and outmoded, for example, having been opened in 1887. It is indecently overcrowded, and the state is under federal court order to improve conditions. Walla Walla has a history of riots and strikes; its population exists in idleness and boredom; "the joint" is wracked by internal violence (two inmates were murdered while McCoy and Hoffman were studying the prison) and largely "controlled" by powerful inmates or factions (veteran inmates who "own" cells peddle space in them to new "fish" with no place to sleep; the fish sometimes pay with their bodies).

A reporter and photographer whose interest in the prison led them to quit their jobs and take on this project, McCoy and Hoffman were given mostly free run at Walla Walla, except that they were not allowed to spend their nights inside. They describe close calls with violent inmates, angry encounters with guards, grotesque prison rites and customs, the difficulties of wrenching their own middle-class attitudes into rudimentary understanding of the vastly different world with which they had to deal.

Mostly, however, their work is a series of valuable studies of certain characters at Walla Walla that, with little variance, probably could be discovered in any prison, at any time. They begin with Fred, a "fish" just encountering the strange terrors of life behind the walls, and go on to Browny, the old hand who had spent his life in and out and in again, to Jackie the reigning "queen," Wino the snitch, Kenny Agtuca, the lifer who rules most of the prison, guard Parley Edwards, and even Yvonne, who visits her inmate husband sixteen times a month and knows more ways than one to make love in the visitors' room.

Their stories and those of others, recounted in McCoy's unadorned prose, together with Hoffman's harsh and direct photographs—nothing prettified here, either—make up about as authentic a picture of prison and prison life as "outsiders" are likely to compile. And this powerful record drives home (although Hoffman and McCoy do not dwell upon them) the enduring questions:

Why do we expect human beings to emerge from such surroundings as better men and women than those who entered?

Why do we continue to send people into these warehouses of violence and despair, knowing it does little good and may well cause *more*, not less, crime and violence?

The answer to the first question, I think, is that no one really does. We don't send criminals away to be reformed but to be kept off the streets and to be punished. Law-abiding people who live in fear (real if sometimes exaggerated) of their lives and property are not to be accused of inhumanity for such a reaction, and for these visceral purposes, prisons serve admirably—if only in the short run.

The answer to the second question, in my judgment, is that we don't know what else to do. This includes even those who believe that prison is at best a short-term and ultimately counterproductive safeguard, who know that most prisoners get out and, when they do, are likely to be more violent and antisocial and less able to make it in the straight world.

I don't mean that various "reforms" are not available, or that we lack theories and good intentions. Indeed, it may be that we have too many views of how to improve things. But no agreed-upon alternative to prison-as-usual exists; those who condemn the present system cannot go to a legislature or to Congress and say confidently, "Instead of *this*, the weight of the evidence is that we should do *that*, upon which we're all agreed."

Rather, sociologists, criminologists, law-enforcement officials, and other authorities speak with many voices, but primarily four:

First, some urge a "rehabilitation model"—more psychiatrists, drug counselors, job training, group therapy, help of all kinds in the "treatment" of criminality. But where such approaches have been plausibly tried, the results have not been encouraging; and if that is owing to a lack of resources, who can believe that the public will ever be willing to finance a range of services for prisoners that is rarely available even in the public schools?

A second group of advocates, many of whom do not believe "rehabilitation" programs can work in a prison setting and when not completely voluntary, favors essentially a "punishment" model—better prison housing and living conditions in smaller, better-controlled institutions, together with shorter, fixed sentences, no parole, and productive work for inmates who want it. But this conflicts with the cost of building modern new facilities and the public's desire to "lock 'em up and throw away the key."

A third line of reasoning holds that prisons should be done away with, save for custody of the relatively few criminals too dangerous to be let loose on the streets. Drawing their conclusions from the documentable failure of prisons over two centuries, these advocates argue for "community corrections," alternative sentencing, victim restitution, fines, probation, community service—a wide range of penalties other than incarceration, combined with emphasis on eliminating the "causes of crime" rather than punishing offenders.

Its considerable merit aside, this "do-gooder" argument enrages conservatives, who consider it "coddling criminals." Owing to the public's fear of crime, it also lacks political persuasiveness to the legislators who'd have to authorize such an approach.

Finally, arguments can be heard for various combinations of any of the above—more humane institutions, shorter sentences, rehabilitation programs, incarcerating only the most violent offenders, alternative sentencing. To some extent, these approaches only heighten the conflict among advocates.

With exceptions here and there, the consequence of no agreed alternative is mostly more of the same—we go on filling up our inadequate prisons, then building more to be filled in turn. A sort of Parkinson's law appears to be at work: inmates increase to meet cell capacity.

A study for the National Institute of Justice concluded that "where new space has been added, it has, on the average, been followed two years later by [prison] population increases of nearly equal size." Similarly, the American Foundation's Institute of Corrections, in a 1976 study of fifteen states that increased their prison capacity by 56 percent, found that their prison populations then increased by 57 percent.

One more comment about the role of prisons in American life. Since their inception, these institutions have been filled mostly with those on the lowest rung of the economic ladder. Once it was the Irish, the Italians, the Eastern Europeans; now blacks and Spanish-speaking people form the majority of the prison population.

Isn't it likely, therefore, that prisons are in part an expression of class distinction in a supposedly classless society? That even Americans *need* some means of designating and segregating the lowliest and most despised among them?

McCoy and Hoffman have not burdened their book with such speculations, or with reform theories and political rhetoric. Their aim was at once more modest and more profound. They went inside the walls, they looked, they listened, they learned, they sought to understand not just the kept but the keepers, and to pass on that understanding in words and pictures.

What results is strangely redemptive. Lowly and despised or not, the human beings in this book are of rich variety and sometimes impressive strength; they may have lived meanly or shabbily, their world may have been a place of nightmare visions and contorted reality, but in these gripping pages they do not fail to make upon us the most human of claims—that there, save for the grace of an unfathomable God, might go any of us.

Tom Wicker
3 August 1981
New York, New York

Contents

Concrete Mama

Prison Profiles from Walla Walla

Introduction

When Ethan Hoffman and I arrived in Walla Walla, Washington, in mid-1977, neither of us had any plans to do a book about prison life. We were beginning our careers in journalism and, like most newspaper rookies, had found our first jobs at small-town paper. Hoffman, a native New Yorker who had just completed a master's degree in photojournalism, had never been to Washington State. Although I had grown up in Seattle, I got my first look at Walla Walla the day that I applied for a job on the *Walla Walla Union-Bulletin*. I was assigned to cover three areas: food, religion, and the Washington State Penitentiary. Hoffman became the paper's chief photographer and photo editor.

Both of us were soon convinced that the penitentiary was the biggest, the most difficult, and the most fascinating story in town. Our convictions, however, were not shared by the newspaper's management, who had adopted the prevailing local attitude that the best way to live with the penitentiary was to ignore it. For more than a year, we told the story as best we could, stringing together news accounts that highlighted prison problems but ignored prison life.

In August 1978, we decided to leave the newspaper in order to do an in-depth report of life inside the penitentiary. With the warden's permission, we planned to spend as much time behind the walls as possible over a four-month period. We sought approval to talk to any inmate or staff member, to wander anywhere in the prison plant, and to walk about unescorted by guards or prison officials. While journalists and photographers had been allowed "inside" before, the extensive and prolonged involvement in prison life that Hoffman and I proposed was unprecedented. While we waited for the warden's answer, we learned what we could about American prisons in general and about the Washington State Penitentiary in particular.

Prison is a relatively modern invention. Until the end of the eighteenth century, the prevailing form of criminal punishment was torture: pillorying, flogging, amputation, and, for the most serious crimes, prolonged and painful public execution. In his *Commentaries on the Laws of England* (vol. 4, 1766), William Blackstone describes an execution in Paris in 1757: the condemned man's "belly was opened up, his entrails quickly ripped out, so that he had time to see them, with his own eyes, being thrown on the fire; in which he was finally decapitated and his body quartered" (p. 89).

The first American prisons in Pennsylvania and New York were designed by Quakers and other humanitarians who believed that criminals could purge themselves of their criminality by spending time in private cells, quietly contemplating their past sins. What criminals required, the reformers reasoned, was work, discipline, and solitude. They called their prisons "reformatories" and "penitentiaries" because they meant them to be places of reform and penitence.

The nineteenth-century reformers argued that imprisonment would serve several ends: It would punish the offender and would satisfy society's need for justice; it would deter the offender from future crime and would discourage others from turning to crime; it would keep the offender off the streets for the duration of his sentence and would reform the offender, returning him to society with the inclination to obey the law and to earn an honest living.

Today, few people are so optimistic. Aside from punishing, which prisons do with a random and unpredictable vengeance, most observers insist that imprisonment falls miserably short of its aims.

Soaring crime rates and the high number of repeat offenders suggest that prisons do little to deter crime. Prisoners may be temporarily isolated from society, but they do not stop breaking the law: They simply select new victims—prison guards and fellow inmates. Robbery, rape, extortion, theft, and assault are everyday occurrences among the inmate populations of most American prisons. The irony of prison life is that the inmates who cause the least trouble are the most likely to be victimized. In the upside-down prison morality, the men at the top of the prison pecking order come from the bottom of society's barrel.

Only the most naive observers would contend that prisons rehabilitate. If anything, prisons encourage crime. The prolonged and exclusive association with other prisoners in an environment that denies men the right to make the most rudimentary choices for themselves erodes socially acceptable behavior and fosters an exaggerated attitude of toughness and defiance.

Over the past fifty years, a series of crime commissions has concluded that prisons not only fail to rehabilitate but actually aggravate criminal tendencies. The 1967 Task Force Report on Corrections by the Presi-

Opened in 1887, the Washington State Penitentiary houses the state's worst and most chronic offenders. The main prison compound covers twenty acres.

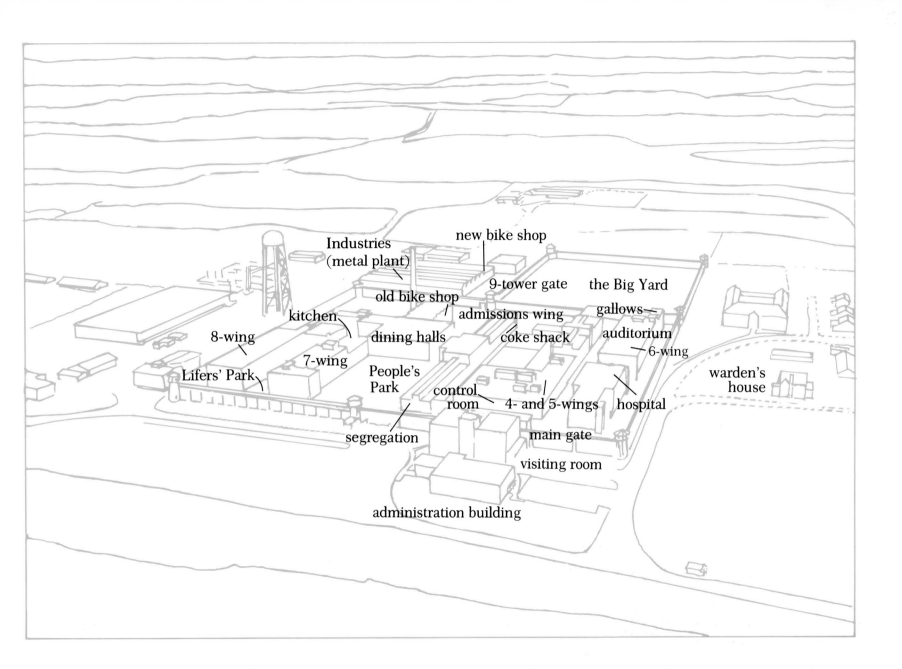

new bike shop

Industries
(metal plant)

9-tower gate

the Big Yard

old bike shop

gallows

kitchen

admissions wing

auditorium

8-wing

dining halls

coke shack

6-wing

7-wing

Lifers' Park

People's
Park

control
room

4- and 5-wings

hospital

warden's
house

segregation

main gate

visiting room

administration building

dent's Commission on Law Enforcement and Administration of Justice, *The Challenge of Crime in a Free Society* (Government Printing Office, 1967), declared that "for a great many offenders, corrections do not correct. Indeed, experts are increasingly coming to feel that the conditions under which many offenders are handled, particularly in institutions, are often a positive detriment to rehabilitation." The 1973 report by the National Advisory Commission on Criminal Justice Standards and Goals, *Corrections* (Government Printing Office, 1973), stated that "the American correctional system today appears to offer minimum protection to the public and maximum harm to the offender." The report recommended that "prisons should be repudiated as useless for any purpose other than locking away persons who are too dangerous to be allowed at large in a free society."

Even U.S. Chief Justice Warren Burger, hardly a man who could be considered "soft" on crime, concluded in his 1980 year-end review of the criminal-justice system that American prisons were "stupid," "expensive," and "out of the 19th century." Burger noted that conditions in many American prisons were as bad or worse as those that had led to the bloody New Mexico prison riot in which thirty-three inmates died at the hands of other convicts. Stressing the need for prison reform, Burger wrote: "To put people behind walls and bars and do little or nothing to change them is to win a battle but lose a war" (*Christian Science Monitor*, 13 January 1981, p. 4).

At the time the chief justice was writing his report, federal courts had ruled that the conditions of imprisonment in twenty-four states violated the constitutional ban on "cruel and unusual punishment." Among those states was Washington.

Ironically, in 1886, a growing public outcry against the inhumane treatment of convicts forced Washington's legislature to make plans to build the territory's first public prison. For the previous twelve years, the territory had turned its felons over to a couple of private contractors named Billings and Smith. The two contractors received seventy cents a day per prisoner and the right to use the prisoners' labor in return for housing and feeding the convicts. Billings and Smith saved themselves the cost of guards by riveting heavy chains around the prisoners' ankles. The chains were left on, day and night, until the prisoner died or was released. Prisoners who talked too much were punished by having their teeth extracted with pliers.

Eventually, the scandalous conditions at Billings and Smith's private penal colony roused the legislature to authorize the building of a territorial penitentiary. In 1886 and 1887, the lawmakers appropriated ninety-six thousand dollars for the purchase of land and the construc-

tion of a cellblock, guard quarters, and a jute mill. They also made plans to build a state university. Legend has it that, as the result of the flip of a coin, Walla Walla, whose name soon became synonymous with the state's meanest prison, got the penitentiary, and Pullman, a rival farming town eighty miles northeast, got the university. Walla Walla, incidentally, had won the toss.

The first prisoners arrived at the new penitentiary in 1887, two years before Washington became a state. A 1901 law prohibiting counties from performing executions also designated the penitentiary as the state's maximum-security institution. The prison at Walla Walla, the law said, would receive the state's most desperate criminals and would hang those sentenced to die.

From its earliest years, the penitentiary was troubled by idleness, violence, and overcrowding.

In September 1926, inmates set fire to the central cellblock and were turned back from the walls with a barrage of tear gas.

In 1930, while Seattle newspapers reported "standing room only" at the prison, the National Society of Penal Information criticized the penitentiary for "overcrowding, the lack of industries and the rigid and repressive discipline." The penal group went on to say that "in few prisons in the nation is the overcrowding more serious and in none of them is less done to reduce the evils inherent to such a condition" (Department of Institutions, Division of Adult Corrections, *Washington State Penitentiary*, 1969, p. 2). The overflow crowd of prisoners slept on cots set up on the tiers or camped in tents in the "Big Yard."

A year later, the Wickersham commission reported to President Hoover that the entire theory of U.S. prison operation was wrong. Only in smaller prisons, where inmates could be segregated and educated, was the rehabilitation of convicts possible, the commission said (The National Commission on Law Observance and Enforcement, *Report on Penal Institutions, Probation and Parole*, Government Printing Office, 1931). Meanwhile, at Walla Walla, 1,339 inmates were crammed into cell space meant for 750.

Prison guards and state police used machine guns to quell the "Lincoln Day outbreak" of 1934 in which one guard and nine convicts died. The warden blamed the riot on "bad food." In 1946, the state auditor found a "surprising lack of competent prison personnel," and a state representative called the penitentiary "a sore spot, old and obsolete" (*Seattle Post-Intelligencer*, 28 February 1946).

On 13 February 1953, a few days after an inmate's bomb killed the prison's business manager, the *Post-Intelligencer* reported that visiting Judge Wilford Richmond had found conditions at the prison "intoler-

able and impossible." Richmond ridiculed the pay that prisoners received for their work—two cents an hour. That September, in the second most destructive riot in the history of the state penitentiary, inmates ripped apart their cells and burned the prison license-plate factory. One million 1954 license plates were destroyed in the fire. Despite the "intolerable" conditions that led to the destruction, a year later the number of inmates rose to an all-time high of 1,805.

Inmates rioted again in July 1955. They set fires, tore apart prison buildings, and seized hostages, including the captain of the guards. Negotiations ended the twenty-seven-hour siege. Appearing before a state legislative committee six months later, Warden Lawrence Delmore, who had formerly been the warden at Alcatraz, blamed the penitentiary's troubles on inmate malcontents; he said that inmates were resisting his get-tough prison policy.

Following the destructive riots of the mid-1950s, the penitentiary settled into the twenty-year administration of Warden Bobby J. Rhay, a tough-talking, con-wise Walla Walla native who had worked his way up through prison ranks to become the nation's youngest warden. A confident, politically astute administrator, Rhay's biggest problems were routine—escapes, attempted escapes, and the occasional desperate man who seized a hostage. Then, in the late 1960s, Warden Rhay had to deal with the "reforms."

The so-called reforms began when Gov. Daniel J. Evans, a liberal Republican, passed over the usual lot of corrections officials and named Dr. William Conte, a Tacoma psychiatrist, as director of institutions. Conte proposed that convicts could best reenter society by establishing closer contacts with the staff of the prison and with the outside community. To do that, he argued, prisoners needed certain rights, such as the right to privacy, the right to speak out, and the right to make significant decisions for themselves.

In 1969 and 1970, Conte announced a series of reforms that radically changed life at the penitentiary. Mail censorship ended. Phone calls were permitted. Work was no longer obligatory. Fair hearings were required before guards could punish inmates for rule infractions. Inmates could dress as they pleased and had no restrictions on the length of their hair or beards. On visiting days, they could interact freely with their families and friends rather than having to talk through glass partitions and screens, and on occasion, prisoners could visit at home and could work outside the prison.

The most far-reaching reform gave prisoners the right to elect an inmate council that had real power in governing the institution. Although other prisons had experimented with inmate advisory councils, no U.S. prison had ever permitted inmate self-government. Warden Rhay went to Europe to study the progressive penal systems of Denmark and the Netherlands and returned hailing a new era of prison democracy.

As the penitentiary embraced the reforms, unexpected changes in the makeup of the larger society affected the prison population. In the late 1960s and early 1970s, the segment of the population that provides the majority of convicted felons—men aged eighteen to twenty-five—swelled to an unprecedented size as the children born in the post–World War II baby boom grew up and had their day in court. Even though judges were sentencing a lower percentage of felons to prison, in terms of sheer numbers, more men were going behind bars than ever before. Between 1973 and 1980, the number of inmates in state and federal prisons grew by more than 65 percent, from 190,000 to 314,000. Moreover, those sent to the penitentiary were a different breed than the men who came in the 1960s. The convicts of the 1970s had been through several unsuccessful rehabilitation and treatment programs. They tended to be more impulsive, more drug-oriented, more assaultive, and more prone to gang together.

The guards were different, too. Veteran officers, alarmed by the erosion of their power and fearful of the growing violence, quit the penitentiary in droves. Their replacements, few of whom stayed more than a few months, were assigned to the most dangerous areas during their first week on the job. The prison continually advertised for "correctional officers."

Warden Rhay's enthusiasm for prison reform soon waned. While he complained that he had had no time to prepare his staff for the changes, planners in Olympia grumbled that Rhay had sabotaged the reforms by allowing them to take effect without proper direction. At any rate, morale plummeted and staff turnover skyrocketed.

Old-line prison wardens, who had watched the Walla Walla experiment with a mixture of curiosity and dismay, found new justification for keeping prison business out of convict hands. "I'm not a believer in any kind of inmate council," declared Hoyt Cupp, the gruff superintendent of the Oregon State Penitentiary in Salem. "We're not running a Greek democracy."

Critics charged that, although the reforms had been designed to humanize prison, they in fact made life inside even more inhumane. According to these critics, acquiescent prison officials had allowed fierce inmate gangs, divided by race and life-style, to war for control of the ten acres of living space inside the packed maximum-security compound. They noted that during the 1970s beatings, robberies, and ho-

mosexual rapes multiplied. The number of inmates seeking asylum from other inmates swelled from a dozen to nearly two hundred. Prison murders increased from three in the 1960s to twenty-five in the 1970s.

But, according to prisoners who had lived under both regimens, the inmate council, the relaxed work and dress requirements, and the increased visiting privileges hadn't undermined the reform experiment. These prisoners maintained that the experiment had failed because the so-called reforms did not address the penitentiary's fundamental problems: the lack of work and training programs, an ill-trained staff, and a poor physical plant with limited means of separating first offenders from the predatory, hard-core criminals.

Meanwhile, the prison plant continued to deteriorate. By modern standards, it was horribly antiquated, with shoddy plumbing, faulty wiring, and poor security. Seventy percent of the inmates lived in four-man cells over which guards had no direct surveillance and little control. Improvements, when they came, were piecemeal and haphazard.

During the final months of the Rhay administration, the penitentiary had floundered badly. On Easter Sunday, 1977, inmates rioted, burning the chapel and looting the prison store, and then suffered the consequences by being locked in their cells for a record time of forty-six days.

Mindful that spending money on convicts was about as popular as spending money on themselves, legislators had scrimped on prison funding. Finally, after the 1977 Easter riot, they appropriated funds for two miniprisons, which were part of an ambitious corrections project designed by Douglas Vinzant, once a Mississippi minister and now penal expert. Vinzant argued that the state's big nineteenth-century penal institutions were obsolete. He insisted that prisoners had the best chance for successful rehabilitation in small, community-based prisons closer to family and jobs. Moreover, administrators would have an easier time controlling the smaller prison populations. But newly elected Gov. Dixy Lee Ray, reacting to public fear of backyard prisons, doomed the project by vetoing the appropriation. Instead, she gave Vinzant a consolation prize: the warden's post at Walla Walla.

Vinzant inherited a penitentiary divided between inmates who wanted to have more privileges and guards who wanted to reclaim their lost power. He took over the top job at the penitentiary in early summer 1977, about the same time that Hoffman and I arrived in Walla Walla to start our jobs at the *Union-Bulletin*.

I first interviewed Vinzant in the warden's office one hot July afternoon. While Hoffman snapped close-ups, I asked questions and tried to figure out what the new warden was up to. Vinzant could purr with Southern charm or could bury you with impressive-sounding crimino-logical jargon. Avoiding specifics, he cautiously suggested that prison ought to be as much like the real world as possible. Inmates should work and should be paid prevailing wages. They should use their earnings to support their families, to pay taxes, and to make restitution to their victims. Also, Vinzant continued, inmates should be shown "a little light at the end of the tunnel" so that they had an incentive to behave.

Vinzant's incentives, introduced over the next few months, were inmate-run businesses, trips outside the walls, and hints of a speedier release. Rather than forcing inmates to stamp out license plates because the state wanted them, Vinzant allowed inmates to rebuild motorcycles, to carve wood, and to sell ice-cream cones because they wanted to. "Let inmates find something to do besides trying to figure out how to beat the system," he said. With Vinzant's approval, a dozen of the prison's toughest convicts formed an interracial committee that persuaded inmates to fight with words or fists instead of with knives.

Guards complained bitterly. They felt that Vinzant was playing into the inmates' hands. They protested that the new warden bent prison rules, ignored inmate disciplinary infractions, and made secret deals with inmate bosses. It unnerved them to see Vinzant, who never called staff meetings, chatting for hours in the inmates' visiting room.

Yet, whether by fortune or skill, Vinzant governed a relatively calm prison. He was there eleven months before an inmate died a violent death. The comparative peacefulness of his administration enabled the reform experiment to continue despite an increasing public sentiment to pursue a hard line and a growing conviction among hard-liners that Walla Walla was a country club run by inmates.

Hoffman and I became more curious about life at the penitentiary as we watched Vinzant carry out his reform program. At the same time, we grew increasingly frustrated by the *Union-Bulletin*'s unwillingness to tell the full prison story. We began to discuss doing a book about the penitentiary. We met with Vinzant one afternoon in July 1978 and proposed our idea. We told him that we would like to spend three or four months hanging around inside the prison, talking to convicts and staff, taking notes and photographs, and assimilating the prison scene. Vinzant agreed and granted us free access to prisoners, staff, and facilities. We told him that we would like to start the project in late August. In the meantime, Hoffman and I gave the *Union-Bulletin* notice of our intentions to resign our newspaper jobs so that we could devote all our time to the penitentiary.

Two weeks after our conversation with Vinzant, he moved to Olympia as corrections chief. He had been named state prison director some months earlier and hence had the advantage of being his own boss at

Walla Walla. He left his right-hand man in charge at the penitentiary.

But Vinzant's new job was short-lived. On 11 August, a mishandled pipe bomb exploded in the prison control room, wounding two officers and maiming Lt. Roger Sanders, who later died of his injuries. In the aftermath, Governor Ray and her top aides decided that they and the public had had enough of the experiment at Walla Walla. Vinzant and his right-hand man resigned. Inmates were locked in their cells, and the prison-reform experiment ended once and for all.

Hoffman and I were afraid that the pipe bomb had also blown away the permission that Vinzant had given us to go inside. We met James Spalding, the new warden, at a press conference on the afternoon that he arrived from the state reformatory to assume command of the locked-down penitentiary.

A former Green Beret and a veteran corrections officer who had risen up through the ranks, Spalding sat awkwardly behind the warden's desk and conducted what was probably his first press conference. He declined to discuss correctional philosophy. He said that he intended to end the excesses of the reform years, to adhere strictly to state codes governing corrections, and to gradually return the penitentiary to the more secure, more custody-oriented institution that it had been in the past. He had been given a mandate to regain control of the institution. He accused the Vinzant administration of "playing games," of arousing unrealistic expectations that inmates could work their way out of prison. "The reality is that many inmates have a hard time dealing with their time," Spalding said.

After the press conference, we told Spalding about our project. To our surprise, he agreed almost immediately and said that he would honor the deal that we had made with Vinzant. He asked few questions and imposed only one restriction: We couldn't stay overnight. It was assumed that we would follow prison rules and would avoid causing trouble. We were free to circulate unescorted anywhere in the penitentiary after the lockdown ended.

The lockdown ended on 28 August 1978. Prison officials asked us to postpone starting our project for a few more days so that they could be sure that tempers had cooled. On 8 September, we began by meeting with a dozen inmate leaders in the prison's visiting room. We explained our plans and asked for their cooperation. We emphasized that we were working independently and that we would tell the story as we saw it.

The convicts showed little enthusiasm. Two of them objected that "street people" could never know what it was like to be locked up. One man complained that reporters always made convicts look like "bad asses." Another merely asked for some free copies of the finished book.

Mostly, they shrugged. Reporters and photographers had gone inside before; it was no big deal.

When the meeting broke up, a lanky, solemn-faced inmate wearing prison-issue denims motioned me aside. He had said nothing during the meeting, but now he seemed anxious to talk. "I'll tell you something about prison," he said, his voice hard and full of controlled anger. "The court sentenced me here to do time. They didn't sentence me to a place so dangerous that I wake up every morning wondering if today I'm going to have to kill—or die." Those words proved chillingly apt. The solemn-faced inmate lived through our brief stay at the penitentiary, but others didn't.

Richard Anderson, a twenty-eight-year-old drug offender, was the victim of a feud between two powerful inmate groups, the lifers and the bikers. A quiet, unassuming bike-club member who had never ridden a motorcycle outside the walls, Anderson was stabbed to death on a crowded prison breezeway, in broad daylight, with guards nearby.

We had met Anderson two weeks earlier at his annual appearance before the parole board. Sitting bolt upright, tense and uneasy, he told the board members that the bikers had taught him how to custom paint and that now he had a job offer on the outside. "Doing more time isn't going to change me any more than I've changed already," he pleaded. "I want my life back."

Soon he was dead.

We also knew Gary Southards, a twenty-nine-year-old convicted forger. A short, wiry inmate, his face often stamped with a sly smile, Southards was a lounger. He and his buddies slumped for hours against the cinder-block wall of the recreation building and watched the breezeway traffic.

But he had no buddies on the morning that two inmates lured him into an unfriendly cell and plunged their prison-made knives into his body, stabbing repeatedly until Southards lay limp and lifeless. He deserved it, some inmates said, because he had cheated some people on a drug deal.

Southards's murder caused so little reaction that even Warden Spalding, a man accustomed to inmate violence, was shocked. "The blood hadn't even dried on the tier yet and everybody was just walking around like, 'How's it going? Everything's cool,'" Spalding told us afterward. "I had a hard time dealing with that. There has to be something more, some value placed on human life."

Saving lives, we learned during our four months "inside," was not a

high priority. Although all but a handful of inmates expected to survive their incarceration, they accepted the fact that the prison code might require them to kill another inmate. Honor, revenge, and power were more important principles than preventing loss of life.

The stark contradictions between life as a prisoner and life as a free man continually surprised us; so did the diversity of the prison community.

Instead of a mass of anonymous men in identical cages, we found an uncommon community with its own language, rules, and code of conduct. It was a society that both mimicked and disdained the larger society that accounted for its existence.

In the eyes of the state, all inmates were equal. Each ate the same food; received the same state-issue clothing; and was entitled to the same visiting, educational, and recreational privileges.

Yet the prison community bristled with inequality. Some inmates were "con bosses," bullies who got their way and enforced their will with a mixture of muscle and patronage. Others were "punks," weak, young guys despised by other inmates because they traded their bodies for protection. Most prisoners were somewhere in between, forever cautious of getting caught in a power play or of being "put in a cross." Some of them protected themselves by acquiring new identities or by refashioning old ones. Bikers paraded in leather jackets and grubby blue jeans. Pushers sported silk shirts, polished shoes, and smartly pressed pants. Those men who by design or misfortune became the prison's women wore lipstick and rouge.

On the one hand, prison was a place of idleness where men with time on their hands loitered on the breezeways or basked in the sun. On the other hand, there was much industriousness, not in the laundry, in the furniture shop, or in the license-plate factory—the places officially labeled "Prison Industries"—but in the cells and club rooms. Men who had never worked on the outside carved jewelry boxes, crafted musical instruments, and designed model airplanes. The most industrious of all were the drug dealers.

There was a great deal of rhetoric about rehabilitation and treatment. The saying was that if inmates "programmed," by participating in work, school, or vocational training, they got out. With the administration's blessing, inmates used their club affiliations to invent jobs with lofty titles such as "internal vice-president" and "public-relations director." They churned out reams of project proposals, newsletters, and self-congratulatory progress reports. Yet when it came to getting a parole date, treatment did not matter. The parole board winked at rehabilitation and then stared at the crime. What the man had done in a moment

of passion, drunkenness, or cunning was what counted, and with some crimes, the law made sure that the punishment never wavered. First-degree murderers did at least thirteen years and four months; no exceptions.

Later, when we became more familiar with the prison, we thought of it as a separate town, a twenty-acre village surrounded by walls. The walls contained a hospital, a kitchen, two dining halls, a library, an auditorium, a school, a gymnasium, a chapel, a laundry, a warehouse, offices, recreation areas, industrial shops, paved walkways, a small playfield, and several hundred residences. But this village was unlike any other. The inhabitants could not leave. The surrounding walls were topped by towers where armed men sat and watched. The several hundred residences were cramped, bathroom-sized cubicles shared by strangers. There were no women or children. There were few jobs.

The men who lived at the Washington State Penitentiary were a special lot. For the most part, they were in their twenties and thirties. Many were the products of broken homes and reform schools. Sixty-five percent had not completed high school. Some were illiterate. Over half of them had histories of alcohol or drug abuse and nearly half were intoxicated at the time of their crime. Ninety-eight percent of them will return to society someday, but 40 percent of those who are freed will be back inside a Washington State prison within five years. Washington does not keep track of how many of its parolees wind up in prisons in other states, but experts claim that only one out of every three prison parolees stays out of prison for the rest of his life.

Minorities were four times more likely to end up at the penitentiary than whites were. In 1978, only 8 percent of Washington's population was nonwhite, yet 32 percent of the prison's population were members of minority groups. Twenty-four percent of the inmates were black, 4 percent were American Indian, 3 percent were Chicano, and another 1.5 percent were Asian or other nonwhite races. Indians, the state's most disadvantaged minority, were the most overrepresented group and were also most likely to return to prison. According to state statistics, more than 80 percent of the Indian prisoners were drunk at the time of their crime.

About half of the inmates at the penitentiary in 1978 were convicted of crimes against people. Twelve percent were serving time for murder, 15 percent for robbery, 10 percent for assault, and 11 percent for rape or some other sex crime. About two-fifths were doing time for crimes against property: Ten percent for burglary, 12 percent for theft, and

7 percent for drug violations. Another 13 percent, the biggest category after robbery, had not been convicted of any new crime. These men had been returned to prison for violating the conditions of their parole.

In 1978, the state paid almost seven thousand dollars a year to keep a man at the penitentiary, less than it cost to house an inmate at any other state institution. The average length of stay was twenty-two months. Every week, about 20 new residents arrived, and if the parole board was willing, another 20 left. Built to accommodate 850 maximum-security prisoners, the penitentiary's population fluctuated between 1,300 and 1,400. Another 300 inmates lived in a minimum-security building outside the walls.

Hoffman and I soon realized that the story of this prison village was too diverse to tell from the point of view of a single resident. Though the walls confined all prisoners to the same small space, the residents led very different lives. We decided to spend time with particular prisoners and staff members, to watch what they did, to ask what they thought, and, in the process, to learn how they dealt with life in prison.

We gathered our material through observation and interviews. On occasion, we used a tape recorder, but for the most part, we used the journalist's traditional tools—pen and paper. The people in this book are real, the quotes are real, and the observations are as fair and accurate as our limitations allowed. Whenever possible, we checked prisoners' stories with court reports, counselors, guards, and other inmates. Despite the popular opinion that convicts are liars, we found that most of what we were told was true. Stories that were inaccurate tended to suffer from errors of omission, perception, or exaggeration rather than bold-faced lies.

In any event, we did not have to depend on stories. We spent days, sometimes weeks, watching the people in the following pages. We singled out those whom we thought could best lead us into a discussion of the subjects central to prison life. For example, in Chapter 1, we watch Fred, the fearful newcomer, or "fish," deal with his first three days in prison. In Chapter 2, Browny, the seasoned veteran, the career criminal, talks to us about the convict code with a perspective that stretches back to the 1920s.

In the rest of the book, we meet men who highlight other aspects of prison life. Kenny, the powerful inmate boss, introduces us to prison politics, while Bobby pushes "biker brotherhood." Jimmy Joe exemplifies the fierce loyalty of the inmate clubs, while Jackie, the prison's most popular "lady," introduces us to the issue of sexuality in prison. Kim, one of the many marginally employed inmates, provides us with an opportunity to discuss work, idleness, and make-work. Wino, Ed, and Don are in prisons within the prison: protective custody, "the hole," and Death Row. Yvonne is our entrée to the visiting room and to those few, fortunate inmates who still see their loved ones. Officer Edwards represents "The Man"—the warden, the courts, the state, and the parole board—the whole custodial and legal apparatus that sends men to prison, keeps them there, and decides when they may go.

Hoffman and I decided to begin our four months inside by spending all our time with the convicts. We felt that they would be more open with us if we kept our distance from the guards. In prison, we soon realized, there is no middle ground. More than one inmate asked us, "Whose story are you going to tell, theirs or ours?" If the inmates saw us being friendly to the guards or thought that we were passing on information to them, we would learn nothing.

The decision to avoid talking with the guards until the end of our stay did earn us animosity from some of the guards. Some of them saw us as "con lovers" and as "bleeding-heart liberals" and treated us like inmates. They barked orders, put up obstacles, and arbitrarily applied the rules. For example, after Hoffman took some pictures of guards shaking down inmates, we were summoned to the associate warden's office. "You're getting in the way," he warned us, adding that he expected us to inform officers of any "life-threatening" situations. It was a peculiar request: Because many inmates were armed and fights were a common occurrence, life-threatening situations happened every day. We told him that we wouldn't interfere with operations, but that we didn't intend to turn in names. He seemed satisfied.

About a week later, a guard burst into a curtained-off cell and caught two inmates smoking hashish. I was with them. The guard seized a hookah cleverly disguised as a bottle of vitamin pills, wrote infractions on the two inmates, and shook down the cell. He searched me, then grabbed my note pad, and made a futile attempt to read my illegible handwriting. Forsaking my First Amendment rights, I didn't object. I wanted to prove that I was clean.

But I also knew that if I wanted to maintain any credibility with the inmates, I did not dare answer any questions. I could not point out the stash of drugs tucked behind the toilet or offer the guard any help in his investigation. The two inmates would do time in the hole; Hoffman and I were ordered to report to the warden's office.

It was the first time that we had seen Spalding since the press conference on the day of his arrival. Already he looked older, haggard, and besieged. Except for two wood carvings made by inmates and a hunting picture, his office was so bare that it gave the impression that he had been too busy to unpack.

Avoiding mention of my presence at the drug bust, Spalding said that he was getting complaints about us from the guards. He asked if we could be done in a week. Amazed by this turn of events, I interrupted. I explained our project again. I reiterated our intentions to abide by prison rules. I stressed our commitment to fair reporting.

He said that we were getting information that could compromise the security of the penitentiary. We replied that all information that we received was kept in confidence. I talked some more, but he seemed to grow weary of our explanations. Finally, he relented and agreed to let us complete the project.

Guards who frowned on our presence objected to their superiors, but the inmates confronted us directly. Prison was a very honest place. Inmates did not mince words or beat around the bush with social niceties. During our first days inside, prisoners grilled us constantly: What did we want? What were we going to do with what we got? Who was putting us up to this?

Many of them who recognized us from our time with the newspaper accepted our answers, but some weren't sure. A few, convinced that we were undercover agents with clever covers, remained suspicious until the end. They thought that their suspicions were confirmed when I began—too early—to ask questions about drugs.

One afternoon in "People's Park," the tattered bit of lawn between the central cellblocks, an angry inmate walked up to me, rolled up his sleeves, and told me to stop asking questions about drugs. "You could fuck up everything we got going here," he said, planting himself squarely in front of me. I heard him out and said nothing, but I did wait several days before asking any more questions about drugs.

There were some inmates whom we never felt comfortable with— violent, manipulative men who tried to use us to their advantage—but there were others who became our friends. There were inmates we looked forward to seeing every day. We kept up with their lives, and they asked about ours. Several sent my wife a card when we had our first child. Yet their prison lives were so different from ours that sometimes we felt like anthropologists visiting a strange society. Usually, we were cautious. Occasionally, we were scared.

On our very first morning inside, a tattooed, leather-jacketed convict who had once been the president of the bikers' club invited us to his cell. A glib talker, he had a reputation as a ruthless enforcer and as a "cold dope fiend." The cell that he shared with three other bikers was painted black, dimly lit, and decorated with swastikas. Two of his cellmates lounged on a lower bunk. Hoffman and I sat on the opposite bunk and watched our host pull up his sleeves to show us the fresh marks of a hypodermic needle. He was high and told us matter-of-factly about beating up club members who got out of line, crunching inmates' fingers in the bike-shop vise, and losing his punk who had flipped out one day and had hung himself from the upper bunk. Since he had introduced the subject of prison sex, I asked him if he had sex with men when he was on the street. "Are you kidding, man?" he shot back, glaring at me as if I'd called him a pervert.

As we were talking, the cell door slammed shut. It was the 10:30 A.M. lockup. The lone guard at the end of the tier had no idea that we were sitting in a dark cell with three bikers. Trying to hide my discomfort, I continued the conversation. Hoffman told me afterward that his mind was racing, imagining the horrors that they could perform on us before the cell door unlocked forty-five minutes later. Like lion tamers in a cage, we knew that acting afraid would only create suspicion and invite abuse. The conversation rambled on, and when the cell door opened again, we casually left, intact.

In the sense that prison is a society like any other society, prisoners do much of what people do in the outside world. They make friends and enemies, they invent ways to avoid boredom, and they find ways to feel significant. An invitation to have coffee in an inmate's "house" was an occasion that many inmates managed with courtesy and generosity. We were their guests. They shared what little they could offer and treated us hospitably.

In general, however, our treatment depended on following two sets of rules: the administration's and the convicts'. Often the rules conflicted and sometimes they simply didn't apply. Because we were "street people," outsiders from the real world, we were given wider latitude by both sides: Like children given "another chance," we could make some mistakes as long as we did not repeat them.

One of our first mistakes was ignoring the importance of the invisible territorial boundaries that divided the penitentiary. The major clubs had members-only rooms and bitterly defended their "turf." While normally trespassing was forceably discouraged, as outsiders, we usually had free access on the unspoken assumption that we would not do or report anything that would compromise club security.

On our second Sunday inside, we attended the annual lifers' banquet, a gala picnic for inmates sentenced to life, their families, and guests. The banquet was held in "Lifers' Park," a rectangular garden enclosed by two cellblocks and a chain-link fence. During the festivities, "Nuts," a scrawny biker ostensibly there by invitation, asked Hoffman to photograph him smoking a joint. Hoffman resisted, unsure about the propriety of snapping a biker brazenly smoking marijuana in Lifers' Park on the lifers' big day. But Nuts assured him that it was okay, and Hoffman took the picture.

Suddenly, Nuts vanished and Hoffman was confronted by an angry Kenny Agtuca, the powerful lifer president. "You blew it," Agtuca said coldly. "If the cops caught you, they'd call off the whole banquet."

Pleading ignorance, Hoffman apologized and returned to the party. At that time, neither of us was aware of the seriousness of the biker–lifer hostility, which would erupt in Anderson's murder two weeks later. Nor did we know until later that Nuts was having the stuffing beat out of him for having dared to jeopardize the lifers' banquet. He wound up in the prison hospital with half of his ear bitten off. True to the convict code of silence, he blamed his injuries on an accident.

Meanwhile, back at the banquet, an inmate whispered to Hoffman, "You're in big trouble. The bikers want to slit your throat. You better leave."

The color drained from his face, Hoffman cautiously stepped through the crowd to tell me what had happened. As we hurriedly decided what to do, two burly bikers wandered over and hovered behind us. Hoffman heard one of them mutter, "Here he is. Let's take care of it right now." We resisted the impulse to run. Fleeing would mean that we couldn't handle it inside. But what would getting killed prove?

Acting nonchalant, we wandered off to another part of the garden where we were within eyeshot of a couple of guards. The bikers didn't follow, but the whispering inmate approached Hoffman again. "Why are you still here?" he asked. "Don't you believe me?" We didn't know what to believe. Was the threat real, or was it simply a biker show of force? When the party ended soon afterward, we walked out through the prison gate with a great sigh of relief.

But the problem that Hoffman had created had to be resolved. The next morning, we headed for the bike shop. Biker president Bobby Tsow said that the bikers were angry, but he proposed a deal: He got the negatives of Nuts smoking marijuana, and we got off the hook. Hoffman agreed in a second. He laughed about it afterward, saying that "criminal" justice was certainly efficient: The administration would have had to go through a long court battle to get those pictures.

Hoffman and I learned from our mistakes. The better we understood convict society, the more we began to fit in. The convicts who wanted us to smuggle in drugs, to buy their handcrafted leather belts, or to hear how they had been framed gradually learned to leave us alone. Other than the photos that Hoffman passed out to smooth our passage, inmates soon realized that we had nothing to offer them.

After the first awkward weeks, we were able to sense when trouble was brewing. We knew what it meant when prisoners walked in groups and friends gave us vacant stares. When crowds gathered to watch two rigidly poised convicts face off, we knew that they were armed with knives. So did the unarmed guards who watched and hoped that they would not have to intervene.

As we became a part of the daily routine, club members stopped whistling a warning to other members when we trespassed on club territory. Rarely did anyone challenge our presence—not even at a closed meeting in which some hotheads proposed storming the segregation unit. Being admitted to the inmates' private councils also made us fair game for their private fantasies. Toward the end of our stay, Hoffman received a love letter of sorts, an anonymous note that he found tucked in his camera bag. What it lacked in tenderness, it made up for in passion. "Bitch," the note read, "I am hip to you walking around here with them camera on your big fine ass. Beggin' to be fucked . . ." Hoffman shrugged it off, although he would have panicked two months earlier.

As we adjusted to life inside, we noticed that our temperaments changed. We both became more abrasive, aggressive, and impulsive. I found my conversation becoming peppered with prison jargon to the point of copying the inmate habit of describing people as some type of "motherfucker." Hoffman told me that he began having violent dreams that ended only when he awoke, sweaty and agitated. In one dream, he robbed a bank and mercilessly beat the security guards with a baseball bat. To his surprise, he enjoyed beating them.

My dream life was more serene, but I temporarily developed an assaultive disposition. If someone dawdled in the supermarket line, I felt like shoving. If another car cut in front of mine, I felt like ramming it. I had to continually check myself from acting out my hostile fantasies.

I remarked to Parley Edwards, the veteran officer who headed the guards' union, how my brief stay behind the walls was changing my disposition. Edwards said that guards experienced the same thing. "Your language changes. Your personality changes. You begin to mistrust everybody," he said. "Up there on the hill you're on the defensive eight hours a day. When somebody drives on you out here on the street, you fire back."

We left the penitentiary in mid-January 1979. It was a time of rising tension and growing violence, cooled only by the frigid Walla Walla winter that tended to make inmates less active. During our time behind the walls, inmates Anderson and Southards had been murdered, two inmates had briefly escaped in the first successful tunnel job in a decade, and three others, including lifer president Agtuca had been halted by shotgun fire as they scurried out another tunnel. These events, however, would pale by comparison with what was to come.

1

Fred: Fish

Out of his mind on a mixture of beer, whiskey, marijuana, codeine, and hallucinogenic mushrooms, Fred Crist aimed his .357 Magnum and fired.

It was a warm Seattle night in August 1978. Fred had been partying. He had blacked out, and when he woke up, he could not find his car keys. Sure that someone at the party had stolen them, he got angry, unpacked his gun, cocked the hammer, and fired. The bullet tore into the body of a sixteen-year-old black youth who was reclined on a nearby couch. The youth died, and Fred was going to prison, convicted of second-degree murder.

Although he was twenty-seven years old, hardly a kid, Fred was scared. He had had brushes with the law before, but he had never done hard time. His previous arrests for driving while intoxicated, assaulting a policeman, being drunk in public, and carrying a concealed weapon had only cost him some fines and a little time in jail. But now he was going to "The Walls."

Awaiting sentencing in the county jail, Fred heard stories about rapes, killings, and gang warfare at Walla Walla. He learned that some inmates forced others to pay for cell space. He learned that "fish," newcomers like himself, had to fight to keep from becoming some convict's sexual property, or "punk."

"I'm going in there with the attitude I'm not going to pay rent or be punked. So if it comes to killing somebody, I'll shank [knife] them before they shank me," Fred said, not too convincingly. Then, his bravado collapsing, he confessed, "I'm worried about having to fight every day. I don't want to have to fight every day."

At the jail, Fred got a warning that compounded his fears. He heard that his victim had cousins in the penitentiary. He heard that they were waiting for him.

Fred's journey to the penitentiary began when he was sent from the county jail to a "reception unit" at the state correctional center in Shelton. During his three weeks at the reception center, Fred was shaved, shorn, fingerprinted, photographed, examined, tested, and outfitted with the blue overalls that later, at the penitentiary, would mark him as a new arrival. He was cooperative, scored well on achievement tests, and faithfully answered questions that he thought were silly ("Do you want to be a girl?" "Do you think policemen are honest?" "Do you hear voices?").

When he appeared before the committee that decided where to place offenders, he asked to be sent to the state reformatory in Monroe. "No, sir," the committee chairman told him. "I can't let you shoot somebody and then go someplace easy."

Like most inmates sent to Walla Walla, Fred "drove up on the chain," shackled to other prisoners inside the big white bus that arrived at the penitentiary's back gate every Wednesday afternoon.

The bus brought new inmates and returned old ones. It delivered them to the 9-tower gate where a group of convicts gathered to check them out. Some looked for easy marks, potential punks, and prospective "old ladies." Others looked for old friends, greeting them with hugs, backslaps, and ready-made cell accommodations. Sometimes the scene looked like a homecoming, as if repeat offenders were returning warriors being welcomed back into the fold. But some inmates who watched the new arrivals coming through the 9-tower gate were simply being cautious. "You better check it out," advised one shrewd convict. "Your worst enemy could be coming in."

When the bus carrying the twenty-five men on Fred's chain stopped outside the gate on a chilly December afternoon, there was no welcome waiting for Fred. Frozen snow crunched under the feet of the eight officers who stood guard, the collars of their uniform jackets turned up against the cold. Overhead, the 9-tower guard leaned his rifle on the catwalk rail and watched. "We beef it up," one guard offered as an explanation for the large number of guards, "in case something happens."

Fred shuffled off the bus hooked to the prisoner next to him by a chain tied around his feet and hands and looped around his waist. He stood slouched forward, subdued, like someone hiding in a crowd. In better times, he had worn his curly black hair and beard in a great shaggy mane. His friends had nicknamed him "Snowman," and to his

delight, the name stuck. He did not like being called "Fred."

What Fred liked, despite the problems that it caused, was getting high. Alcohol and drugs had forced him out of high school, had cost him an undesirable discharge from the marines, and had destroyed both of his marriages. "When I start drinking, I don't know when to quit," Fred admitted. He conceded that he had a problem but boasted about getting stoned as if he were a teenager on his first big bender. It seemed as though, underneath his boasting, he had a nagging suspicion that sobriety would unravel his shaky self-image and would kill the Snowman.

When the guards undid his chains, Fred thrust his cold hands deep into the pockets of his blue overalls and shivered silently. A prison sergeant called out the names and numbers of the new arrivals, checking them off on a clipboard. Some of the names had notes scrawled next to them indicating who was violent, who was crazy, and who needed protective custody. After checking the names, the sergeant waved the prisoners down a fenced walkway to the clothing room where they gave inmate workers their clothing sizes.

In the morning, each of them would receive his state-issue clothing inside a mesh laundry bag printed with his convict number. Fred would get a pair of crepe-soled shoes, three handkerchiefs, two pairs of denim jeans, two T-shirts, three pairs of socks, and two blue work shirts. But for now, all the clothing room provided was a pair of high-topped tennis shoes, a bedroll, and a brown paper bag containing a razor, soap, tooth powder, matches, rolling papers, and a box of Roll-Rite tobacco.

Fred sat next to another fish, a six-foot, 230-pound army veteran nicknamed "Ajax." A sullen, sober-faced fellow with a gray-flecked crew cut, Ajax was forty years old. He had been convicted of a sex crime. Sex criminals were sometimes harassed by other prisoners, but Ajax did not anticipate any trouble. "I don't look like I'm the greenest turkey off the streets," he said.

Fred and Ajax had struck up a friendship at Shelton where the two of them had worked in the kitchen together. They had made plans to get a cell together at Walla Walla. "The way I figure it," Fred had said at the time, "me and Ajax can kick ass if we have to."

Except for hearsay, Fred, Ajax, and the other first-timers knew nothing about the penitentiary. The prison staff provided no handbook, no map, nor even any oral instructions. Waiting for some indication of what to do, the newcomers sat on their bedrolls or leaned against the clothing-room wall. They could not go anywhere until guards completed the "count," a tally of all the penitentiary's inmates. Guards as-signed to cellblocks and work areas counted inmates three times a day, at 7 A.M., 4 P.M., and 9 P.M. During count times, no inmate moved out of his cell or work area until every inmate was accounted for.

While the count continued, a smooth-talking, redheaded prisoner representing the penitentiary's inmate government addressed the new arrivals. "The institution is crowded," he announced. "People know that, so most of them won't say anything about you moving into their house. There's no cell moves tonight. Tomorrow, you can look for cells. If you got a problem tonight, come to the Resident Council office after dinner. After dinner, you'll be released from your wing. You can go around and do what you want to do."

Nobody asked any questions, so the redhead kept talking. "The best way to find a cell is to get to know people during the next few days. Talk to people. It ain't hard to find houses. Tonight, if you don't know people, stick together, go to chow together."

Dismayed, Fred clutched his bedroll. He realized that he and Ajax would be assigned to different cells. "We'll be scattered all over tonight," he mumbled to no one in particular.

One fish told the sergeant that there was bad blood between him and another inmate and asked to go to protective custody. The sergeant granted the request. "We don't need a stabbing over in 6-wing," he muttered to another officer.

When word came that the count had cleared, a guard read out the names and the cell assignments. Fred and Ajax were called out for separate cells in 8-wing, the four-hundred-man cellblock that housed the penitentiary's unruliest inmates. Motioning to them and to the others who drew 8-wing assignments, another guard conducted them out of the clothing room, down the fenced-in walkway, through the 9-tower gate, and into the maximum-security compound.

It was colder now and dark, a crisp, moonless night. The pale prison lights cast uneven shadows in the yard. Fred quickened his pace, ignoring the blank faces of the inmates who brushed past him on their way to dinner. Outside the door to 8-wing, the burning contents of a garbage can lit the night sky with an eerie glow. Fred's group entered the cellblock.

Fred pressed close to the wall, staring at the cells stacked three tiers high and marveling at all the noise: stereos, televisions, guitars, people yelling at each other. On winter evenings especially, the din in the cellblock was fearsome, as if the accumulated racket of hundreds of households was compressed into a single concrete and metal room where sounds reverberated in a maddening roar.

"Steve, you back. About time you got back," an inmate called to one of the new arrivals standing near Fred. "Welcome home," an 8-wing guard taunted another returning convict. An Indian inmate rushed past Fred to hug another Indian who was back for another prison sentence. A solidly built black man leaned over a stair railing and studied the new arrivals. He wore a scarf around his head, mascara, lipstick, and a short print dress.

The guard who had escorted Fred's group from the clothing room to the cellblock disappeared, and the 8-wing officer took over. "If any of you don't have a mattress on your bunk, let me know," he said. Pointing in various directions, he read off the cell numbers. Fred's was number 1, A deck.

Eight-wing's A deck, the bottom tier on the west side, was "owned" by the bikers, the prison motorcycle club. A tough group of outlaw motorcyclists and hangers-on, the bikers claimed the tier's seventeen four-man cells as their territory. They decided who lived there and who should pay to live there.

Although prison rules prohibited the buying and selling of cell space, the guards felt powerless to enforce them. "There's no way we can prevent it," shrugged Lt. Joseph Colombo, the officer responsible for assigning cells. "That's the problem with multiple cells. You see, the guy who tells me about buying cells is liable to get his head cut off. If I knew about it, I could lock up the other three, but then the guy has to testify against them. If he does, he can't live out there."

A slim, affable, white-haired man in his fifties, Colombo wore a Playboy-bunny belt buckle and a grin that said, "I've seen it all." He worked in a small office in the "control room," the cluster of offices housing custody's nerve center inside the walls. He kept track of inmate cell and work assignments on a revolving board with pull-out tabs. The tabs were color-coded by race: white for whites, red for Indians, blue for Chicanos, and green for blacks.

Colombo was convinced that inmates preferred to live with their own race, and he tried "to keep 'em happy." He went along with most inmate requests for cell changes except for those that looked coerced or exploitative. Accepting the facts of prison life, Colombo put punks in the same cells as their "jockers," aggressive, macho inmates who played the male role in homosexual relationships. "With these weak kids, one guy will get a hold of them and then the kid's going to be protected. There won't be ten to fifteen guys driving on the kid," he reasoned. When possible, he put the elderly, the lame, the retarded, and the mentally disturbed in one-man cells. When an inmate claimed that his life was in danger, Colombo had guards move the inmate and his possessions to asylum in protective custody.

When Fred meekly introduced himself at the barred door of cell number 1, he did not know that A deck was biker territory. "I guess I'm in here, guys," he said, peering into the dimly lit ten-by-twelve-foot cage.

Inside were two bunk beds, a table, two wooden stools, a sink, a lidless toilet, piles of clothes, an extra mattress flung on the floor, a wall papered with *Penthouse* pinups, a couple of pornographic books, a black-and-white television set, and two of the cell's three occupants. One of them was the cell's owner—Smiley, a stout, bearded biker wearing a plaid lumberman's jacket. Smiley owned the cell because he had lived in it the longest.

"We got a 'bro' coming out of the hole [an isolation cell]," Smiley said, objecting to Fred's assignment to his cell.

Fred hesitantly stepped inside. "I thought they told everybody that we'd be moving in," he apologized.

Grunting, Smiley motioned toward a littered upper bunk and told Fred that he could sleep there for the time being. Fred threw his bedroll on the bunk, ignoring the Harley-Davidson emblems and the pictures of spread-eagled women taped on the wall.

"There ain't nobody going to hassle you tonight. We'll get it straightened out," Smiley said. Fred stood next to the bunk, crossed his arms, and looked around the cell. After a while, Smiley introduced himself and, pointing toward the man sprawled on a lower bunk, he added, "That's Spike."

"I'm Snowman," Fred responded stiffly. Nobody shook hands.

Two more bikers appeared at the cell door asking Spike and Smiley to join them for dinner. They nodded slyly at Fred, as if to say, "Who's this chump?" Smiley handed Fred a padded jacket to cover up the blue overalls that spelled "fish" and indicated that he could come with them.

Trailing behind Smiley and the three other bikers, Fred plodded off to the south dining hall, a sterile, tiled room where inmate servers dispensed measured quantities of steam-heated food from aluminum pans. Dinner was roast beef, beans, rice, and a sweet roll. Fred and Smiley sat together at one of the eight tables that the bikers claimed as theirs. Another fish, who sat at a biker table without being invited, was told to leave. Fred saw Ajax a few tables away but did not acknowledge him. He sensed that convicts did not do a lot of visiting in the dining hall; too many people were watching.

Despite his misgivings about Fred, Smiley figured that he was stuck with him for a few days and might as well make the best of it. However,

as he left Fred in the phone room, Smiley warned him, "What happens when you come out of my house and move into somebody else's, that's your responsibility."

Fred had wanted to call his mother but became discouraged by the long line of inmates waiting to use the phone. Trudging back through the crowded recreation area, he ran into Ajax and four other men who had arrived with them. The newcomers huddled together and exchanged observations. "This place isn't as big as I thought it would be and it's dirty," Fred said.

A squat, middle-aged Chicano nervously confessed that he had already blundered by walking unannounced into the black prisoners' club. "I feel like I'm walking on soft-boiled eggs," he whispered. Then, as an afterthought, he added, "I think 98 percent of these people belong here."

The Chicano's buddy, another fish, said that he had been warned by his new cellmate not to show his face in the cell except at count times. "You know why I can't go back till nine," he said, his face pinched with disgust, "because the guy's got a homosexual in there."

Fred listened to the conversation, but his attention was elsewhere. He gazed around the recreation area, scanning the faces of the card players and of the men who stood at their backs watching them play. He was relieved to spot J. C., a gabby, seasoned convict who wore cowboy boots and fancied himself to be an undiscovered country-and-western singer. Fred and J. C. had met at Shelton where J. C. was quickly processed and routed back to the penitentiary. Fred asked J. C. if he could help him find a cell. "I'll try," J. C. promised, "but this fucking place is jam-packed full."

Glad to find somebody who knew his way around, Fred pumped J. C. for information. He asked about the mail; about jobs, laundry, and lockup times; and about which TV stations reached Walla Walla. Fred was exasperated by the day's ordeal and by the uncertainty of his situation. He asked J. C., "What are we supposed to do in the morning?"

But by the next morning, Fred felt better. After lockup, he and Smiley had talked and Smiley had given him some advice: "Stay away from lifers and niggers and don't fuck around with drugs until you know people. If you talk to cops, stay at least ten feet away. Otherwise, you'll get pegged for a snitch."

Smiley even invited Fred to "prospect" for the bikers' club. Fred said, "I could slide right in." The conversation and the invitation must have been reassuring because Fred felt safe enough to undress and sleep in his underwear. Some fish sleep in their clothes for months.

Despite his new biker friends, Fred ate breakfast with Ajax at a table well outside biker territory. Over tin plates of eggs and soggy pancakes, the two fish had a brief, guarded conversation about their situations. Fred left on his own, wandering up to the country-and-western club room where J. C. hung out. J. C. wasn't there, but Dave, a pudgy repeat offender who had arrived on Fred's chain, was walking around in the corridor. Fred told Dave that he was thinking about joining the bikers' club.

"Ahh, come on," Dave replied. "You don't have to do that to be a bad ass." Dave told Fred that he had some marijuana, and the two of them ducked outside where they shared a joint.

The marijuana made Fred feel indecisive and edgy. He didn't know what to do with himself. He had expected to have a prison routine of work or school or to have guards telling him to do this or do that. But "The Man" wasn't telling him anything.

It was too early for lunch, so Fred roamed the breezeway, hoping to run into somebody who knew about an available cell. He ran into the fish whose homosexual cellmate had barred him from their cell. "I know where there's a cell for sale," he said, "for $350, completely furnished. You give the guy $350, and he moves out."

"I know where there's three for sale," responded Fred, who was still determined not to pay. "I hear there's one guy in here who owns twenty-one units."

"Yeah," muttered the other man, "the state sends you up and then you got to buy a place to live. Ain't that a bitch?"

If Fred did have to buy a cell, he would have to borrow money from other inmates. His money, like that of all new arrivals, was still frozen in an inmate account at Shelton. Transferring it to the penitentiary took two to three weeks. In the interim, the newcomers either went without cash or borrowed from convict loan sharks. The usual interest rate was 50 percent, compounded weekly.

Prison loans were a risky business. Creditors with insufficient muscle or backing were likely to get taken for what they loaned. Borrowers who were slow to repay their debts invited bodily harm from their creditor or from the creditor's hired "bill collector." Payment was made in cash, prison-issue scrip, drugs, food, clothes, electronic goods, favors, or flesh. "Some guys end up paying out of their asses," explained one convict loan shark.

Fred decided to borrow. He wanted to buy some Marlboros, so that he wouldn't have to smoke the state-issue tobacco that inmates called "horseshit." J. C. introduced him to a loan shark, a menacing, muscular

black whose tough demeanor was softened only by the silk scarf that he wore wrapped around his forehead. Fred borrowed ten dollars and promised to pay back fifteen.

He figured that he would have no problem repaying the debt. He expected to receive eighty dollars a month from his mother, one hundred dollars a month from his father, and "whatever my old lady can afford."

The loan shark referred Fred to Trig, a wiry young black who owned a cell in 6-wing, the cellblock that housed most of the penitentiary's blacks. Trig's cell had an empty bunk because the previous occupant had run up some bad debts and had checked in to protective custody. Trig told Fred that he could move in on the condition that he provide the cell with a television set. Fred agreed.

He filled out a "kite," a form requesting an interview with Lieutenant Colombo. After a couple of perfunctory questions, Colombo approved Fred's move to Trig's cell.

A week after his arrival at the prison, Fred was called before the penitentiary classification committee. The committee, composed of Colombo, two prison counselors, and a prison teacher, determined an inmate's custody level, recommended school and work assignments, and inquired about problems.

"You've been confined to close custody inside the walls," one of the counselors told Fred, who sat alone, facing the committee across a wide table. "Your good-time release date is 1985. But you're going to have to work your way out."

The counselor told Fred that, on the basis of the tests that he had taken at Shelton, the committee recommended that he earn a general educational development (GED) degree and that he work in the building trades.

"Fred," interjected the teacher, "I think you should get high school knocked out."

Colombo asked Fred if he had ever done any carpentry work. "Yeah," Fred replied. "Okay," Colombo said, "I'll put you on the list."

Concluding the brief interview, the counselor told Fred that he should participate in the prison's alcohol-treatment program and gave him the director's name. Fred asked no questions and was excused. His five-minute interview with the committee was his first personal contact with prison staff. Unless he broke the rules, he was unlikely to talk to another staff member for months.

After the interview, Fred returned to Trig's cell, climbed into the upper bunk, and stretched out. Besides Trig, his cellmates were a "big black dude" and "an old white man." The black protected the old man, Fred explained, and in exchange, the old man gave the house coffee, cocoa, and fifty dollars a month for marijuana and cigarettes. "The old man never goes out at night," Fred said. "He's scared."

"In here, everybody shares everything," Fred went on, describing his new living arrangement. "If you ain't got no cigarettes, you smoke somebody else's. Trig is keeping me in weed."

The etiquette was the same in most cells. The tenants shared, but the owner decided who cleaned the house and took out the laundry, who had first rights to the sink and the toilet, who got the lower bunks that had a better view of the television set, and, finally, who paid and who got kicked out.

"So far," Fred said, "I ain't had to pay nothing to nobody." He planned to cover his drug debts by smuggling "white money"—regular cash—through the visiting room. He expected his mother to sweeten her first weekend visit with a little hard currency. "I'll take some Vaseline and keister it [insert it in his anus] if I have to, or I'll cut a hole in my coat," Fred said. "I'm going to buy weed with it. That's all you can do."

Thanks to Trig and pudgy Dave, Fred claimed that he was getting high every day. "Everybody's got dope," he declared, amazed that drugs were more plentiful in prison than they were on the street. "Even the old men got it. Most of it's just weed, some yellows [Valium], and cough syrup. I think, unofficially, they just let 'em have weed in here."

Tucking a pillow under his head, Fred found a comfortable position and lit up a cigarette. He looked as though he knew what he was talking about. "You know," he remarked, "a lot of the stories I heard were bullshit. There ain't none of that guy's cousins out to get me. They don't fuck with you here."

Reviewing his first week in prison, Fred said that he'd learned two things—"to hate queers and snitches. Otherwise," he continued, "everything's pretty mellow. I just stay out of people's faces. I thought I was going to have to come off the bus fighting. But it's not rough and tough like people were saying."

Fred took a long drag on his cigarette and exhaled slowly. When he spoke again, he sounded smug like an old con. "I was walking down the corridor the other day," he said, "and I was thinking, 'This motherfucker ain't no prison. It's a college. And you ain't got to pay for it.'"

Every Wednesday, a prison bus carries a load of prisoners from the "reception center" to the penitentiary. A tower guard, his rifle ready, watches as the new arrivals get off the bus. Another guard unlocks the chain that binds Fred to the two dozen other "fish."

After picking up their first-night necessities in the clothing room, Fred, Ajax, and the other new inmates wait silently during the count. After the count has cleared, Fred and the others assigned to 8-wing are led through the 9-tower gate, down the breezeway, to their cells.

Fred eats his first prison meal with Smiley at a table in "biker territory." Smiley owns the cell to which Fred has been assigned. The next morning, Fred starts a letter to his "old lady" but is too worried about finding another cell to finish it.

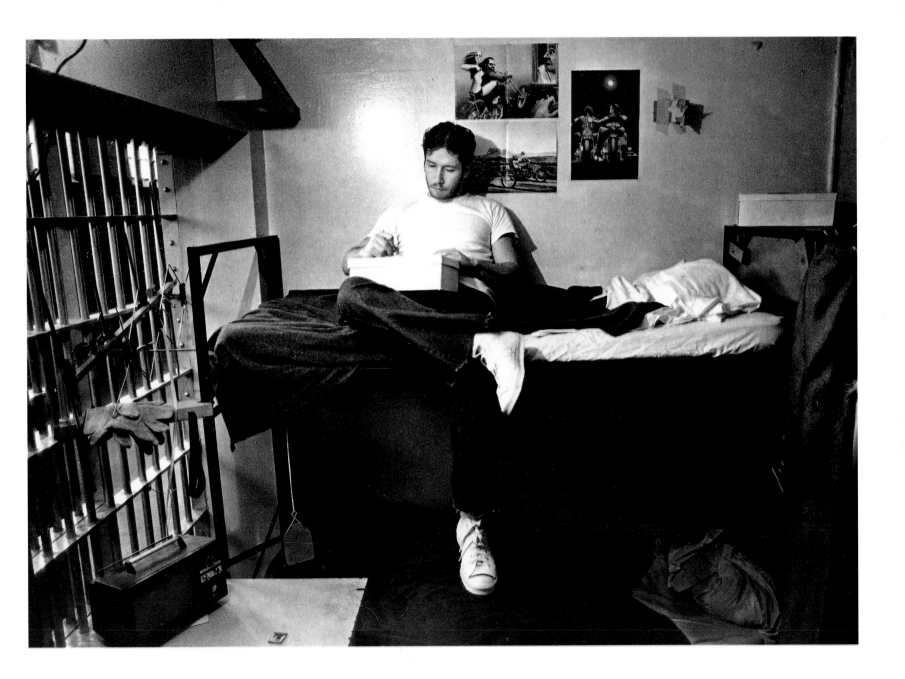

Having no routine to follow and not knowing what else to do, Fred roams the breeze-ways. A week after his arrival, in a five-minute interview with the penitentiary classification committee, he is told to finish high school and to join the alcohol-treatment program.

2

Browny: Convict

Love sent Browny back to prison at an age when most men are retired—love of a thirty-five-year-old woman who turned out to be a junkie.

"I was afraid if I didn't support her habit, she's going to leave me," Browny said, recalling the events that led to his latest conviction. "I was madly in love with her."

Though he abhorred drugs and distrusted junkies, Browny was persuaded to renew his criminal connections to buy some heroin. His girl friend said that they could make a lot of money. "Oh, Browny," she said, "I know half the hypes [heroin addicts] in town." But she poked most of the profits into her arm. Then one of their pushers turned them in to the police. Browny's girl friend got off lightly, but Browny, with a prison file four inches thick, didn't. He got fifteen years: ten for possession of heroin; five for possession of a gun by an ex-felon.

So, at sixty-nine, Browny was back inside the penitentiary that he had first seen as an eighteen-year-old boy. "Yeah," he admitted, "I'm a seven- or eight-time loser." Browny puzzled over his career as a strong-arm robber and thief. "I wish I could have figured out why I started out thieving," he said. "It's almost like it was an inborn thing."

Born Darrell Brown, the second son of "a chippie chaser who later got religion," Browny grew up in East Los Angeles. His earliest recollections included stealing change out of milk bottles and Salvation Army canisters. Twice convicted of auto theft as a juvenile, he was caught red-handed burglarizing an Oregon drugstore in 1926 when he was sixteen. He went to the Oregon State Penitentiary under the alias "James Mason." Everybody called him "Jimmy." "I only looked about fourteen," Browny remarked, recalling how the guards would call each other over to stare at him. "Some of the older cons would pat me on the butt, but I'd clout 'em."

Paroled a year later, he robbed a couple of gas stations and then got caught holding up a Seattle hotel. "We only got a hundred dollars altogether. It was just crazy," he said. "Crazy," he repeated, as if the memory of the ornery kid who victimized gas stations for small change amazed the gray old man who passed his days pacing the prison yard.

In 1927, Browny was convicted of the hotel robbery and was sent to Walla Walla. Five years later, he was back on the street in Salt Lake City, where he and a partner pulled a twenty-thousand-dollar payroll robbery. Six months later, in San Francisco, they were ready to rob the biggest bank in town when their luck ran out. Police burst through their apartment door and caught them with an arsenal of pistols, rifles, explosives, and even a machine gun. Browny went to Folsom Prison.

Out again in 1936, he took a one-fifth cut of seventy-three thousand dollars, the loot from the robbery of a Salt Lake City department store. But an earlier, two-bit, grocery-store holdup linked him to the big robbery. This time, he served six years at the Utah State Penitentiary. "I always thought if I had a good score, I'd buy into a good business," Browny said. "But it never worked that way. I'd always blow it. I was a damn fool, that's all I was."

From Utah, he went to Nevada where he did time for robbery and escape, then to Idaho where he served time for grand larceny, then back to California where a post-office robbery got him a seven-year sentence at Alcatraz in the company of some of the nation's most notorious criminals. Alcatraz transferred him to the McNeil Island Federal Penitentiary near Tacoma. Paroled from McNeil in 1963, he was soon caught robbing a nightclub restaurant in Los Angeles. The judge revoked his parole and returned him to McNeil. Then California claimed him for the nightclub holdup and sent the old man to Soledad in the midst of the murderous race wars then erupting in California prisons.

In 1975, Browny was free once more. "I didn't think I'd ever break the law again," he said, "never again." But he was wrong.

Like many older convicts, Browny lamented the way that prison and prisoners had changed. He had little use for prison reform and had even less use for the "sniveling crybabies" he saw coming through the gate. These guys were a new breed, he said. They ratted, they ganged up, they ripped each other off, they wanted to destroy everything, their word was no good. Browny did not understand it. He lived by the old convict code like the men he had known in prison fifty years ago. "In

those days, a guy would take his life to protect a friend," Browny said one afternoon as he paced a corner of the prison yard.

The comment reminded him of "a hype who found himself in the county slammer." The police wanted to wheedle information out of him: Who were his partners? Where did they get their drugs? Where did they sell it? So they laid a fix, a needle, and a syringe on a chair right outside the door to his cell. The man, who was seriously addicted, was afraid that he might break down and tell the police what they wanted to know, so he hanged himself. He wrapped the bed sheet around his neck and snuffed out his life to protect his friends. That's how strong the old convict code was: Better to die than to snitch. "No," Browny said, shaking his head, "convicts aren't like they used to be. In those days, nobody told The Man nothing."

The wind had come up, chilling the afternoon air, and Browny walked hunched over against the cold. He wore only prison-issue clothing—the lightly padded denim jacket and the loose-fitting trousers that were available to all inmates but were worn only by those who were too poor or too indifferent to have their own clothes. The denims sagged on Browny, who was only five foot six and a half inches tall. He weighed only 135 pounds and said that he had trouble keeping his weight up.

Yet Browny retained the tidiness of the dandy that he had been when he was young. He wore his gray hair parted neatly on the side and slicked back above his ears like a singer in a barbershop quartet. His complexion, sallowed by years spent in damp cells without sunlight, had the color and texture of beeswax. Browny spoke with a raspy voice that rose from his throat as if a lifetime of cigarette smoking had numbed his tongue and lips. On bright days, he protected his watery blue eyes with a pair of dated sunglasses with clear plastic frames. But that afternoon was overcast, and Browny's sunglasses were tucked neatly into the breast pocket of his prison jacket.

The more he talked, the more animated Browny became, as if explaining his code of conduct would somehow make others abide by it. "You never tell on anybody even if somebody snitches on you," Browny insisted. "Even if you're innocent and somebody does you dirt, you never tell nothing. But if you do get snitched off, either you or your friends get back at the rat. Somebody takes care of him even if it's just putting a snitch jacket out on him."

Browny lived in 4-wing, a block of five-by-eight-foot, one-man cells housing those who were old, disabled, insane, or too cantankerous to get along in a four-man cell. In comparison with other inmates' cells,

Browny's "house" was threadbare. He had no radio, tape recorder, television set, coffeepot, or pinups. His cell contained just the necessities: a few toiletries, a couple of library books, a mirror, a calendar with the days crossed off, some envelopes printed with the prison's return address, the small stool that served as a chair for the writing table, and a ladder for climbing into the five-foot-high concrete alcove that held his bunk. Browny offered his occasional guest the wooden stool while he retired to the only other sitting place in the cell—the toilet. He had covered the tiny writing table with a blanket to keep the metallic cold from penetrating his elbows. Overall, his cell was nearly as empty as it had been the day that the state gave it to him. "I travel light," he explained.

When the prison upholstery shop folded in September 1978, Browny was out of a job. Unemployment bothered him. He had spent his evenings planning the next day's work, figuring out how he would fit the cloth to cover a certain chair or couch. Now the days were long and boring. "Not working, I just can't get myself a routine," he sighed. "That's what a fellow needs, a routine, a schedule, something to do."

He whiled away the idle hours reading "a lot of trash fiction," taking long walks, and watching other inmates play sports, particularly baseball. He loved baseball. At McNeil, he had taken a course and had earned his card as a member of the National Association of Umpires. "If umpires are officiating good," he said enthusiastically, "they help to make a good game."

By choice, he was a loner. Unlike so many others, he did not get involved in the scheming for the prison highs—marijuana, pills, and "pruno," an ersatz wine quickly made by combining yeast, sugar, and fruits or vegetables and allowing the mixture to ferment. "I don't want to get high in here," Browny said flatly. "What would I do?"

When he spoke with other inmates, he was cautious. "I never ask a guy what he's in for," he said, "but I try to find out. Just because a man isn't a stool pigeon doesn't mean he's all right. You see, normally I don't talk to rapos [rapists]. In fact, most of your thieves wouldn't have anything to do with rapos in the old days."

In the evenings, Browny went to the television room, a small, brick-walled enclosure where wooden benches faced an elevated color TV screen. There were never many viewers since most inmates had television sets in their cells or club rooms. Those who watched in the television room had to strain their ears to hear above the din that spilled over from the adjacent recreation area. Browny came to watch the

news. On weekends, he altered his television habits by going to the movie shown by the recreation department. Wallace Beery was his favorite actor.

The Black Prisoners Forum Unlimited showed racier films, even some X-rated movies like *Deep Throat,* but they charged admission. Since losing his job in the upholstery shop, Browny had no income. He was content with the free films, which were far better than the ones that he had seen at Alcatraz. "Oh, God, they were horrible," Browny recalled. "They'd show these phony musicals where the guy would just be about ready to kiss a girl and then he'd break out in song."

Browny's biggest vices, he said, omitting mention of the armed robberies that kept returning him to prison, were smoking and women. He smoked hand-rolled cigarettes—soft, gummy creations that he fashioned from the free tobacco provided by the state.

Though he had had many girl friends, Browny had never married. "When I got out, I'd find a woman and we'd shack up together," Browny said, "but I couldn't jeopardize her or any kids by getting married."

The woman whom Browny really tried to woo was his mother. He had seen her sporadically over the years, but their feelings for each other were complicated by Browny's transgressions. The last time that he had talked to her was in 1963, when he was paroled from McNeil. She was living in a California "old folks' home." He said that he imagined her in a wheelchair in a balcony room that looked out on a long driveway lined with trees. They seldom corresponded, so his memories of her were colored by dreams. He telephoned her once, long-distance, asking if he could visit. They had a brief conversation. He had never forgotten it. "The people here think I only have one son," his mother had told him. "I'd like to keep it that way."

Browny no longer knew if she or anyone else in his family was still living. It was likely that his parents, at least, were dead, but no one had ever told him so. The years in prison, the disgrace of continually returning there, and the wandering, wastrel life of the armed robber had severed Browny's contacts with the outside world.

But in the prison world, Browny had earned the respect of his peers. They had to respect a convict whose criminal career had taken him through nearly every prison west of the Rockies. Younger, tougher inmates gave him a leeway that others did not merit. A few even addressed him as "Mr. Brown." "If I do something they don't like," Browny noted, "they'll say, 'You know better than that, Browny.' They won't punch me."

But the attitudes of many younger prisoners puzzled Browny. They seemed so strange. "Guys who break the law got to expect to do time," Browny figured. "If I was foolish enough to get caught, then it was my fault. What else are they going to do with me? Let me go out and rob somebody else? . . . These prisoners nowadays, they blame the police because they got caught. Well, what are the police supposed to do? Not catch 'em?"

Aside from all the "snivelers," Browny went on, "there's prisoners ratting all the time. And the ones that don't rat all the time, they'll hush up until something big happens, then they'll rat. On top of that, there's the radicals, who are down with this, down with that, down with everything. But they can't come up with anything better."

Browny's sentiments were shared by many of the older convicts, men in their forties and fifties who had no use for the young, impetuous men unable to make their peace with the world. The older men liked to be called "convicts." They resented those sweet-sounding names—"resident," "inmate," "offender"—that were made up by people who wanted to pretend that prison was not prison.

These euphemisms had become the basis for a sort of status system. "The resident," explained Jesse, a wizened Alabama black who spat out the word as if it had a foul taste, "is somebody who's just here. An inmate is between a resident and a convict. He's a guy who sees something and may or may not say anything. And a convict is a guy who minds his own business. If he sees someone get his throat slit, he'll step right over him without a word. But, on the other hand, if it's the convict's beef and he gets pushed too far, he gets the motherfucker right then. He cuts his damn head off." Jesse said that the problem with "these residents is that they got a hard-on for the judge, the prosecutor, and the rest of society. They're always crying bum beef. Me, I know I'm paying debts to society for what crime I committed. I believes in punishment. I made seventy thousand dollars on my last caper and this is just part of the cost of doing business."

Arlin, a crew-cut, middle-aged robber who boasted of once running 8-wing without a single stool pigeon claimed that the penitentiary had no more than "two hundred who are still old convicts all the way through." He blamed the reforms for helping to create the "militants, extremists, and rats." "I've seen the thing completely turn over just like an airplane when it sputters and runs out of gas," Arlin said. "That's what happened with this inmate self-government trip. What they ought to do is march us out in the yard, gut the cells, and take out all the crap.

If I were running this joint, I wouldn't let 'em have all this bullshit." Arlin even objected to "contact visits," a visiting-room reform that did away with screens and partitions and allowed inmates to touch and caress their loved ones. "I don't like to see a motherfucker getting his prick sucked off," he growled.

Since Browny never had any visitors and hence was never called to the visiting room, the other inmates' visiting-room activities did not disturb him. But he was conservative about sex. He was repulsed by the practice of having a "kid"—using another prisoner like he was a woman. "I couldn't even get an erection," he said.

He was also bothered by the advent of female guards. So far, none of them worked in the cellblocks, but there were rumors that they would. "They're throwing sex at you," Browny said, marveling at the foolishness of hiring women to control men who were denied women. "It's just not healthy. I don't approve of it at all."

Browny blamed much of the penitentiary's violence on the clubs—the cliques of inmates who grouped around con bosses or divided along racial lines in an effort to protect themselves, to manipulate others, and to secure whatever privileges the administration bestowed. In the strongest clubs, if one member had a beef, they all had a beef. "They egg each other on," Browny said. "A guy's friends will say, 'Don't take that dirt. Go in there and get that son of a bitch.' Then somebody ends up getting stuck."

Because he refused to belong to any club, even the innocuous Senior Citizens' Club, Browny was on the periphery of penitentiary politics. He owed no allegiance and got no spoils. By the same token, he refused to patronize the club concessions. "The men are using each other," he objected. "They all want to make a fortune off of us."

More than anything else, Browny blamed drugs for destroying the convict code. "These guys, they'll lie and cheat each other for a fix. They'll stick a shiv [knife] in their best friend," he said. "You didn't break your word like that years ago," Browny continued, shaking his head. "When you told somebody something, it had to be it. Your word had to be good. If your word wasn't good, you went down as not able to be trusted. Your word was your bond. It was all you had to stand on. But now, 80 percent of these guys in here, their word don't mean anything."

Unlike many of the younger inmates, Browny had no quarrel with the guards. He even had a grudging respect for some of them and silently took their side when some kid yelled, "Hey, motherfucker, open my door."

When Browny was first sent to Walla Walla in 1927, convicts did not go around cursing the guards, "because if you did, you went to the hole and you were liable to get an awful, awful beating. There were none of these courts or hearings. If a cop said you did it, you did it."

In those days, if the guards really had it in for a convict, they exiled him to "Old Siberia." A cement block of six cells that was roofed but was otherwise open to the elements, Old Siberia stood alone in the corner of the Big Yard. "It was colder than hell out there in the winter," said Browny, remembering how Old Siberia's tenants jammed newspapers into the cracks around the cell doors. "Sometimes a guy would spend a couple years there."

Browny appreciated the veteran officers who would turn the other way when convicts caught another con prowling around their cells. The old guards knew that the convicts would take care of the guy, he said. Real convicts might steal the state blind, but they did not steal from each other. "You never touch another con's stuff," Browny insisted, "never."

With a fortitude that most cons lacked, Browny endured prison as if it was something that he deserved for getting caught. He was a special kind of convict, one who had the wisdom to stay out of prison but not the will to use it. He understood prison and adapted to it far better than he had ever adjusted to free society. Like many repeat offenders, he suffered from what one prison wag called "the concrete-mama phenomenon"—the habit of returning to prison like a child comes home to mother.

After all, prison offered what mother offered: authority, familiarity, dependence. Unlike mother, prison was cold and hard, but even so, the cold prison mother often nourished inmates who, in the real world, had nobody and were nobody.

Within her walled womb, they acted out their fantasies. They ran rackets, bossed clubs, became titled leaders in prison politics. They developed a camaraderie that in the end made them the heroes and everybody else the villains. Even inconspicuous inmates like Browny, who did their time quietly, earned in prison what they were denied on the streets—respect.

Some inmates became so enamored of mother prison that they could not leave. Guards noted that inmates on the verge of release often committed infractions that would ensure a longer stay. Sometimes, seemingly for no reason at all, men would walk away from the minimum-security building, an offense punishable by up to five more years in prison. Prison counselors said that they did it because they were

afraid of going out in the real world. "I've been released from this institution three times within the past fifteen years," explained one weary convict. "Each time, I found the problem of reentry into a free society more difficult. I found that becoming a normal citizen grew more and more complicated and strengthening old family ties was merely a dream."

A few inmates insisted on serving their full sentences and refused parole. Generally they were people who knew nothing but prison, like "the Spoonman," the grizzled old black who sat near the 9-tower gate selling gum, cigarettes, and notions, his huge portable radio playing at his side. He died in his bunk when he could have been free.

But Browny had no intention of staying in prison any longer than necessary. He had suffered two minor heart attacks at Soledad and was worried about his health. He did not want to die in prison. He did not want one of those public-assistance funerals where nobody came except for the prison guards who had been appointed as pallbearers. He did not want a numbered gravestone in "9-wing," the patch of consecrated earth between the prison hog farm and the dump.

Although he had at least five years left on his minimum sentence, Browny hoped that the parole board would make him eligible for work-release. He had written to three places in Seattle asking about jobs. Every day, he waited in line at the mail room, hoping to receive a favorable reply. "Right now I have about five prospects," he said one morning on his way to the mail room. He was confident that somewhere there was someone who would employ a sixty-nine-year-old high-school dropout who had spent most of his adult life in prison. "Even if they just give me a janitor job, I don't give a damn."

Pausing a moment, Browny leaned back on the heels of his polished prison shoes and stared through his sunglasses. He seemed to be looking at something far off in the distance, beyond the walls.

"Ya know," he said, "my biggest quarrel with the system is that guys get too much time. Putting in a large amount of time, it only makes you bitter."

Was he bitter?

"No, not anymore," Browny said. "I'm not bitter. I just want to get out before I die."

Eight-wing—an unruly, 408-man cell-block that has a reputation for escape plans, riots, and murders. Unlike Browny, most inmates share cramped, ten-by-twelve-foot, four-man cells.

33

34

The dirty, dangerous, and flooded showers in 8-wing are open three hours a day and serve more than four hundred men. All cells have their own toilets, but stall-less communal toilets are also provided in the recreation areas.

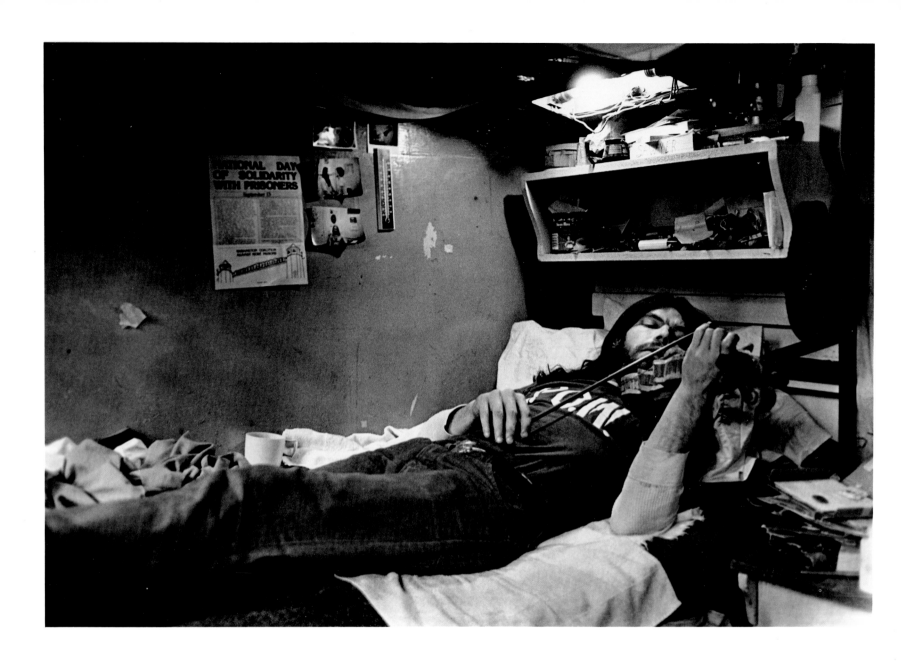

"Doing time" means filling a lot of empty hours. Eddie taught himself to make and play the violin. Inmates who can afford them are allowed to have radios, television sets, and other electronic time-passers in their cells.

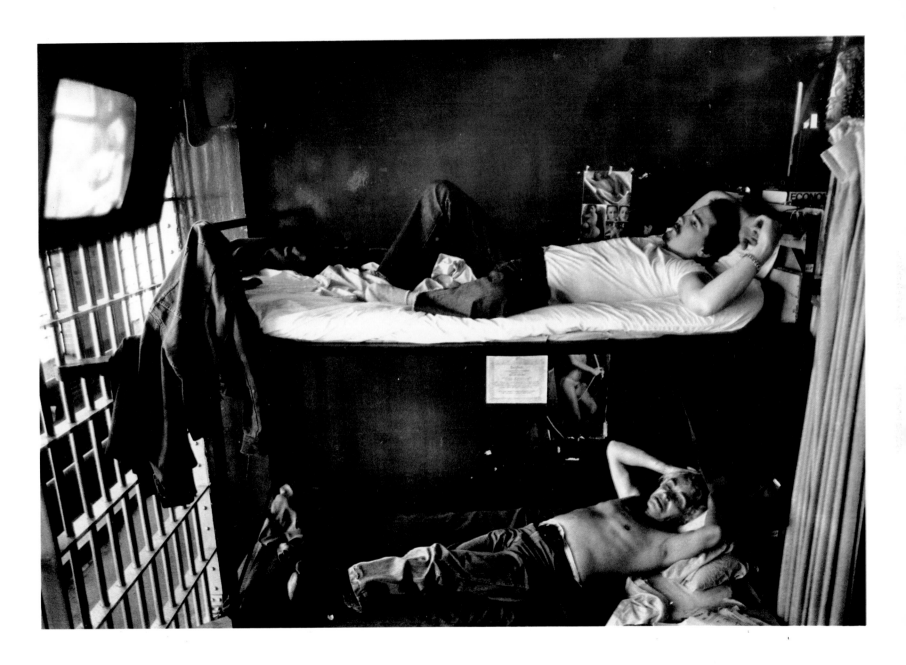

Some prisoners spend hours playing dominoes in the black prisoners' club room. Other inmates work out with weights to pass the time.

Inmates with bulging muscles are less likely to be hassled and more likely to get their way. Many inmates have exceptional physiques.

3

Kenny: Con Boss

Kenny Agtuca was behind bars not so much because of a crime—though there were many of them—as because of an attitude that he characterized as "doing the opposite of whatever I was told to do."

A natural leader and an adept organizer, Kenny tolerated no authority but his own. From his position as president of the lifers' club, the twenty-six-year-old habitual criminal ran life inside the walls. He had the power because he had "backing"—the ability to muster scores of other inmates behind him and to shape those inmates to his will.

On the street, he had a record that included vandalism, burglary, assault, and "a whole slew of robberies." His record inside the walls included rioting, hostage taking, assault, attempted escape, and, according to some, murder. Kenny's power increased as his list of prison exploits grew.

His reputation as a prison hero was established shortly after he was sent to Walla Walla as a teenager. On 4 July 1973, he and two other inmates scaled the penitentiary water tower and frustrated prison officials by refusing to come down until their demands were met. They stayed aloft for forty-three days.

Five years later, Kenny leaned back in his office chair, lit up a cigar, and recounted the water-tower episode with obvious relish. He had begun that day in segregation where he was being confined for punching a guard. During exercise hour, he and another inmate had tricked a rookie guard into taking them near the door. At the right moment, they burst out, climbed the eight-foot wall surrounding the segregation unit, and, as warning shots rang out, sprinted to the Resident Council office.

"We locked the door with our own lock," Kenny recalled. "Then we stripped down an electric typewriter, wiring it to the door to create an electric shock. But still, we were stuck down there, looking a loser, when someone suggested we climb the water tower. So, we went back outside. Half the population got around us and took us out to People's Park."

To discourage such climbs, the legs of the tower were sheathed in sheet metal rubbed with grease, and the ladder going up the tower was cut thirty-five feet short of the ground. Kenny and his companions overcame that problem by throwing garden hoses over the ladder's lowest rung then climbing up hand over hand. "About twenty-five to thirty guys tried to get up," Kenny said, "but only me, Gaze, and Harstad made it. Custody made a couple of attempts to stop us, but everyone ran 'em off."

Rather than rush the tower with guards, Warden Bobby J. Rhay decided to ignore the trio and wait them out. For a while, he managed to joke about it, saying that the three convicts had climbed the tower to get a better view of the town's annual fireworks display.

Meanwhile, other inmates used rope slings to transport provisions to the tower-sitters. They sent up food, chairs, blankets, magazines, a radio, candles, and marijuana. When guards tried to halt the supply line, Kenny and his two companions used slingshots to bombard them with rocks, lug nuts, eggs, and doughballs. The three of them lettered a huge banner that they hung from the tower railing. Visible from miles away, it read: "FREEDOM."

"We smoked weed, listened to tapes, went swimming in the tank, and cooked steaks over a little bit of gasoline in an Almond Roca can," Kenny said. "We even made pruno and lowered it to the ground so people could get drunk."

Tired of pretending that the six-week tower episode was a joke, the prison administration capitulated, meeting the trio's demands for amnesty and for release from segregation. Soon afterward, the water tower was dismantled and was moved outside the walls. Kenny had won.

There were some inmate bosses, tough guys jealous of their own power, who claimed that Kenny was just one of them, a strongman among strongmen. They argued that all the "club heads," the presidents of the penitentiary's rival groups, controlled the temper of the prison. No way, they said, could one guy decide "what goes down."

But that view was not shared by the guards nor by most of the inmates. It was certainly not shared by those inmates who had crossed Kenny or his fearsome sidekick, Al Gilcrist. A two-hundred-pound muscleman with a Fu Manchu mustache, the twenty-three-year-old Gilcrist

was the "business manager" of the lifers' club. "Kenny and Al are running the joint now," said a cautious convict who kept close to his cell. "You don't mess with them. When they're mad at you, you can't talk to them. Kenny and Al, they just don't care."

"Murder power" made Kenny influential, according to an inmate who had once contended for control of the lifers' club and who now languished in protective custody. "He'll kill you if he wants to," the inmate said. "He's not afraid of sticking anybody."

Guards agreed. "Agtuca and Gilcrist are powerful because they're willing to off you, even in the face of insurmountable odds," said a veteran officer who had guarded the two during their long confinements in the hole. Other guards said that, when Kenny got angry, he literally foamed at the mouth. Even Gilcrist, whose cool anger showed itself in brute strength, admitted, "Yeah, Kenny nuts out."

"I have a very bad temper," Kenny conceded one morning as he thumbed through the paperwork on his desk in the lifers' club office. "All my life I've been that way. I get so mad I want to kill somebody."

Some people said that he had killed and gotten away with it. Seven inmates had been ready to testify that Kenny had fatally stabbed another inmate in a June 1974 dispute over a domino game. But, when one of the witnesses was later stabbed, testimony evaporated. The day before the trial was to begin, another inmate confessed to the killing. Although the prosecutor called the confession a "phony," he dropped the murder charges against Kenny and shelved the case.

Kenny would have been charged with murder again in November 1976, if the victim, a "friend" that he and Gilcrist had lured too close to the bars of their segregation cells, had died. But, miraculously, the inmate recovered from thirty-two stab wounds, and so Kenny and Gilcrist were convicted of assault. At the trial, during which a booby-trapped cigarette lighter blew off a guard's fingers, they repeatedly disrupted the proceedings by spilling water, ripping their clothes, and jangling their chains. "We were mad," Kenny recalled.

There were rumors that Kenny had set up the September 1978 slaying of Richard Anderson, the biker who had been stabbed to death as he and his bike-club "bros" marched past Lifers' Park. Some said that Kenny wanted to avenge a beating that a group of bikers had given a lifer. Others said that Kenny wanted to serve notice to the rival bikers that he and the lifers were ruling the prison.

Kenny admitted that he knew about the murder plans beforehand. He said that he'd tried to dissuade his people from violence. "But some people on the fringes didn't honor their word," he said. "Richard got cut off. Somebody saw an opportunity to dust him and they dusted him. In institutions, the innocent are notorious for being the victims." Though no one accused him of wielding the fatal knife, one guard claimed that Kenny was the man who stepped in front of Anderson, thus cutting him off from the rest of the bikers.

Two days later, Kenny spoke before an inmate assembly hastily called in an attempt to calm the tense prison. "The lifers' club takes the direction of cooperation with everybody in the institution," Kenny said. "The direction for all of us should be outside the gate. All we're doing with rumors is pulling our own trigger." Smooth and self-assured, Kenny spoke hoarsely in a deep, guttural voice that commanded attention and, sometimes, caution. It was not the kind of voice that invited questions.

Kenny was short, compact, and sinewy. He retained some of the Filipino characteristics that he had inherited from his father—brown eyes, thick lips, and wavy, dark hair. For a while, he had boxed, working out in the prison gym under the tutelage of an ex-prizefighter. His one-man cell in the admissions wing was crammed with an opulent wardrobe of sport clothes, including a stylish white suit that he wore on special occasions.

Kenny directed operations from his office at the lifers' club, officially called the Lifers with Hope Club. Ostensibly open to all inmates sentenced to life imprisonment, the club had a membership roster of more than four hundred convicts. But in practice, Kenny, Gilcrist, and their coterie of henchmen were the only ones who regularly frequented the premises. Running unopposed for a second term as club president, Kenny took the credit for reviving the club. "I don't think there's anybody else who can keep the wolves out of here," he said.

His second-floor office in what had been a prison dormitory was furnished with a couch, television set, radio, typewriter, adding machine, and pool table. His office window overlooked Lifers' Park, where inmate monitors were stationed to warn him when guards approached. Two prison transvestites, one hired as a secretary and the other as a maid, staffed an outer office where people waited to see the boss. At the old dormitory's first-floor entrance, a notice read: "Non-members must be escorted at all times. No exceptions." The notice was signed "Kenny Agtuca and Al Gilcrist."

"We've got people all over the joint that inform us of what's happening," Kenny said, explaining his operation. It was true. Within seconds,

his runners could summon other inmates to his headquarters. They came quickly, sometimes half-dressed and half-showered. Kenny did not like to wait.

Besides having power over other inmates, Kenny had clout with the prison administration. He frequently asked for and usually got impromptu meetings with the associate warden in the control room. Kenny used the meetings to press inmate grievances about food, visits, segregation procedures, and any number of other topics. He was fond of saying that he and his men "kept the lid on" the prison, implying that if things did not go his way, the lid would come off.

Guards grumbled that Kenny used his leadership of the lifers' club to blackmail the prison administration. Even Warden Spalding conceded that "there have been some people that you better not lock up in segregation because it was going to create problems." The problems occurred when guards went to arrest a club president and found him surrounded by his troops. "I could abandon the club concept today and they'd still have power," Spalding said. He saw the clubs as an extension of the traditional inmate "con boss," the tough, intimidating guy who decided that he was going to run things. "If you've got a con boss who decides he's in charge of the kitchen and he's going to hire and fire, what do you do to stop him?" the warden asked.

Spalding faulted past administrations, frustrated by the lack of work and educational programs, for using the clubs as a management technique. "When you sit down and negotiate, you lose control," he warned. Yet Spalding continued to attend weekly "agenda meetings" with inmate leaders. Kenny said that the warden had to come because the inmates, not the guards, ran the penitentiary.

Spalding did not dispute that statement. "It's a well-known fact that the inmates control the inside of the institution," he said. "If you've got five hundred inmates standing in front of the front gate and five hundred inmates standing in front of the back gate, you aren't going to get in. The staff doesn't own a piece of ground in there, not an inch. Unfortunately, that's why we're in a constant negotiation process."

Spalding's predessor, Warden Vinzant, had allowed Kenny and some other lifers to put together an interracial group of persuasive inmates euphemistically known as the Race Relations Committee. The RRC, as it came to be known, tried to prevent disputes from erupting into gang warfare by allowing the disputants to settle their differences one-on-one with their fists rather than with shanks [homemade knives]. If the RRC heard that two enemies were "packing iron," Kenny explained,

"we'd bring 'em to a secluded place along with their cliques of friends, make 'em put down the shanks and fistfight. Everybody can learn to shut up if they get a fist crammed in their mouth enough."

In theory, RRC intervention allowed the belligerents to save their lives while protecting their honor. After all, Kenny pointed out, "If someone calls you a stool pigeon or a faggot, you got to fight." When the fight was over, the RRC sought assurances that the score had been settled.

Some inmates were skeptical about the RRC's role. "All they want to see is a fight," contended a young burglar. "They aren't going to make no big effort to straighten it out."

While Kenny and his lifers ran the penitentiary in fact, the eleven elected members of the inmate Resident Council ran it on paper. In the heady days of prison reform, the council had achieved near parity with the prison administration, setting up a virtual commonwealth of convicts. But a 1978 "memorandum of agreement" signed by both parties restricted the council's powers. The memorandum stated that "penitentiary residents will be afforded a meaningful and responsible role in the decisionmaking process which affects their lives, to the maximum extent consistent with the legal duties of the Division of Adult Corrections and the Penitentiary."

The president of the council was Joe Allen, a likable, conscientious, fifty-four-year-old habitual criminal who readily admitted that he had been "a pretty successful gambler, pimp, and dope fiend." Easily tired, he walked with a limp, favoring a left foot crippled in infancy by polio.

With the support of Kenny and the lifers' club, Allen had squeaked into office by less than fifty votes. A lifer himself, he called Kenny and the other lifer heavyweights his "surreptitious police force" and relied on them for the backing that he lacked.

As council president, Allen was burdened with much of the legitimate prison business that bored Kenny. Allen was the man whom inmates badgered with gripes about the visiting room, poor pay, shoddy food, faulty light or heat, lack of medical attention, and a host of other problems. "They figure I got more juice with The Man," Allen said. "I'll take it up with the associate warden or the shift lieutenant if it's not bullshit. But it often is bullshit."

By virtue of his position, Allen signed the hundreds of memos that inmates and clubs generated in hopes of securing permission to do what they wanted. There were memos clearing special visitors, memos permitting inmates like Kenny to be out of their cells during the count,

memos authorizing purchases of cake and cookies or granting approval to plant rose gardens.

Allen knew that many of the memos would get nowhere, but usually he signed them rather than argue. "Look," he explained, "a lot of these guys are used to shopping in a supermarket, just grabbing the things they want. They won't listen. I just can't believe the shit some of them are asking me. They're just like little kids. And a lot of them are stupid. They tear up their houses. If they want to tear something up, why don't they go out to Industries and tear up the fucking license plates?"

Noting that he took "more flak from convicts than anybody else," Allen figured that inmates would win few favors by cursing or threatening the prison administration. He believed in playing the game by at least some of The Man's rules. "If you go in there demanding something and they say, 'Fuck you,' what have you got left?" he reasoned. "When it comes down to it, the only two options you get in here is lockup or riot. And that lockup is a whupping."

One of Allen's biggest headaches was overseeing the inmate store, a windowless cinder-block building commonly called the "coke shack." The store sold cigarettes, soft drinks, popcorn, and potato chips as well as products like peanut butter, honey, cookies, coffee, marshmallows, flavored orange drink, shampoo, and mouthwash. Its profits went into the Inmate Welfare Fund, an account administered by the Resident Council.

Allen, the other council members, council clerks, and store workers drew salaries of up to $125 a month from the account. Yet despite an average daily gross of $2,000 and a hefty markup of 18 to 25 percent, the store often lost money. "There's some guys we have to let go," Allen said, conceding that some store workers pilfered too much or, pressured by inmates whom they either feared or favored, gave too much away.

While Allen ostensibly presided over inmate government, Kenny and his pals ran a thriving illegitimate business in drugs, protection, extortion, loansharking, debt collection, real estate, and sex.

The legitimate tip of the business was the franchise that the lifers' club had to sell candy bars and soft ice-cream cones. Kenny pointed out that the lifers pumped $550 a month into the inmate economy by employing candy and ice-cream vendors, office help, and gate men and grounds keepers for Lifers' Park. "If we didn't give the guys a job, they'd be out on the breezeway," he argued. But most of Kenny's men were usually employed making drug deals.

Although possession of drugs was a serious infraction of prison rules,

marijuana was so common that it was a basic unit of the inmate economy. In 1978–1979, a "nickel bag" of marijuana—two tightly rolled joints—equaled $5.00 in cash, or $7.50 in prison-issue scrip or in a cash transfer (an authorized form that moved money from an inmate's personal account to a club's account). Prison dealers preferred hard currency or "white money" because they needed it to buy drugs from their connections outside the walls. "Say you want to buy some weed," explained an inmate who regularly purchased marijuana from the lifers. "You tell the gate man and he'll let you in. You go upstairs and you pay for it with scrip, white money, or a cash transfer."

A lifer more candid than Kenny described how the club's drug business worked: Kenny and company collected eight hundred to twelve hundred dollars to buy a pound of marijuana on the street. After they smuggled it inside, they each took an ounce for personal use and then broke the rest into nickel bags. The passed the nickel bags on to the dealers who kept one bag for each three that they sold. "The lifers triple their money on the dope deal," he figured. "They cover their debts and the rest they split up. Then they kick back in their cells and things are cool."

Candy and ice-cream sales were used to circumvent the prison rules that prohibited reselling scrip, possessing cash, or transferring funds from one inmate to another. When necessary, drug purchases were disguised as candy purchases. Scrip legitimately collected for ice cream was sold back to inmates at a 50 percent markup. Cash transfers were written for candy and spent on drugs. Sometimes the lifers strong-armed weaker inmates into signing cash transfers as "donations" to the club. "They forced one guy to sign a five-hundred-dollar cash transfer at knife point," one guard recalled. "Then they gave him some candy."

Prison staff tried to monitor the clubs' financial transactions, but the inmates found ways to outsmart them. It was hard to tell whether checks drawn on the Lifers with Hope account and innocently endorsed by the club's civilian sponsor were being paid to a legitimate business or were being laundered through a third party to buy drugs.

Kenny and his lifers were willing to let the other clubs have a piece of the drug action, but free-lance dealers who let their business get bigger than their backing bothered them. One free-lancer whose business got too lucrative recalled how the lifers moved in on him. "Me and another guy were talking about getting three pounds of weed. We would have split fifteen thousand dollars. But then other people started to get involved, people who had a reputation for stabbing somebody at the

drop of a hat." To get out of trouble, the erstwhile dealer set himself up: He told a friend to tell the guards that he was carrying a knife and waited to get caught. Guards hauled him off to the segregation unit where he was punished with ten days of isolation. By the time he got out, the heat was off, and he was out of the drug business.

"If a dude is out there doing business and he ain't got no backing, he's going to get burnt," explained one experienced dealer. "If the lifers want our dope, they're going to get it. They'll take guys right out of the visiting room and make them shit it out."

Even with backing, the drug business can be an "ass whipping," said another dealer. "If you're going to sell dope, you got to be ready to kill somebody. Because if somebody owes you something, you got to collect or stab them. Otherwise, people will walk all over you. And you always got to be watching your back. Anyone who's got a pocketful of weed on him is susceptible to being robbed. That's why the population knows out front that when you're dealing drugs, you're packing steel."

Inmates slow to repay drug debts not only risked their lives but often found themselves owing new debts. "I owed some money to Kenny and Al for crank [amphetamines]," one speed freak recalled. "Actually I bought it from somebody else and he put me in a cross. So they jammed me one day and said I'd suck cock. I paid up."

Kenny acknowledged that "people in the club make money selling weed." He even admitted to dealing a "little weed" to friends, adding that "being in the position I'm in, I don't have to purchase any." But he denied that the lifers controlled the marijuana market like the bikers used to control the market in heavier drugs. "Most people who smoke weed have their own and sell it," Kenny insisted. Yet guards were convinced that Kenny had a hand in any big drug deal. "Power in here is the drug traffic and the muscle," said veteran officer Parley Edwards. "The surest, easiest, and quickest way to make a grubstake is drugs."

While marijuana made Kenny and his friends a tidy sum, harder drugs like amphetamines, cocaine, Ritalin, and heroin were more profitable. Inmate dealers sold amphetamines in twenty-dollar "papers" that contained five to eight tablets. "Angel dust," the tranquilizer PCP, was sold in ten-dollar papers. Users got more for their money by crushing the tablet, mixing the powder with water, and injecting the solution.

The heroin supply was irregular. Substantial sums of hard cash, sometimes two thousand out of the estimated ten thousand dollars inside the penitentiary were needed to set up a delivery. "It's like fucking," said one part-time junkie, "you get it when you can."

Inmates normally got inferior Mexican brown heroin that had been diluted so many times that it was less than 10 percent pure. Inside the walls, dealers diluted it even more, cutting it down to 2 or 3 percent purity with milk sugar or amphetamines. "Christ," remarked one user, "I've even seen them cut it with Ajax. It paralyzed a guy."

Like amphetamines or PCP, heroin was sold in papers. "You can determine how much is in the institution by the breezeway price," observed one officer. In 1978, penitentiary heroin averaged about fifty dollars a fix.

As many as fifty inmates paid that price when a supply of heroin came in. But the high, like the supply, was short-lived. Times had changed since the mid–1970s when an inmate "godfather" smuggled in thousands of dollars worth of heroin a week. "When I had dope," recalled a convict who had held the godfather's supply or "bag," "they used to line up at my cell like it was chowtime."

Heroin trickled into the prison, but marijuana came in in a flood. It got inside in hundreds of ways. It came concealed inside milk cans from the prison dairy, in provisions from the prison warehouse, in boxes of motorcycle and auto parts, in baseballs thrown over the prison wall, in the pockets of guards and other prison employees, in the vaginas of female visitors, and in balloons swallowed into the stomachs or "keistered" up the anuses of inmates returning from the visiting room.

Guards told stories of recovering keistered drugs by forcing inmates to bend over, spread their cheeks, and squat so that "their assholes wink at you." Inmates told stories of new guards who showed up to work, carried pounds of marijuana inside, and a month later left with ten thousand dollars and a new Cadillac. There was truth to both sides' stories. Drugs, especially hard drugs, often came in through the visiting room, and guards, especially young, rookie guards who spent far more time with the inmates than with their middle-aged superiors, had been persuaded to become "mules" who sneaked marijuana into the prison. "It's not strictly money. It's a friendship relationship," explained a convict whose mule charged him seventy dollars a lid. "The guy feels sorry for me."

Both sides agreed that stopping the drug flow was virtually impossible. "There's no way they can stop the drug business unless they lock us down twenty-four hours a day and there's no contact with guards," said one inmate.

After marijuana, the most common high was "pruno," a hastily fermented concoction of yeast, sugar, and fruit or vegetable matter. To

minimize the risk of detection, pruno was consumed as soon as it was ready. A batch made from tomato puree, a favorite, was ready in eighteen hours. Connoisseurs, however, preferred the three-to-five-day "wines" made from jam or jelly.

Some inmates made pruno in their cells, hiding the good stuff and leaving out a decoy batch for guards to find. Most of the time, however, pruno was fermented in the kitchen, where inmate workers had easy access to all the ingredients.

An inmate dishwasher famous for his "grape wine" used a kitchen washing machine. "I put the plastic container inside the machine," he explained. "Then I take some clothes, sprinkle them with baking soda, and put them around the top. The cops don't fuck with it because nobody can smell it. When it's done, I take a cup and just dip it in. I like to drink two or three cups each time, just enough to get a good glow on."

Pruno, which cost from five to twelve dollars a gallon, was cheaper than marijuana but more awkward to sell because it was bulky, hard to conceal, and unsavory if the yeast got stirred up. Even so, plenty of inmates drank it. It was not uncommon to see inmates staggering drunk in People's Park or passed out in the segregation "drunk tank." On occasion, pruno drinking led to fights, to assaults on guards, and to general chaos. "I've seen the kitchen crew so fucking drunk, they had to postpone chow," said one old-timer.

Kenny didn't bother with the pruno business. He claimed that he had quit drinking following "some drunken stupidness that led to a beef with some blacks." He had to conduct himself in a sober fashion, he pointed out. "If I go in and see The Man drunk, there goes my credibility."

But in the last weeks of 1978, whatever credibility Kenny had had with prison officials was exhausted. On the evening of 5 December, Kenny, Gilcrist, and Arthur St. Peter, a legendary convict whom they both revered as a father figure, dropped down a hole in Lifers' Park, scurried across the dirt basement of 8-wing, and crawled thirty feet through a tunnel that a dozen lifers had bored under the penitentiary's west wall. The guards were ready for them. When Kenny and Gilcrist failed to halt, they were stopped with shotgun fire. Wounded, they were carried back inside, first to the prison hospital and later to the hole.

Nursing a leg wound in his segregation cell, Kenny said that he had to escape because the Spalding administration had dashed any hope of an early release. "I thought the odds were in my favor," he said of the failed tunnel attempt. "But too many people were aware of what was going on."

In an October issue of the *Lifers' Newsletter,* Kenny had written: "If your foundation has rats, deal with it in a vigorously prosecuted manner." Convinced that "rats" had ruined their escape, he and Gilcrist drew up a "hit list." Some of the candidates were lifers.

Kenny, Gilcrist, and St. Peter remained confined in segregation, but others did their bidding. On 9 February 1979, a lifer was stabbed to death near Lifers' Park. Earlier he had told the associate warden that he knew his name was on the hit list. That killing was followed by another stabbing, by several assaults, and by rumors of another impending murder. Consequently, on 15 February, Warden Spalding locked down the penitentiary. Guards shackled Kenny, Gilcrist, St. Peter, and five other lifers, loaded them on a van, and transported them to Shelton.

A month later, Kenny Agtuca, the one-time tyrant of Walla Walla, was just another inmate in a federal penitentiary three thousand miles away.

Kenny presides over a lifers' club meeting.

Because of his position, Kenny is allowed into protective custody to assure some inmates who have "checked in" that he will guarantee their safety if they come back out. He also has ready and frequent access to the associate warden.

Inmates can make something dangerous out of practically anything, as this sample from one guard's collection of confiscated weapons shows. The source of Kenny's power is his control over the other lifers—his "murder power." He often reminds prison officials that he and his men "keep the lid on" the penitentiary.

Reddog claims that the diamond in his tooth marks him as a cocaine
dealer. Drugs, particularly marijuana, are so common that they are a
basic unit of the inmate economy. Many inmates smoke "weed" daily.

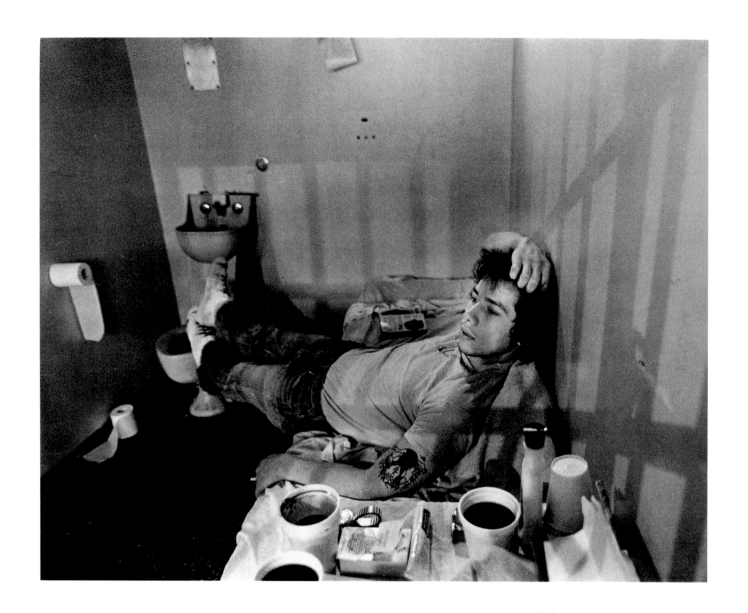

After his attempted tunnel escape, Kenny is confined to a segregation cell. He and Al Gilcrist, his enforcer, wait to appear in court, where both are convicted of being habitual criminals.

4.

Bobby: Biker

The best thing that ever happened to him, Bobby Tsow said, "was coming to the joint the first time." Being in prison gave him the opportunity to become a biker. Becoming a biker gave him an identity, a "big family of 'bros,'" and a commitment to the thumb-your-nose-at-the-world cause that he had admired for years. As a boy growing up in a series of foster homes and juvenile institutions, he had been fascinated by "those big, old, burly motherfuckers jamming down the freeway with a joint in one hand and a fifth of Bacardi in the other."

Before he went to prison, he said, he had been a lonely nobody, a two-bit robber, and a junkie. His criminal record included truancy, shoplifting, auto theft, and armed robbery, but he claimed that becoming a biker had helped him to clean up his act. Paroled in 1976, he moved to Seattle. He bought a 1968 Harley Sportster and joined the Gypsy Jokers, a club whose bylaws prohibited shooting heroin. "You get strung out on dope and you're liable to rip off your brother," explained Bobby, who credited the Jokers with keeping him off the needle and out of trouble.

But his trouble-free days with the Jokers ended in a tavern parking lot in January 1977. Bobby said that he had knocked out a guy's front teeth after the guy had ripped "my old lady's blouse." But the prosecutor said that Bobby and a partner had beaten and robbed an older man after offering him a girl for the night. The jury believed the prosecutor's story, and Bobby was returned to the penitentiary, convicted of second-degree assault.

It was 4:00 P.M. Friday, count time, and the Big Yard was closed to everyone but the bikers. Once a week, prison officials permitted up to five bikes and ten bikers to make test runs in the empty yard.

While most inmates sat out the count in their cells, the bikers powered their big Harleys around the quarter-mile track. Under the watchful eyes of the armed tower guards, they took turns riding the huge machines, stopping, starting, punching the accelerator, drag racing each other on the straightaway, banking hard on the turns. The yard's red-brick walls reverberated with the roar of their engines.

After tinkering with a gear adjustment, Bobby mounted his 1951 panhead Harley-Davidson and stomped on the starter. The engine caught fire immediately, and the leather-jacketed president of the Washington State Penitentiary Motorcycle Association, Inc., gunned the glossy black bike out into the yard. Circling and recircling the perimeter track, he sat low in the saddle, leaning back as if he had the throttle wide open on a long, lonely stretch of highway. "When you're riding on them bikes," Bobby said afterward, "you almost forget you're in the penitentiary—almost."

Though he grew up as a poor white, Bobby looked Mexican or Indian. He had an olive complexion and often wore his long black hair tied back with a red bandanna. He was big—six foot one and a shade over two hundred pounds. But, despite his size, Bobby was not as imposing as some of his predecessors. He did not have the cocksure, ruthless manner of some past biker presidents nor did he have the "murder power" attributed to other inmate leaders. His tough demeanor, exaggerated by his dark sunglasses, seemed thinner and less sure.

Like many of the bikers, he dressed in black. Under his black leather jacket, he wore a black T-shirt printed with the picture of a jester outlined in white. The T-shirt, like his bike and his tattoos, bore the abbreviated motto, "G.J.F.F.G.J."—"Gypsy Jokers Forever, Forever Gypsy Jokers."

Like the Hell's Angels, the Devil's Disciples, the Bandidos, and the other "outlaw" bike clubs, the Gypsy Jokers numbered themselves among the "one-percenters" who embraced biking as a life-style rather than as a hobby. "We're real bikers," growled Blinky, one of Bobby's Joker buddies. "We're not like them weekend warriors. Fuck those guys in the ass."

On the street, the outlaw clubs were often warring rivals, but behind the walls, united under the bike-club banner, the old hostilities were supposed to be forgotten. "In here, the bike shop comes first," Bobby said. "We're like a big family. We trust each other. In here, you know that you can kick back and forty people will be watching your back."

Regarded as the prison's closest-knit club, the bikers advertised their allegiance. Besides the leather coats and the club T-shirts, they wore heavy boots and dirty, sleeveless, denim jackets adorned with swastikas, flags, and their club patch.

Many sported tattoos of coiled snakes, of nude women, or of slogans

like "Born to Raise Hell." They called each other by nicknames such as Nuts, Kickstand, Spike, Face, Tugboat, Bulldog, Boogeyman, and T. Tommy Tuck. Sometimes, they publicly kissed each other on the lips "to freak out the rest of the population."

Bobby kept a biker "family album." It contained snapshots of Harleys, naked girl friends, and a New Year's Eve party where everyone was drunk, undressed, and giving the finger. "Bikers do what most people haven't got the nutsack to do," Bobby explained.

Like street bikers, the inmate bikers saw themselves as the last desperadoes of the Wild West. They scorned the hippie generation as much as they scorned middle America. Society, they said, was phony and two-faced. They took Hitler, history's most hated man, as their hero and defaced penitentiary walls with "ftw," the initials signifying their motto, "fuck the world."

In theory, the bikers' club was open to all races, but in practice, its members were white. Past biker presidents hailed the club as the prison's "white ethnic group." Its first bike, acquired in 1974, was dubbed "the nigger killer." Prisoners familiar with political ideology called the bikers "the Fascists."

What made the bikers tough, other convicts said, was "ratpacking." Even when the prison was calm, the bikers hung together in groups of three or four. When things were tense, they marched en masse. "There's no member gonna lose a fight. We believe in that," a brawny Bandido swore. "If one of us falls, there's going to be somebody there to help him get back up."

Yet ex-bikers hiding out in protective custody claimed that the club's profession of brotherhood was bunk. A former probationary member, tired of "them seeing how much shit I could take," said that the club's real motto ought to be "fuck your brother in the name of brotherhood."

A paunchy Devil's Disciple said that he had asked for protective custody when he finally got fed up with the bikers' pressuring him and his girl friend to smuggle drugs into the prison. Then he incurred their wrath by agreeing to testify in a prison murder case. "They put out a five-hundred-dollar contract on me," he said. "I'm sitting up on that tier waiting to be stuck. Every night I dream about waking up with holes in me."

Bobby dismissed bikers who checked in to protective custody as "rats." "The easiest thing in the joint is to make the bike shop the scapegoat for those stool pigeons," he said. Nevertheless, the bike-club president conceded that "a lot of guys checked in around the shit that

came down" in the mid-seventies. "From 1972 to 1976, it was killings, robberies, rapes, and fights," Bobby said.

In those years, the club's membership roster was full of toughs who could scarcely tell a Honda from a Harley. The club was a haven for enforcers, debt collectors, breezeway robbers, extortion racketeers, contract killers, and drug dealers—especially drug dealers. During 1975, the bikers demanded a cut of all prison drug transactions; if they didn't get paid, somebody got thumped. Years later, stories still circulated about bikers who tortured other inmates in the bike-shop vise, sodomized them in the darkened prison auditorium, or threw Molotov cocktails into their locked cells.

But in 1976, a genuine street biker took charge of the club. He banned heroin shooting and kicked out those who had no real interest in motorcycles. As one prison teacher delicately put it, "The bikers went into an industrial phase."

Under its new leadership, the bike club set up classes in engine repair, in cycle construction, in welding, in electronics, and in custom painting. The Vinzant administration helped the club to arrange to do upholstery, painting, and body work for outside companies. At the same time, the club mounted a vigorous campaign to convince prison officials and the public that they had forsaken their evil ways in favor of vocational rehabilitation.

A little bribe in the inmate editor's hand got the club front-page coverage in issue after issue of the sporadically published *Voice of the Prison*. Under a banner headline, the *Voice* reporter lauded the Washington State Penitentiary Motorcycle Association Schools, Inc., for its "remarkable record of leadership, unity and Brotherhood." The public-relations campaign even won favorable comment from state legislators who wrote back praising the club's "high training standards," "self-improvement efforts," and its "well-written and well-typed letters."

Some people, however, were suspicious of the bikers' transformation. Guards said that the bikers' good behavior and newfound interest in work were clever ploys to draw off the heat so that they could smuggle in more drugs. "Why should they let some guy go out on the breezeway and rob a little old man of his Timex watch when they can play goody two-shoes and make thousands of dollars in drugs?" one guard asked.

When Bobby became the bike club's president in the fall of 1978, the bike shop had more motorcycles than ever before, nearly two dozen of them. Most were heavy-chromed Harley choppers, painstakingly restored with scavenged or makeshift parts. One, dubbed "Brutus," was

a restored 1936 Harley worth ten thousand dollars, Bobby said.

But, while the club had more bikes, it had fewer members and less clout. Warden Spalding had taken advantage of the lockdown that he had inherited from his predecessor to move the bikers' workshop out of the maximum-security compound. Actually, he had had little choice: Guards demanded that the bikers' workshop be moved to a more secure area and threatened to walk out over the issue. With Spalding's approval, they stripped the biker clubhouse of cycles, tools, spare parts, gasoline, cutting torches, grinders, and welding equipment, confiscating some of it and moving the rest to a more easily supervised shop in the prison industrial area. Spalding hoped that the move would slow down the manufacture of prison weapons.

Keeping weapons out of inmate hands was a never-ending task. Convicts could make something dangerous out of virtually anything. They made bludgeons by putting a bar of soap wrapped with electrical tape in a sock; garrotes by attaching a sharp metal edge to a neck-sized loop of surgical tubing; chako sticks by using a short string to connect two wooden bats that, when twirled effectively, could club an opponent into unconsciousness. Other inmate weapons included "thumpers," short metal bars held in a tight fist; spears, broomsticks with razor blades fastened to the end; zip guns, pieces of pipe loaded with powder to fire bullets made from melted tobacco tins; and pipe bombs, short pieces of pipe stuffed with an explosive mixture of match heads, crushed Ping-Pong balls, and a nitroglycerine compound scraped from the backs of playing cards.

The main prison weapon, however, was the "shank"—a knife fashioned from a screwdriver, fork, spoon, steak bone, piece of wood, file, steel ruler, radio antenna, or practically any piece of scrap metal. "Anyone who don't have a goddamn shank when the heat is on is a fool," grunted Manny Parejo, the burly ex-boxer who headed the Chicano club.

The best shanks were sharp, double-edged blades that allowed the fighter to cut both ways. "The sharper it is, the less it hurts," explained a convict whose favorite weapon was an ice pick. "That way you can get one of those vital organs without getting a lot of screaming and shit."

The most feared weapons were guns. Guards and inmates alike estimated that there were a half-dozen pistols in convict hands. "It used to be when two convicts got in an argument, they said, 'Well, go get your shit,' and they were talking about a shank," a longtime guard remarked. "But an old convict told me, 'I'm scared to go and get my shank because I might come around the corner and meet a .38.'"

There were stories of disassembled pistols entering the prison through the visiting room and being carried back into the cellblocks in the inmates' anuses. But there were easier ways. "A guy on work-release picks up a gun downtown," suggested a sergeant. "He passes it to somebody who works in the dairy. That guy wraps it in a plastic bag and suspends it in a milk container. The guy inside who services the milk machine takes it out and hands it over to the guy who ordered it."

Although most guards and inmates accepted shanks as a fact of life, some convicts were as anxious as the guards to keep guns out of inmate hands. "There shouldn't be no guns in here," objected a tall, reserved convict scarred from shank fights. "These motherfuckers get too crazy." The tall convict said that he had bought a .22 caliber pistol on the breezeway for a hundred dollars, then quietly sold it for two hundred dollars to an inmate whom he knew would turn it over to the guards. That roundabout method enabled the tall convict to get rid of the gun without looking like a stool pigeon.

In the bikers' new workshop—a cluttered garagelike shed sandwiched between the prison laundry and the furniture-refinishing shop—there was still plenty of weapons material. But without a clever scheme, shanks and zip guns were unlikely to leave the shop. To get to their new workroom, the bikers had to pass through the 9-tower gate where guards checked their names, patted them down, and walked them through a metal detector. Cyclone fencing separated the approach to the bike shop from the walkways to the laundry and the metal plant. Despite this increased security, no guards patrolled the bike shop itself. A "point man" signaled the approach of guards or visitors so that club members inside the shop could quickly snuff out any marijuana cigarettes. Except for an occasional "shakedown crew," the bikers were left undisturbed.

Since the coming of the Spalding administration, however, they did not have much work. The new administration did not like all the activity generated by the bikers' custom-paint and cycle-seatmaking business. Guards argued that every part, motorcycle, or car that came into the bike shop could contain a stash of drugs. Bobby's denials were to no avail. "No drugs have been brought in by motorcycles or cars," he insisted. "There are plenty of ways to get drugs in without destroying our program."

But most of the bikers' program had dried up when Spalding canceled

escorted inmate business trips. With no one able to drum up business outside the walls, there were no sales.

Although their business had essentially folded, Bobby argued that club members were still getting an education in mechanics. He said that one Spokane transmission shop would employ any biker whom the club said was qualified. "Nobody in here wants to press license plates," Bobby said, frowning at the mention of it. "I want to give a guy something he wants to do in a good atmosphere where he can learn something and go out and get a job."

Bobby himself was not interested in a job, not even a job as a motorcycle mechanic. "I don't like to work," he said. He planned to return to the same business that he had run before he "got popped on the assault beef." He said that he had managed "a stable of four or five girls" who table-danced in topless bars. Though Bobby lost his stable when he went to prison, he figured that there were plenty of other women willing to work for him. "Women are a dime a dozen," he said, "and they are naturally fascinated by motorcycles. That opens the door. Then if you take a broad that looks right and teach her conversation, that's all it takes. You got to bring her what she wants to hear, what she wants to do, and what she wants to feel. Then you turn that around and she'll be doing that for you. Love and all that shit, that ain't about nothing."

Without much real work to do, the bikers spent most of their days lounging around the shop, drinking reheated black coffee, and smoking marijuana. A few tinkered with their bikes or rummaged through the spare parts stacked high on the shelves. The littered shop floor was crowded with Harleys in various stages of completion, some merely frames, others fully equipped with sidecars. "The biggest thing in here is boredom," complained Blinky, a gray-bearded biker who wore a black cap with a Harley emblem. "It creates a thousand conspiracies a day."

On weekends and evenings, when the industrial area was closed, the bikers hung around their old quarters, a cavernous brick structure that had once been the prison powerhouse. With the cycles and work tools gone, the old clubhouse looked bare and forlorn. The furniture was sparse: three couches faced a fuzzy television screen, a long table was strewn with outdated electrical catalogues, several chairs surrounded a worn table where the bikers played dominoes. A concrete staircase led to a loft where empty student desks were arranged before a sign that said, "WSPMA School, Walla Walla." A huge canvas picturing a fat Mexican bandit, the emblem of the Bandidos, separated the desks from Bobby's office and from some file cabinets. The cabinets contained "evaluation reports," biker-prepared forms that advised the parole board that club members had learned new skills in prison. The files were in disarray.

Two "prospects"—inmates who worked as servants until they were voted into the club—fetched coffee, supplied cigarettes, mopped floors, and generally waited on the needs of the other bikers. If they were accepted for membership, the prospects would be doused with crankcase oil and awarded a WSPMA patch. Bobby remembered his eleven weeks of prospecting as "a real whupping."

Fewer prospects, the genuine emphasis on motorcycles, and the uncontested move to the industrial area had all weakened the bikers' position as the most powerful prison club, but their failure to avenge the murder of Richard Anderson signaled their fall from the throne. Kenny Agtuca's lifers had been able to cut down a biker on a crowded prison breezeway, and the bikers had done nothing about it. More than one convict concluded, "The bikers ain't worth shit no more."

The slain "bro" was a sore subject with Bobby. "The night he got killed, I had to make a thirty-second decision not to let more happen," Bobby said, his voice hard and distant. "The guys in here wanted to go. But there's a time and place for everything to happen. I'm not going to have somebody die because of some stupid move. If I send somebody to deal with that, it's going to be a never-ending battle."

Bobby had his own reasons for not putting club lives on the line: His sentence was short, and he was eligible for minimum-security and for work-release. "My objective is the gate," Bobby said. "I'm not a career convict. I'm a motorcycle rider."

"Bulldog," a bike-club member and a Bandido.

63

This Bandido in full regalia is a visitor at the annual "Bikers' Banquet."

The prison bikers' club includes members of the Gypsy Jokers, the Hell's Angels, the Bandidos, and other "outlaw" motorcycle clubs. Rivals on the streets, they claim to be "bros" behind the walls.

Bobby shares a quiet moment with the bike club's
cat, "Knucklehead." "Nert" and "Kickstand" share a cell.

The prison rules that prohibit tattooing are often ignored.
Bikers are particularly fond of decorating themselves with
swastikas, four-letter words, and their club's name.

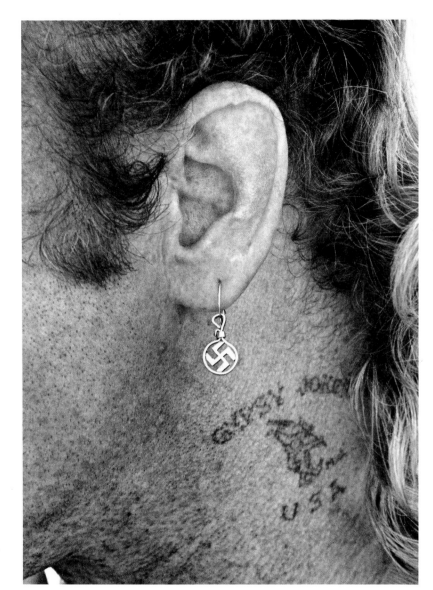

Bikers' lives revolve around their motorcycles. J. J. made this miniature chopper out of Q-tips and the aluminum foil from cigarette packages. Bikers only get to ride their bikes on Friday afternoons, but they spend hours in the bike shop tinkering on them.

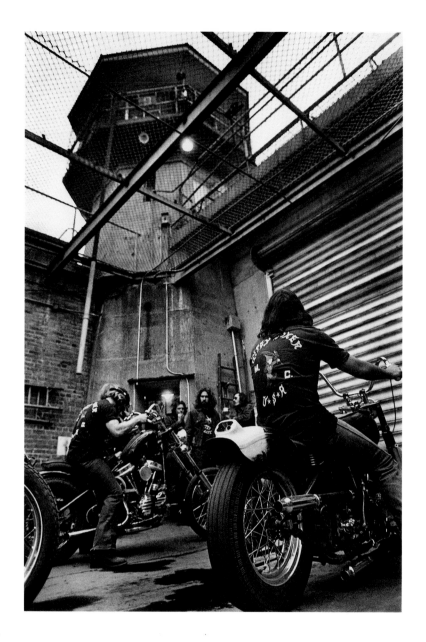

"Blinky," Danny, and Bobby joke while waiting for a prison biker's supreme moment —a chance to run his bike in the Big Yard.

5

Jimmy Joe: Ethnic

Jimmy Joe Lucero never figured that "trying to get a little respect by going upside some dude's mouth" would send him back to prison. As a matter of fact, the jury acquitted him on the assault charge but convicted him of burglary—Jimmy Joe had forced his way into the man's house in order to hit him. It was the kind of crime that would have gotten most people a suspended sentence and probation, but with Jimmy Joe's record, there was no doubt that, at the age of forty-one, he was going back to prison.

"Man, this isn't what's happening," Jimmy Joe groaned about being behind the walls again. "I been through hell. I been whipped on, jumped on by convicts and The Man. Fuck, I ain't no twenty years old."

Yet prison was Jimmy Joe's most familiar home. He got his first taste at fourteen when, unable to understand English, he skipped school, got arrested for truancy, and was packed off to a New Mexico reform school. "I was into a low-riding bag," he recalled. "When I got into the spoon [began shooting heroin], I really cut loose."

A joyride at eighteen led to eight months at the New Mexico State Prison, where his father had once done time for murder. Jimmy Joe went in remembering his father's advice: "Don't be a rat and don't be a fruiter [homosexual]."

Later, another auto-theft conviction sent him back to prison. Free again at twenty, he stabbed his brother-in-law in Nogales, Mexico. He was awaiting trial when he eluded a deputy's grasp, sprinted three blocks, and crossed the border into the United States. "You talk about a Mexican kicking up dust," Jimmy Joe said, laughing. "I got to the other side, turned around, and flipped the finger at them."

Armed with a syringe and a .44 caliber pistol, Jimmy Joe continued his career as a drug addict and robber. He served two years in the Colorado State Penitentiary for auto theft and followed that with a five-year sentence for robbery in New Mexico. "I did every fucking day of it," he said.

Paroled for Christmas 1965, Jimmy Joe returned to his boyhood home in Los Angeles where he drove a cab for a year. Then he quarreled with another brother-in-law. "He had an L-wrench and sent me to the hospital, but I killed the dude with a bone knife. I stabbed him thirty-two times," Jimmy Joe said without regret. The Los Angeles sheriff's office arrested him for murder but could not collect enough evidence to prosecute. They released him without charge.

For the next two years, Jimmy Joe traveled around the West—Seattle, Montana, Oklahoma City, San Antonio—trying to mend his marriage and keep a step ahead of the law. "I didn't believe in settling down," he said. "My thing was robbing, shooting dope, and dealing dope. I pulled robberies when I had no more to deal."

In 1967, Jimmy Joe was arrested in Albuquerque for shoplifting, burglary, and possession of heroin. New Mexico turned him over to California, where he was wanted for burglary, grand theft, robbery, and assault with intent to commit murder. Convicted of robbery, Jimmy Joe began a six-year sentence in the California corrections system.

While awaiting sentencing in the Los Angeles County Jail, he first encountered the Mexican Mafia, a fiercely loyal, cold-blooded gang of Chicanos who grew up in the prisons of the Southwest. "They asked me to join because they knew I was the type of person who didn't give a fuck."

They tested Jimmy Joe's mettle by ordering him to stab a member of a rival Mexican gang. He did it. Later, when he had a score to settle at the Chino Correctional Center, Jimmy Joe recalled, "I personally told the brothers, 'You take care of that dude.' Then I told that dude, 'You just signed your death warrant, you stupid motherfucker.' The guy never even got to his cell."

As a result of the stabbing, Jimmy Joe was transferred to San Quentin and then to Folsom Prison, where he "stuck another dude who hit a brother." He was paroled again in 1975 to the home of a forty-five-year-old nurse who had befriended him. "She bought me a 1970 Mark I Continental," Jimmy Joe said. He seemed amazed at the nurse's stupidity. "She fucked up. She shouldn't have bought me a car." He took off to Seattle to live with his wife.

In Seattle, Jimmy Joe claimed that he was finally starting to go straight. "I got in a methadone program, was getting welfare, paying my rent, and going to school day and night," he said. "I pulled only one robbery to send my old lady to visit her mom."

But a fight over a wristwatch led to the assault charge, the burglary conviction, and a twenty-year sentence at Walla Walla.

When Jimmy Joe arrived at the penitentiary in January 1978, he found the Chicano club an embarrassing disgrace.

The pliant inmates who ran the club were letting the bikers use the Chicano clubhouse as if it were their own private cantina. The bikers and their friends trooped into the gaily painted club room and made themselves at home. They ignored the pencil-and-ink sketches of club members, the wall slogans saluting Chicano power, the paintings of galloping gunfighters in wide-brimmed sombreros, the stern posters of Pancho Villa and Emiliano Zapata. The carnival atmosphere that they created made a mockery of the challenge printed below Zapata's somber visage: "What are you doing to defend the conquests for which we gave our lives?"

While a "point man" kept a lookout for guards, the intruders dimmed the lights and turned up the music. They sat at the tables, sipping pruno, smoking marijuana, and catcalling at inmates who put on a floor show. Prison queens, decked out in lipstick and rouge, go-go danced, shaking their hips to the tunes playing on the club's jukebox. For ten dollars, a customer could take a queen into the workshop and sodomize "her" beneath a mural of the Virgin of Guadalupe. "It was like a fucking nightclub," Jimmy Joe said, "with the bikers selling whores, weed, and pruno."

If guards came near, the point man yelled "Bulls!," so customers could hide their intoxicants, pull up their pants, and act discreetly. If the guards left without incident, the show went on.

"The Chicanos in here before couldn't handle it," Jimmy Joe said, recounting the club's humiliating past. "So when me and some guys from California drove up, things turned around. I cleared the books. The guys who had smut on them, I kicked out. I told the biker president that things were going to change, that he and anybody else got to be announced before they come into the club." When Jimmy Joe assumed the club's presidency, a sign appeared at the door: "Cultural Center," it read, "you can enter only with escort."

A dark, slender man with sunken cheeks and tight skin, Jimmy Joe looked as if the needle that he had stuck into his arm for so many years had sucked something out rather than put something in. Tattoos of eagles, coiled snakes, and lovers' names hid some of his scars but could not mask the two missing teeth on his lower jaw. A sharp dresser, Jimmy Joe fancied polyester pants and buffed black shoes. In the winter, he wore a three-quarter-length checked coat with a fur collar, the kind that an Ivy Leaguer might wear to a football game. Like many Chicano inmates, he secured his long black hair with a bandanna. In his four-man cell in 8-wing, he hung his bandannas on a wooden rack alongside a washrag embroidered "J. J." When on club business, he carried a green binder scrawled with the same notation that appeared on many of his belongings: "La EME."

"EME," the Spanish pronunciation of the letter M, was shorthand for the Mexican Mafia, whose cause Jimmy Joe carried like a badge of honor. It was a cause that worried state officials. Jimmy Joe said that one parole-board member had lectured him: "You're a hit man for the Mexican Mafia. They got you down for six stabbings. But listen, if you think you're going to get a Mexican Mafia in this prison, you're sick."

Jimmy Joe figured that the prison administration had him pegged as the joint's "godfather of the EME." But they were fooling themselves, he said. "To be honest with you, I'm the only EME in here. I swear on my mother. The other Chicanos here, they don't have the fucking balls to be members of the EME. They want to go home."

The EME's deadly enemy was a rival Chicano gang called Nuestra Familia ("Our Family") or NF. Both groups recruited in prisons, but their members came from different backgrounds. The EME's roots were in the Latino ghettos of Los Angeles, San Diego, and San Jose, while the NF's were in Mexico and the rural Southwest.

Jimmy Joe referred to NF members as "hicks" and hated them intensely. "If an NF guy drives up, he's dead," Jimmy Joe vowed. "I'd kill him in front of the warden. I'd kill him in front of Jesus Christ."

When Jimmy Joe did time in California prisons, the EME allied with the Aryan Brotherhood (the AB), a tight society of tough white convicts whose natural enemy was the blacks. The blacks allied with the NF. Each group advertised its allegiance with distinctive tattoos. The AB wore the lightning bolts sported by Hitler's SS stormtroopers. The EME wore the crouched Mexican eagle. The NF wore the "Pachuco cross," a Maltese-like cross whose origin went back to the Mexicans who had started the "zoot suit" riots in Los Angeles in the 1940s. AB members tattooed their affiliation on their necks, while the two Chicano groups wore their allegiance tattooed over their hearts.

One knowledgeable guard insisted that the blue teardrop tattoos worn by some Chicano inmates indicated membership in the EME. But Jimmy Joe, who had no blue teardrops, swore, "That's bullshit." Others said that the teardrops meant "I killed a nigger," or simply, "I did time."

Ruthless, fiercely loyal gangs like the EME, the NF, the AB, and the

Black Guerrilla Family (BGF) were feared by convicts and prison officials alike. At Walla Walla, penitentiary staff were thankful that their inmate clubs were the homegrown variety and not part of the national network of convict gangs that had turned California prisons, for example, into warring camps. Yet they recognized that convicts like Jimmy Joe could sow the seeds of wider, more violent gang warfare. "Look," explained a guard who had worked in the California prison system, "the majority of the people in a penitentiary never had people who gave a fuck about them. An EME guy pats another guy on the back and says, 'You're an all right motherfucker,' and he'll do anything for him."

Jimmy Joe ran the Chicano club until the summer day that Manny Parejo got out of the hole. A pugnacious ex-boxer whose massive shoulders tapered to a narrow waist, the twenty-five-year-old Parejo became club president as soon as he left "Big Red," the red-brick building that housed the prison's segregation unit. Parejo, who spoke no Spanish, used his muscle and his meanness to claim power. A habitual criminal convicted of rape and kidnapping, he said that his ambition was to be a "gangster."

Sheepishly, Jimmy Joe explained that he had agreed to step aside for Parejo. "I was just taking care of the club till Manny came back," he insisted. He would not say that he resented Parejo's rule because he knew that he did not have the muscle to overthrow him. So the two men maintained an uneasy peace.

Parejo boasted that, under his surly leadership, the Chicanos had become the most disciplined club in the prison. "Mess with us and it's like fucking with a rubber ball," he said. "We're the baddest motherfuckers there ever was."

Parejo said that the club was open to the penitentiary's seventy-odd Chicano inmates, except for snitches and those "who don't have heart." But after he took over from Jimmy Joe, the club's active membership shrunk to a dozen California Chicanos. On some afternoons, Parejo, shirtless, doped up, and sprawled in front of the color television set, was the only one in the club room. The others stayed away. "There's a lot of guys who don't go to the club since Parejo took over, because the first time you turn him down, him and his pals beat your ass," said a recently arrived Texas Chicano. A timid, middle-aged thief, the Texan had been assigned to live in Parejo's cell. He was kicked out the first night. "If you don't have no drugs or money, you got no business living there," the Texan said.

A Mexican national who quit the club complained that Parejo's California clique tried to control everything. "And they do it shitty," he said. "They make some people pay out of their ass to belong to the club. They don't get down honestly. They fucking stab you from behind. And any money the club makes goes in somebody's vein."

In the fall of 1978, Parejo's clique was allied with the lifers. The alliance gave the Chicanos backing that far exceeded their numbers in the population. It also ensured the lifers' cooperation in setting up drug deals, particularly deals for heroin. What the lifers got in return, guards said, was some cheap, but very able, hit men. Guards said that the Chicanos committed at least two inmate murders for their lifer benefactors. There were no convictions for either murder.

While the Chicano club dealt drugs and carried out enforcement contracts, the Indian club—officially the Brotherhood of American Indians—was undergoing a spiritual renaissance. Lawsuits won by Indian advocates had established that Indian inmates had the right to practice their native religion. In search of what they called "the old spiritual ways of our people," the Indians had obtained the prison administration's reluctant permission to erect a sweat lodge on the penitentiary grounds.

In early summer 1978, the Indians built their first sweat lodge on the grassy no-man's-land that stood in the lee of the prison wall. It was a simple domelike structure, scarcely eight feet in diameter, constructed of willow saplings and covered with canvas.

Whenever they could scrounge enough firewood, the Indians sweated. They began by rewrapping the saplings with the canvas sheets, overlapping the sheets several times. "You can't have any light coming in," said a young Makah Indian who wore a small leather "medicine bag" containing dirt, tobacco, and hair.

Satisfied that the lodge was dark inside, the Indians stripped naked, left their clothes bundled against the prison wall, and walked around the lodge in a clockwise direction. "You always go to the left," the young Makah explained. "It represents the circle of life."

Once the others had entered, he handed in a bucket of water and shovelfuls of rocks heated in an outside fire pit. The men inside picked the rocks off the shovel with a pair of antlers, dropped them into a hole, and sprinkled them with water, creating a cloud of steam.

The young Makah then joined the others in the lodge. There was

silence. Then, softly, they began to pray aloud. They prayed for Frankie's little girl, for the brothers in segregation, for guidance in the club. They concluded with a chant to the Great Spirit, whom they addressed as "O Grandfather" and "O Great One."

The teachings of the Great Spirit came to the penitentiary in the form of itinerant medicine men—elderly, white-haired Indians who arrived with weathered suitcases full of blankets, feathers, and leggings that jangled with bells. The medicine men spoke at "powwows" held in the club's "lodge," an isolated third-floor room in the admissions wing. On the walls were unsmiling portraits of Geronimo, Crazy Horse, and Sitting Bull. At the door, there was the usual admonition that nonmembers needed escorts.

On ritual occasions such as a medicine man's visit, several members beat a large hide-covered drum and chanted. Others, dressed in beads, feathers, bells, and moccasins, danced. One medicine man told the inmates that there were only two Indian commandments: Walk straight and talk straight. "The Great Spirit can give you wisdom," the old man said. "He can make you walk solid rather than in sand."

The club for black inmates, the Black Prisoners Forum Unlimited (BPFU), was also trying, as one club president put it, "to bring people up on their identity." Although all the penitentiary's 350 black inmates were nominal members, the club was disorganized and struggling.

"A bunch of niggers are never gonna be organized," Parejo snarled from the safety of the Chicano club room. "They're all down there chucking spears or something. We're disciplined. They ain't."

During late 1978 and early 1979, the BPFU existed primarily as a social club operating out of a small hall that was once the prison library. Black inmates came to play dominoes, checkers, and chess or to smoke marijuana. The hall's dreary brown walls were relieved by a huge, canvas theater flat depicting a street scene in which a slick-looking pimp and his woman posed in front of the "Southside Pool" hall.

Perhaps one reason for the BPFU's chronic disorganization was that several potential leaders were Muslims. A devout group of predominately black inmates, the Muslims shunned the punks, the partying, and the pill popping that characterized the BPFU. Although they occasionally held their *jumah* prayer service in the BPFU hall, the two black groups had little in common.

"A lot of people want to see more material things, more madness in the hall," said a frowning Aquil Ameer-Mateen, the inmate *imam*, or Muslim leader. "They still have that mentality of partying, and they'll need a lot of insight because they're still hung up on that black thing."

Aquil, born Larry Owens and formerly known as Larry X, presided over the Muslims' weekly prayer service where he delivered the *khutbah*, or sermon. A twenty-eight-year-old convicted drug dealer, he was a handsome man with a smooth complexion, a mustache, and a wispy goatee. He was also an extraordinary speaker.

"We've followed every kind of leadership there's been: Huey Newton, Eldridge Cleaver, Bobby Seale," he lectured the three dozen Muslims gathered for prayer one November afternoon. "But we were not following the light and guidance of the almighty God Allah. It's his truth that will set us free. When we didn't have the truth and was out there pimping, robbing, and selling drugs, we lost the money as fast as we got it."

Pausing, Aquil cocked his red skullcap to one side. The responses from the audience began to come, slowly at first, then loud and vigorous—"That's right." "Teach it." "C'mon, here come the reality."

Aquil grasped both sides of the lectern and gazed intently at the solemn faces before him. "Until we have the truth of the almighty God Allah," he said, his voice skipping an octave higher, "we're going to be in prison either physically or mentally. Without the truth, this prison you're locked up in today is only a minute compared to the prison the almighty God Allah is going to lock your mind up in for all time. It's very plain to me here today that the wrong you've done comes back on you."

"As-Sallam-Alaikum," Aquil concluded, bowing slightly as his voice trailed off into spontaneous applause. "Wa-Alaikum-As-Sallam," the audience responded.

As he left the podium, Rashid, a thirty-eight-year-old inmate born a Yugoslav Muslim, stepped forward to lead the chanting in Arabic. One of only two whites in the group, the diminutive Rashid was the *muezzin*, or prayer caller. Successively standing, kneeling, and bowing, he directed the other Muslims in prayer. At certain times, they pressed their hands to the floor, brushing their lips on the carpet remnants that served as prayer rugs. Then they rose and cupped their hands to their ears. When prayer was over, they left as unobtrusively as they had come, quietly and with dignity.

During the early seventies, the prison Muslims had been regarded with suspicion. They wore kitchen outfits—long-sleeved white shirts and white pants—and narrow-billed, red baseball caps decorated with

a yellow star and crescent. While many blacks were growing Afros, the Muslims shaved their heads. Behind closed doors, they drilled and studied martial arts.

When they walked around the prison, they marched in military formation. "Drilling was a form of discipline," said Aleem S. Abdul-Jabbar, a Muslim inmate who remembered the time of the "silly red baseball caps." "We drilled so that when you left here you didn't forget what you were taught."

Despite their misgivings, prison officials did not interfere with Muslim activities. "The Muslims never caused any problems," a prison staffer pointed out. "Their cells were clean, they were rarely tagged for infractions, they shied away from confrontation. Yet the threat was always there." One penitentiary teacher recounted how several Muslims, unhappy because he had expelled one of them from class, assembled in uniform at the classroom door. They stood tall and stone-faced, saying nothing.

Elijah Muhammad, the prophet and founder of the black Muslims, taught a doctrine that mixed Islam with black supremacy. He preached that whites were devils and that blacks would rise from white dominance to build a separate nation of Islam. But when he died in 1975, the ideology of the militant black Muslims died with him. His son and successor, Wallace D. Muhammad, pursued new paths of harmony with white people and of accommodation with world Islam. At the prison, whites began to show up at the *jumah* prayer service.

In accordance with the dietary strictures of the Koran, prison Muslims cooked and served their own evening meal in the prison's dining hall. They avoided ground meat, pork, and pork by-products and soaked red meats in vinegar and water to draw out the blood. For some Muslims like Aquil, the evening meal on "the Muslim line" was all that they ate. "The less you eat, the longer you'll live," Aquil said.

The Muslims avoided hassles with guards and other inmates by "keeping each other in check and letting each other know when we're off base," said Aleem, a slender, studious ex-*imam* who wore owlish glasses. "We follow the guidelines of the Koran. We don't use our fists and we avoid being the aggressor." Aleem said that the Muslims "try to stay in a zone of wisdom by steering clear of fools."

While guards generally praised the Muslims and tolerated the Indians' search for spirituality, they were under no illusions about the activities of the "Chicano Cultural Studies Center." Parejo's Chicanos, guards argued, did as much contract work as Kenny Agtuca's lifers.

Some contracts were for murder, but most, they said, involved "enforcement" and extortion.

"Enforcers" were toughs who made deals with other convicts to provide protection, collect bad debts, or square old wrongs. Some inmates paid for protection voluntarily. Thinking they were in trouble, they wanted the population to know that someone with a mean reputation was "backing their play." Big-time drug dealers, who could afford it, considered hiring a couple of beefy bodyguards a sensible precaution not a luxury.

When an enforcer collected an unpaid bill for a drug dealer or a loan shark, he usually took half of whatever he collected. If he was unable to collect and failed to beat or stab the debtor, he lost his credibility. As one enforcer put it, "You ain't got no business backing nobody unless you're going to do it."

A creditor unable to recoup his loss had to back up his threats to protect his business. "He wants you to know that you can't burn him and get away with it," said an inmate who got thumped for being "bum pay." "If you're going to buy dope, you better be able to pay for it."

More often than not, enforcers who sold protection were extorting rather than protecting. "You'll get three or four guys who look for the weak guy," one guard explained. "They'll say pay us or we'll take you over to the BPFU and they'll fuck you." Sometimes, the guard remarked, enforcers were in cahoots. A couple of them would create a problem for an inmate, two others would offer to protect the threatened inmate, and the four of them would split the protection money.

Enforcers also extorted money from an inmate's family. They called or wrote family members threatening reprisals against the inmate unless a certain amount of money was sent to a certain post-office box. Penitentiary officials said that they received complaints about such extortion plots about once a week.

Sometimes, enforcers inside the prison had parolees, ex-convicts, or friends on the outside break windows, slash tires, or otherwise pressure people whom they hoped to milk for cash or drugs. Visitors, particularly those who had smuggled drugs or cash into the prison in the past, were especially vulnerable to extortion schemes. Those who told prison officials about such plots risked putting a "snitch jacket" on their loved ones.

Jimmy Joe readily conceded that he had done "other people's dirty work." "But if I do that now, I'll just catch another beef. I don't want to see any more problems," he said, claiming that he had defused some

tense situations by "going around and picking up weapons."

Patting the green binder that he often carried with him, Jimmy Joe said that he now used "the WAC rules to help the 'bros.' " He used the rules to gain access to inmates in segregation where he was admitted for brief visits as a "lay adviser." He also used the rules to defend Chicanos appearing before the prison disciplinary committee. "I focus a lot of attention on my brothers," Jimmy Joe said, "because I see a lot of things they don't see."

If a club member were charged with a crime inside the walls, he could count on Jimmy Joe to testify favorably in his behalf. For example, despite ample evidence to the contrary, Jimmy Joe testified in a February 1979 trial that a fellow Chicano charged with murder was nowhere near the murder scene. Following his testimony, Jimmy Joe stretched his handcuffed arms and clasped the defendant's hands in a salute to brotherhood. The accused killer was acquitted.

Some inmates, however, were unconvinced by Jimmy Joe's purported conversion from hit man to jailhouse lawyer. One Chicano griped that Jimmy Joe and two of his buddies "took a contract out on an old man. They moved in cheaper than me. I didn't like that."

Even Jimmy Joe himself still felt that there were some wrongs, like membership in the NF, for which people deserved to die. He told how he had dealt with a relative who had snitched on him. "I had a friend blow his car window out on the West Seattle bridge. He didn't try to hit him, just scare him," he said. "That way the dude knows it's Jimmy Joe. If he gets busted and goes to Monroe, I'll have him killed."

After all, Jimmy Joe concluded, it was so easy to murder people, even free people. "To kill a guy on the street," he said, nodding toward a nearby phone, "all I got to do is make a call."

Manny Parejo, Chicano club president, poses in front of his self-portrait in the Chicano club room. Parejo, an ex-boxer, usurped Jimmy Joe's position.

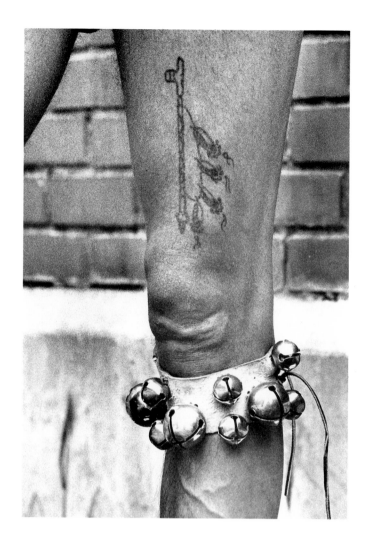

Indian inmates have won the right to practice their native religion. They dance; meet in their "lodge," a cellblock dayroom; and observe the ritual of the sweat lodge.

Elwood Koshiway, a visiting medicine man, and an inmate dance at a Saturday "powwow" in the lodge. Indians believe that the sweat-lodge ritual purifies them physically through sweating and spiritually through praying.

85

Aquil Ameer-Mateen, born Larry Owens and once known as Larry X, is the imam, the religious leader to the penitentiary's Muslims. Devout Muslims abstain from drugs, pruno, and prison sex and pray to Allah several times a day.

Rashid, an Arabic-speaking Yugoslav Muslim, leads his fellow inmate Muslims in prayer. Aleem S. Abdul-Jabbar, a quiet, bookish ex-imam, recalls the days when the penitentiary's Muslims subscribed to the black-militant philosophy of Malcolm X.

6

Jackie: Queen

A shapely, smooth-faced black whose sheer, sleeveless blouse accented her pert nipples, Oaland "Jackie" Graham was perhaps the most desired lady inside the penitentiary. By her own admission, "a day doesn't go by in here that a man doesn't ask me for some sex."

Jackie had beautiful, moist brown eyes; glowing, luxuriant skin softened by creams and lotions; and a vulnerable, girlish walk that invited male companionship. At twenty-six, she was still young and firm. Conscious of her alluring charms, Jackie wore clothes that accented her femininity: a snappy knit cap, white bone earrings, a petite gold watch with a narrow band, sleek tops that flattered her developing breasts, and neatly pressed jeans that clung tight enough to outline her bikini panties but were loose enough to hide the bulge of her male organ.

One of nearly a dozen prison "queens"—men who dressed and behaved like women—Jackie did not deny her male anatomy. That's the way she was born, she said. But in her head, she had always felt like a woman. "I always had my little girlish ways," she said softly, unable to remember a time when she didn't want to be a woman. "I put on a wig, panties, and earrings and that's how I felt comfortable."

Jackie talked with a woman's voice, referred to herself as "she," and expected to be treated like a lady. She shared hormone pills smuggled inside by another queen but had decided against a sex-change operation. "If somebody can't accept me how I am, that's their problem," she figured. "If God truly wanted me to be a female, he would have given me all the female equipment. I know I can be happy and loved without a sex change."

Until Jackie came to prison, there wasn't much love in her life. She left a troubled, fatherless home at fifteen, "wanting to be free to be me." She and a female companion named "Big Mama" headed for the big city—Seattle. After a couple dead-end jobs in fast-food restaurants, Jackie decided to work as a prostitute. "I made my own choice," she insisted. The money was good, but Jackie ran afoul of the law. Arrested for shoplifting and prostitution, she spent six months in the county jail. Then in February 1976, a quarrel in a cocktail lounge led to a second-degree murder conviction and to a twenty-year sentence in the penitentiary.

Jackie claimed that she had acted in self-defense. She said that the victim had gotten rough with her because she was leaving the lounge with another man. She drew a knife, swung wildly, slashed his aorta, and killed him. "I feel bad about that," she said. "It's something that will always be with me."

When Jackie arrived at the penitentiary in the spring of 1976, she fell in love with a shrewd black convict who found her a cell and kept her in clothes and jewelry. In return, she kept him in money by turning tricks. Depending on the prostitute, the customer, and the sex act, a prison trick cost from $7.50 to $30.00. Attractive and vivacious, Jackie commanded a high price and set her own terms.

Her cultivated femininity notwithstanding, Jackie could handle her own affairs with her fists, if need be. She once traded blows with an inmate who had slapped her and had called her a whore. "He was discriminating against me and wanting my body at the same time," she huffed. Moreover, Jackie refused to be bought, sold, or swapped by inmate "wolves" who dealt in gays like plantation owners once dealt in slaves.

But Jackie also liked her menfolk to take care of her. She liked to receive gifts, to hear her man talk sweetly in her ear, and to watch him prove his concern for her by admonishing inmates who treated her with disrespect.

In the fall of 1978, Jackie's man was Percy, a handsome, strapping, soft-spoken black whom she called her husband. "We've been together since March 9," Jackie said proudly. "That's our anniversary." Since her "marriage" to Percy, Jackie claimed that she had stopped tricking and "chipping"—sneaking sex with inmates besides her "main man."

When Jackie pranced down the breezeway, other convicts yelled good-natured comments like, "Hey, baby, I love you," or "Hey, sugar, how about a roll." Jackie pretended to ignore their remarks, but secretly she loved the attention and favorably compared her fanfare to the lesser adulation aroused by the other queens. "A lot of guys come on to me, but I use that to my advantage," Jackie said slyly. "They aren't going to pressure me into sex because they respect Percy. He's made it clear he's not going to let anybody disrespect me."

Jackie, Percy, and another inmate lived in a tidy four-man cell that Percy owned on an upper deck in 8-wing. Jackie had decorated the walls with magazine photos of male fashion models. Because the double bunks were pushed forward until they were flush with the cell bars, there was room for another mattress behind the black curtain draped across the middle of the cell. The extra mattress was for lovemaking.

Prison rules prohibited sex acts, but unless guards literally caught inmates with their pants down, there was no evidence to support an infraction. Consequently, Jackie and Percy were openly affectionate, often cuddling and caressing in Jackie's forward bunk, oblivious to their cellmate as well as to guards and inmates who passed on the tier.

Jackie was more modest about bathing. Unfortunately for her, the car-wash-type communal shower, with its plugged drains and flooded floors, was down three flights of stairs at the far end of the cellblock. For Jackie, wrapped in a fluffy towel, the trip to the shower occasioned catcalls and snickers from other inmates. She preserved her dignity—and hid her gender—by showering in a pair of bright bikini panties. Even so, she said coquettishly, "I'm embarrassed."

Jackie spent her days in a small second-story office in the admissions wing. The room overlooked People's Park, a view that Jackie and the other queens took advantage of by eyeing the men below and bantering with their favorites. Although the queens often quarreled bitterly, they shared a similar pursuit. "Deep down inside we all like the same thing, and that's men," Jackie said flirtatiously.

The office was headquarters for a prison club called Men against Sexism (MAS), most of whose dozen members regarded themselves as ladies. Jackie, the de facto queen of the queens, was president.

Newspaper clippings and posters covered the office walls. One clipping, circled in black, read, "If you are a gay in prison, you are a piece of goods, or property. You are bought and sold, passed from hand to hand, as an object, not a man." Nearby hung an innocuous poster of a smiling frog. The caption read: "You have to kiss a lot of toads before you find your prince." The bookshelf that divided the room held newspapers with titles like *Changing Men, Seattle Gay News, The Burning Spear* (published by the African Peoples' Socialist Party), *Open Road* ("the magazine devoted to total anarchy"), and *The Pentecostal Evangel*. The papers lay dusty and neglected. On the office door, Jackie had fastened a fresh, hand-lettered sign: "Condemnation without investigation is truly the height of ignorance."

Founded in 1977 as a radical gay-rights group, MAS sought to protect gay and weak inmates from sexual harassment at the hands of prison wolves. The group's original leadership had mounted a campaign to confront prison bullies, to secure safe cells for gays, and to oust the Protestant chaplain, who had condemned homosexuality as sinful. They had also laid plans to use an MAS party as a cover for an armed escape attempt. Guards discovered the arms, the escape attempt collapsed, and MAS's leadership was given an extended stay in segregation.

Jackie stepped in. "I really didn't understand anything about sexism, gay rights, and discrimination," she confessed. "But I had to take a leadership position when they locked everybody else up." Jackie credited MAS with "raising my consciousness level. I used to think that what the man says, goes."

Although Jackie and the other queens still espoused gay rights, they ran the MAS office as a tailor shop. They mended trousers, sewed on buttons, stitched hems, and even made quilts out of prison-issue clothing. On the wall opposite the frog poster was a list: Hems—$2; mending—75 cents; patches—$1; drapes—$2; buttons—25 cents; cuffs—75 cents per leg; hats—$7.50; dye jobs—$2.25; winter scarves—$5.

During the day, customers and visitors wandered in and out of the MAS office. Some helped themselves to reheated coffee from the coffeepot in the corner, ignoring the sign that requested fifteen cents a cup. Others sat around on a few broken chairs, listening to scratchy recordings by the Temptations and ogling the queens. "Most of the fellas like to hang around where the girls are," gushed Leomy, a tall, colorfully dressed black with rouged cheeks and a singsong Caribbean accent.

If the crowd got too thick or somebody came in whom Jackie did not like, she ordered them out. When Jackie wanted her way, she raised her voice and shrieked like a fishmonger. "This is not a hangout for nonmembers, so please state your business and leave," she barked.

Guards periodically entered the office checking for contraband and for illegal sexual activity. They probed the desk drawers, dumped the lipstick and mascara out of purses, and patted down the queens. Jackie barked at them, too, accusing them of harassing homosexuals. One officer, who suspected that the queens were less indignant than they seemed, maintained that the ladies liked to be shook down. "They hope the guards will get embarrassed," he said.

According to Jackie, MAS used the tailor shop's profits, if any, to rescue gays who had been claimed or bought by "jockers," aggressive, macho inmates who forced weaker inmates to play the female sex role. If a jocker was especially cruel to his gay partner, MAS tried to buy the gay's freedom by purchasing him from the jocker. "We'd rather give somebody fifty to a hundred dollars than have somebody else lose their

life," explained Jackie, who had no objection to jockers if they treated their human property with respect.

Although new inmates invariably expressed surprise at "the guys dressed up like women," most of them soon subscribed to the fiction that Jackie and the other queens were the exaggerated women that they pretended to be. Convicts called them "broads," "bitches," and "cunts" and treated them with the flattery or contempt that they held for real women. Some made straightforward, serious statements declaring that women—meaning the queens—had the right to be treated with respect.

For their part, the queens, men who had come to prison with the idea that they were women, had varied experiences. Some, too helpless or too cowed to use their feminine attributes to their advantage, were bought, pimped, and, occasionally, gang-raped. Others like Jackie, plucky queens who exploited their femininity, flourished in prison, vying for male attention, flitting from man to man, seemingly head over heels in a succession of "marriages" and love affairs. Many enjoyed selling themselves. Besides making good money, prostitutes received proof that they were the desirable women they wanted to be. Many of them received more attention inside the walls than they had ever received on the street. Even some prison staff members admitted to being sexually attracted to some of the queens, particularly Jackie. In a bleak, all-male world, the queens looked good.

Some prison gays, like Jackie, chose their "main man" and seduced him with flirtatious behavior and sexual come-ons. But in most cases, the jockers did the choosing, snatching up good-looking boys on the day that they walked through the prison gate. One of those boys was Tina, a fresh-faced, nineteen-year-old blonde, who claimed to be "the best thing that walked into this penitentiary in a long time."

At the state reformatory, where she had done time before coming to Walla Walla, Tina had dressed and acted like a man. "But here I couldn't argue with the system," she sighed, shrugging as if the system was not all that bad. "If you don't want to be bought or sold, you either get beat up or you 'check in' to PC." Tina had no desire to live with the snitches in protective custody or to have her pretty face marked up, so she accepted the prison transformation from "him" to "her."

A convicted burglar with long, flowing hair, Tina called herself "a fairy—a young lady with a major malfunction. I got a part I don't want." She liked being called a fairy rather than a queen because she thought that the queens looked too much like "bull dikes." She was hesitant about undergoing a sex-change operation because she had heard that such operations aged people five years. Despite the rough talk that she affected in prison, Tina wanted to be a little girl. Inmates said she had the "pink look"—cute, fragile, and well-scrubbed. She dressed in a corset-shaped, powder blue silk blouse with a bow at the front, pressed blue jeans, or, on special occasions, a leather miniskirt. "I would wear a bra if I had any tits," she said. Often she exaggerated her tender age by twirling a yo-yo or sucking a lollipop. She had to shave every morning, ever since prison staff seized her hair remover; they also confiscated her mail-order panty hose.

Tina was "married" to a three-time convicted murderer who had a reputation as a man you didn't cross. He also had a reputation for collecting young men, but Tina insisted that her relationship with him was special.

Two months after she moved into his cell, she made, without vows or ceremony, "a marriage commitment" in which she agreed to be truthful and to clean the house. As a result, she claimed that she had quit prostituting herself and had earned some respect. "I don't fuck for money or marijuana no more because I got too much love for my husband," she said, blinking the black eye that she had suffered in a marital spat. Despite Tina's protestations of marital fidelity, other prison gays said that she still did a little chipping on the side. "She'll give it up if the money's right and she's got her old man's okay," another gay inmate contended.

Tina said that before her marriage she had endured months of forced prostitution and abuse at the penitentiary. She had belonged to a biker whom she had thought would be her salvation. "But I got abused there, too," she groaned. "If he came in and wanted a fuck, I had to do it. If the bikers wanted something, they got it." Tina credited her husband with "pulling me out because he knew I was being abused and cared enough to help me. If it wasn't for him, I'd be getting burnt."

Being married to a notorious convict had its advantages. Her husband's knife-wielding reputation allowed Tina to wander unmolested. She lived in a handsome cell, lavishly furnished with a color television set, naughahyde upholstery, and a reel-to-reel tape recorder for playing a shelf full of jazz recordings. "My husband has helped me out more than anybody else in my life," she said.

Although the prison ladies like Jackie advertised their sexual inclinations, most gay inmates hid their homosexuality. Jackie estimated that there were only about fifteen "out-front gays." But based on their observations, the guards claimed that at least a third of the inmate population was actively homosexual by preference, not because of the

prison environment. Beyond that, commented one sergeant, "With the men being pushed into these circumstances, I'd say about 80 to 90 percent use other men for sexual favors."

Sometimes sex was a mutual proposition. Sometimes it was one or more men forcing themselves on another. Sometimes it was purely a trade-off. "If I'm horny," a veteran convict explained, "I look for guy who needs money and say, 'Let's fuck.' Then it would come down. He's doing it for money or weed. I'm doing it to fantasize."

Like a nickel bag of marijuana or a half-gallon of pruno, sex was also a form of prison currency. One queen, whose misconduct regularly resulted in segregation time, promised sex for cigarettes. She yelled through the screened windows to anyone in the yard, "Hey, baby, you want a piece of pussy? Send me in a pack of smokes and I'll fuck you when I get out."

Most sexual activity occurred in cells, shower rooms, club areas, the chapel—which many straight prisoners avoided for fear of being labeled gay—or at the weekend movies in the darkened prison auditorium. "At the movies," one inmate remarked, "the lights go out and you can look down the rows and see the heads go down."

Aside from the queens, convicts distinguished between two types of homosexuals: faggots and punks. Faggots were inmates who had identified themselves as homosexuals before they came to prison. Punks were inmates whom jockers forced into homosexual acts. The jockers did not consider themselves to be gay. Priding themselves on being supermasculine men, they always acted the male part, disdaining the "flip-flopping" practiced by the faggots. "I'm a heterosexual who fucks punks. I'm not ashamed of that," said a jocker who was more candid than most. Generally, punks were young, weak, or naive prisoners who decided that it was safer to "switch than swing." Once adopted by their jockers, they were known as "kids."

Some kids emerged as "jailhouse turnouts," inmates who discovered their homosexual or even female tendencies in prison. Sometimes, as in Tina's case, an inmate entered the penitentiary as a man, noticed that other prisoners found him attractive, and decided to encourage that attraction by taking on effeminate airs, wearing lipstick and rouge, and answering to the feminine name that a jocker gave him. More often than not, however, it was the jocker, fulfilling his fantasy of having a kept woman, who insisted that his kid wear lipstick and rouge. Even so, unless they nursed feminine inclinations, most kids balked at wearing makeup.

Often sex offenders became kids. A thirty-five-year-old convicted rap-ist who lost several teeth defending himself from sexual attacks explained the rationale: "The convict figures that a sex offender could have been diddling his daughter, therefore he's going to give it to him. He's going to make the sex offender play the role of the rapee. That's his form of justice."

Lynn, a twenty-three-year-old convicted forger, was a faggot, an inmate who had thought of himself as gay ever since puberty. Slender and pale, he had a curly, bouffant hairdo and a sly, tentative smile that suggested that he knew more than he let on. He eschewed relationships in which "I'm told what to do" and refused to dress as a woman. He liked to wear snug printed T-shirts. He had one of revolutionary hero Che Guevara and another of a smiling frog nestled on a lily pad. The frog croaked, "I'm so happy here I could just shit." Despite the shirt, Lynn hated prison.

He hated prison more than most convicts because his frank homosexuality and his upper-middle-class background made him especially vulnerable. Taught by a governess and reared by a wealthy gay uncle, Lynn had made a career of accompanying rich businessmen on travels to Miami, Hawaii, Canada, Rio, Bermuda, and the Bahamas. Arrested at eighteen for writing bad checks, he came to prison unprepared. "I had a pretty sheltered life," he realized. "I had never been exposed to an environment like this. I thought it wasn't bothering me that much, but it was bothering me a lot inside. You might think you're doing all right and handling this place okay, but you don't know what you'll do when you get back in society."

At the corrections center in Shelton, Lynn said, he was so persecuted by "weight-lifter types" that he decided to escape from minimum security. During his three months of freedom, he met a gay in Toronto. "The man wanted me to penetrate him," Lynn said, quietly telling the story. "I blacked out and when I awoke I realized I'd tore him open with my hand. I had pushed my fist in his rectum. When I took him to the hospital, I realized I did this because of all the harassment from the jocker-types. I wonder what prison does to other people."

The evening that Lynn arrived at the penitentiary, he met Danny, a big, bruising inmate who wore carefully slicked hair and studded jeans. "We went to the lifers' club and talked. He seemed nice and polite," Lynn recalled. "I moved in with him and we had an intimate relationship."

When the authorities transferred Danny to the Idaho State Prison, Lynn was in trouble. "A lot of people were jamming me up, trying to get me into trick bags," he said. On Danny's advice, he moved in with Vergil, a wheeler-dealer who was famous for collecting punks. Only

later did Lynn find out that Danny had sold him to Vergil for three hundred dollars.

Vergil never abused him sexually, he said. "Instead, he used me like a fluorescent light to increase his popularity. If you're with a brand-new gay person, you're going to be popular. We used to go for walks all over the institution. I was his advertising, and he gave me anything I wanted."

But Lynn soon tired of being a showpiece. "I felt like I was being degraded. I felt I should work for what I want," he said. After a week with Vergil, he moved into a four-man cell in 8-wing.

"I don't have a relationship here," he insisted, gingerly sitting on the edge of a neatly made lower bunk. "I keep their house clean and they will take care of me. They will defend me. I take the clothes to the laundry. I make the beds. I make sure they have clean towels, just like a maid, and I clean the neighbor's for fifteen dollars a week. I feel unappreciated, but it occupies my time, and it keeps me away from other people."

Lynn argued that most of the penitentiary's gays were unwilling to come to grips with their homosexual tendencies. "Most of them have it forced out," he said. "When I lived in 6-wing, I used to hear them scream at night. I call them pen punks."

Ken, a skinny, fair-skinned, twenty-one year old with crooked teeth and soft, woeful eyes, was a pen punk. Until he went to jail, his sexual experiences had been with women. In the county jail, where he was serving a sentence for burglary, he and a cellmate sodomized another inmate. Ken claimed that his victim had enticed him, but the jury did not believe him. Convicted of second-degree rape, he arrived at the penitentiary scared, naive, friendless, and nineteen years old.

Within hours of Ken's arrival, a well-known wolf introduced himself, warning Ken that the bikers were after him. The wolf offered to protect Ken and invited him to live in his cell. "I was stupid enough to do it," Ken recalled, wishing now that he had slugged the wolf squarely in the face. That evening, the two of them went to the BPFU club room to smoke marijuana. "We smoked up and then three guys raped me," Ken said, nervously picking at his prison denims. "I didn't say anything. I was afraid to go to the cops."

From then on, Ken became the property of a series of black inmates. He was bought and sold—for a hundred dollars, for a leather jacket, for merchandise ordered from a Sears catalogue—and passed from cell to cell. White inmates called him "niggerpunk." Afraid to resist and afraid of the consequences if he complained to the guards, Ken meekly accepted his fate.

Then he developed a genuine affection for one of his jockers, a quiet black loner named Gilbert who came to regard Ken as more than a sexual plaything. Gilbert got Ken a job in the prison library and sparked his interest in books. Long after Gilbert's parole, Ken was still plowing through Immanuel Kant's *Critique of Pure Reason*.

"Gilbert says there's only two types of persons," Ken said, fondly quoting the man whom he still telephoned once a week, "an acquaintance and the person you bed down with." Though Ken bedded down as a woman in his relationship with Gilbert, he did not feel misused. "It beats jacking off," he said, arguing that "there isn't but a handful of motherfuckers in here that haven't done something at some time. It's the environment. Eventually, you settle in."

When Gilbert was paroled, however, Ken was in a predicament. "Some blacks started driving on me to see how I'd react," he said. For a while, he hid out in the library, avoided the dining hall, and walked quickly down the breezeway. Still, they found him. They pushed their angry faces at him, telling him over and over again that Gilbert had left some unpaid debts that Ken was going to settle by moving into a black cell. Ken escaped their grasp by hooking up with Gilbert's friend John, an older white convict who used his clout to ward off Ken's pursuers.

Ken insisted that his newest relationship was different. He did not live with John, and he did not always play the female role. John, a chunky convicted murderer who had spent nearly two decades behind bars, agreed that he and Ken had an unconventional prison relationship. But, to keep other convicts from tormenting Ken, John said that they had to project the appearance that he was the traditional jocker and that Ken was the traditional kid. Maintaining that fiction might even "come down to him getting a black eye," John said.

Despite appearances, John noted that there were many long-term intimate relationships between prisoners. "It's not the sex, it's the contact that's important," he said. "When Ken gets uptight, he needs somebody for comfort. His goal is the contact, not getting his rocks off. There's a massive amount of tension in here. If he can hold on to me for ten minutes, it relieves the tension."

Listening to John explain their relationship, Ken nodded approvingly. "I've gotten so uptight with tension, I've chipped teeth," he said.

"It's lonely in here," John concluded. "Everybody needs somebody. Everybody pairs off."

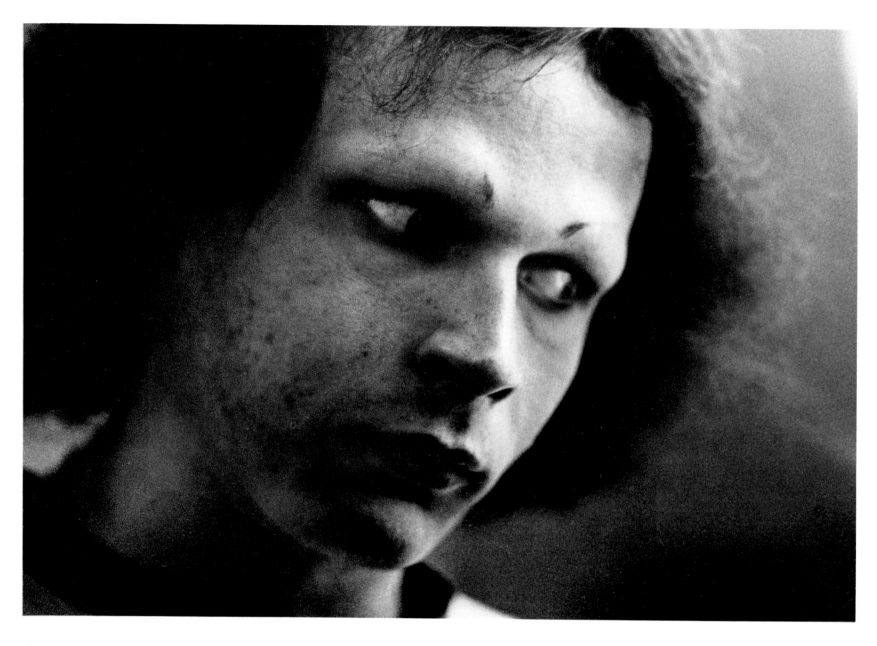

Three expressions of prison sexuality: "Rachel," a queen who works as a maid in the lifers' club; David, a boxer, a lifer, and Rachel's jocker; and "Star," a convicted pimp who became a prostitute in prison.

Many homosexual relationships in prison are casual, but some are considered to be "marriages." "Tina," who calls himself a "fairy," is the private sexual property of a tough, older convict. Tina's jocker gave Tina a black eye for "chipping" and bit an ear off the inmate who had dared to have sex with "her."

While the prison queens openly exploit their feminine attributes, other inmates are forced into homosexual relationships. Ken was once sold to a jocker for a hundred dollars and a leather jacket.

7

Kim: Idler at Work

A chance rendezvous in a West Seattle tavern on a hot July night in 1976 put Kim Simon on the path back to prison.

Twenty-six-year-old Kim and a buddy he met in California were hitchhiking to Alaska. They had leaned their backpacks against the tavern wall and were seated at a table enjoying a pitcher of beer when a woman walked in . She was intoxicated and upset, having just quarreled with her boyfriend in a nearby bar. She did not object when Kim and his buddy moved to her table and poured her a glass of beer.

After a few more beers, the three of them hitched a ride with another tavern patron who dropped them off at Lincoln Park where they intended to go for a swim. They smoked some marijuana, drank a bottle of wine, and got so loud and boisterous that the police came by and suggested that they leave. But instead, they moved back into the woods where the men unrolled their sleeping bags and made advances on the thirty-four-year-old, blue-eyed blonde.

Kim's buddy had sex with her first.   Then Kim said that it was his turn."I fucked her five times," he said. "She said how she never had sex with a black man before and wanted to take us home and meet her mother," Kim later told the police.

But the woman's story was markedly different. She said that Kim had threatened her with a machete and then, using a bayonet and his fists, had forced her to have sex with him and his buddy. Both men talked of cutting off her breasts and her head, she said. Kim hit her in the face, called her a "Communist pig," and lay on top of her all night, preventing her escape until dawn.

The next morning police found Kim and his buddy still asleep in the park. Nearby was a bayonet and a machete. "The cops and a doctor testified she got beat up. But who beat her up? I didn't," Kim protested. "Maybe her boyfriend did."

Nonetheless, on the advice of his attorney, Kim pleaded guilty to second-degree rape. His buddy was convicted of third-degree rape and received a suspended sentence; Kim got a maximum of ten years at the penitentiary.

It was not his first conviction. The prosecuting attorney's report to the judge noted that Kim had served several sentences in Maryland prisons on convictions of tampering with a motor vehicle, carnal knowl-edge, escape, arson, and larceny. Kim claimed an even more extensive criminal history.

Born in Brooklyn, New York, he grew up being shuffled among a number of foster homes in Baltimore. "After I finished junior high," Kim said, "I became a stickup man and sold narcotics."

He used a .45 in his armed robberies, he said, because he liked the gun's "knockdown" power. "You hit somebody with that and he been stung." Kim said that he and a female partner ("she was *bad*") robbed cleaning stores, groceries, and small loan companies. "The most we ever made was six grand off of one of the loan companies," he said.

Disguised in a ski mask, gloves, and overalls, Kim never let his victims see his face. "I'd wear a suit underneath the coveralls, then hit the nearest alley and drop the coveralls," he said. Kim laughed at the "cowboy-type" robbers with whom he was doing time at the penitentiary. "Man," he said, "90 percent of these guys in here had their face showing, no gloves, putting fingerprints all over the place. Then they wonder why they got caught."

Although the presentencing report did not show it, Kim maintained that he first went to prison for a drug-connected murder. He said that he jammed the muzzle of his .45 into his victim's mouth and pulled the trigger. "I blew the dude away," Kim said. "He owed me fifteen hundred dollars, and I had to pay my boss. The only way I can take care of it is kill that motherfucker or be killed. The man I was dealing for, he was so big I couldn't take care of him."

At the Maryland State Penitentiary, Kim said that he spent eighteen months in the hole for stabbing a jocker who had made a pass at him. "I whipped out my shank and asked the motherfucker if he still wanted some buns," Kim bragged.

Paroled in 1975, Kim said that he moved to Washington, D.C., where he worked as a hotel cook. "I played it real straight," he said, "but I couldn't support myself. I bought a kilo of weed and made my living dealing. I had nice, nice fancy clothes and a fancy new car. I wasn't hurting nobody. I was just dealing weed. Tell me what's wrong with that?"

One night, Kim got into an argument with a federal officer and punched him. He was bailed out on the assault charge and decided to

run. "I didn't stop running till I got to California," he said. "I met this white dude who says 'let's go to Alaska.' We get up to Seattle and we get a fucking rape charge."

Prison provided inmates with few opportunities to constructively pass the time they were sentenced to serve. Jobs were few. Some of them were accompanied by relatively high pay or by "perks" that could make an inmate's life more comfortable, but most were scarcely above the level of make-work. Because there were not enough jobs to go around, some inmates, like the leaders of the clubs and self-help groups, who were not content to idly watch the world go by, made up their own.

Kim was one of the few inmates who had been assigned a permanent prison job. When he was at work, which was not often, Kim operated a machine that applied reflectorized tape to rolls of aluminum. As the tape unwound from a spindle, Kim was supposed to make sure that it threaded through the machine and adhered to the uncoiling metal roll. Other inmates manned machines that cut, embossed, painted, and baked the light, rectangular metal pieces—the license plates for all the motor vehicles in Washington State.

License plates were the penitentiary's most important and most lucrative product. Working with specialized machinery in the prison's metal plant, less than two dozen inmates could stamp out five thousand plates a day. At $1.52½ a set, the prison sold more than $1 million worth of license plates to the Department of Motor Vehicles every year. One out of every $2.00 grossed by the sale of penitentiary-manufactured goods came from license plates.

In fact, license plates were the only product manufactured inside the walls that showed a profit. The license-plate operation underwrote the cost of making other prison products like desks, lockers, chairs, couches, and cabinets. The prison's license-plate business, of course, also enjoyed the distinct advantages of a guaranteed market and no competition.

"Where do they make license plates other than here?" demanded Kim, who complained that he was learning a useless job. "The only reason I'm here is I don't want to be out on the breezeway," he said, shouting over the clackety-clack of the cutting machine. "Because if I'm out there, I'll be smoking dope, chasing little boys, or sticking somebody."

A shuck-and-jive, street-wise hustler, Kim wore a blue slouch hat and a grin that glittered with silver and gold. He was twenty-eight, wiry, five feet nine inches tall, and 130 pounds. "But I still hit like I weigh 170," he insisted. Posing and posturing like a fighting cock, he punctuated his conversation with arm waving and finger popping. He called himself a "lobo," a "lone wolf" because "nobody in jail qualifies to be my friend. Society can't trust 'em, so how the hell can I trust 'em?"

Kim loved to talk about sex and the topic rarely left his conversation. "I'm young and I got to come," he said. "If I don't come, I get angry." He boasted that he had a "dame" who visited him on weekends, a queen who took care of him inside, and the run of any "cute little kids" who came in on the chain. "I do that because I don't have no women in here," he said. "Bend over, I'll fill 'em up just like Texaco. I know it ain't the natural thing, but I got to get my nut off somehow. If a man's built like a woman, I got to have a piece. I don't like beating my meat."

Kim's "inside lady" was Leomy, a tall prison queen who spoke with a Caribbean accent and wore a nose ring. Because she wore a size eleven shoe, Kim teased her by calling her "Big Foot." The couple had had its quarrels: Kim had spent thirty-seven days in the hole following a fight in which he punctured Leomy's lung with a knife.

Despite his remarks to the contrary, Kim had plenty of time to hang out on the breezeways, dawdling the afternoons away with Leomy. On warm days, they would find a place in the shade of the prison wall where she would braid his hair while he watched the goings-on. Nearby, idle inmates loitered in groups, laughing and backslapping, eating popcorn, and drinking soft drinks purchased at the open-air "coke shack," the inmate-run concession stand.

Opposite the coke shack, on a concrete slab that marked the remains of an earlier prison laundry, sat the Spoonman. A stout, elderly black, he always wore the same blue overalls and striped railroad cap. He sat in the same place every day, his huge portable radio at his side playing soul music. A sort of one-man variety store, the Spoonman displayed cigarettes, gum, fingernail clippers, and other notions, but inmates said that he sold everything from light bulbs to Chivas Regal.

The Spoonman was not the only sidewalk entrepreneur, but aside from "The Breezeway Bon Marche," he was the most visible. Inmates selling marijuana or pills lingered quietly, neither showing nor hawking their goods. "The Breezeway Bon Marche," named for the big Northwest department store, was run by a pushy, loudmouthed wheeler-dealer who retained a taste for the flamboyant clothes that he had worn as a pimp. He hung his goods—form-fitting shirts, flared trousers, trendy jackets—on coat hangers hooked on the breezeway's cyclone

fencing. Some of the clothes were his; others were being sold on consignment.

Kim often skipped work for days at a time. He had laminated so much aluminum that he was days, perhaps weeks, ahead of the cutter. In turn, the cutter—the quick, flawless machine that sliced the rolled aluminum into license-plate-sized pieces—was weeks ahead of the embosser. The cutter worked so fast that a wall of laminated aluminum plates, stacked five feet high, sat waiting. "I don't have to show up until they print every one of those plates," Kim said, pointing at the large stack. "You don't even lose your pay as long as someone takes care of your card."

Working in the metal plant, Kim had one of the better-paid inmate jobs. His base wage of forty-nine cents an hour was supplemented with a thirteen-cent-an-hour bonus if his time card showed that he had worked 125 hours that month. He made sure that his time card earned him the higher rate.

A new metal-plant worker started at twenty-five cents an hour, or at thirty-three cents if he earned the bonus. "Lead men," inmates whose work the civilian supervisors judged to be "truly exceptional," earned eighty-four cents an hour or about $135 a month. In terms of legitimate income, they were the best-paid inmates in the penitentiary. Some jobs, tier porters, for instance, paid as little as $10 a month.

Kim, who had waited nine months to get a job in the metal plant, griped that older white convicts monopolized all the high-paying jobs. "They don't allow us black guys to be lead men," he complained. "I ain't jiving, look around. These motherfuckers here wouldn't give a black dude nothing. The only thing I learned since I been in here is how to hate," he went on. "I ain't no model prisoner. For one, I'm doing ten years for nothing. How am I supposed to get rehabilitated behind that?"

Kim had no illusions that operating a tape applicator would help him to get a job after he was paroled. He did not want a straight job, anyway. He planned to sell drugs. "I can make more money in a half-hour standing on a street corner than you can make in a year," he boasted. He planned to make his fortune back East. "I ain't going to stay in this motherfucking cowboy state no longer than it takes me to get my dick wet and keep moving."

On the mornings when he showed up for work, Kim arrived in the metal plant between 8:00 and 8:30. If there was work to do, he would run his applicator machine for a couple of hours. If there was no work,

or if there was too big a backlog, he and the other license-plate workers busied themselves in other ways.

Some bathed or washed their clothes in the comparative comfort of the tiled showers provided for metal-plant workers. Unlike the car-wash-type stalls in the cellblocks, the metal-plant showers were safer and more private, and those who washed their own clothes didn't lose them, a problem that inmates who sent their clothes to the prison laundry often had to put up with. The metal-plant workers dried their laundry by hanging it on license-plate hooks and running it through the paint-drying booth. Kim, however, never had to bother with doing his laundry at work. He had Leomy wash his clothes.

The inmate workers began shutting down for lunch about 10:00, an hour before mealtime. They knew that the security check at the 9-tower gate would delay them at least a half-hour, and they were determined not to be late for lunch.

Since inmate workers had access to all sorts of tools, guards checked them carefully when they passed from the industrial area into the main prison compound. Nevertheless, despite the metal detector and the body searches, contraband slipped through.

Kim said that he sometimes taped a small bottle of paint thinner to the inside of his thigh and walked through undetected. "One thing they won't do is feel around your dick," he said. Back in his cell, Kim would pour the thinner into a plastic bag, stick his head inside, and come up "screaming and hollering."

If lunch was served on time, Kim and his co-workers returned to work about noon. But if lunch was late, they sometimes straggled back as late as 1:00 P.M. In the afternoons, there was generally an hour or two of work until the lead men began shutting down the operation about 2:30.

On a hard day, the license-plate workers would be at their posts for about four hours. But even then, most of them were idle. "Look over there," said Kim's boss, a jolly old convict with a big belly and a straw hat. He pointed to a group of inmates lounging around the embossing machine. "I got two men working and seven sitting around." Regardless of the hours worked, inmates drew pay for an eight-hour day.

Meanwhile, in the adjacent welding shop, a half-dozen inmates sat on steel-frame chairs and looked at girlie magazines. "I haven't worked in three months," said one of the welders. "There's nobody doing nothing. We haven't had any orders."

In the past, prison workers had frittered away slack time by playing

cards or by "hobbying," using the shop's tools and supplies to make cribbage boards, necklaces, rings, bracelets, hookahs, and other items. They sold their handicrafts for scrip or for marijuana. "Nowadays," the welder complained, "they say they'll fire us if we don't do some work because they got too many people. See those lockers. We stack 'em one way one day and later they stack 'em another way."

"When there is work to do," another inmate welder piped up, "only two or three guys do it and the rest watch." There was not much to learn anyway, he added, because the welding machinery was inadequate and out of date. "I spend three-quarters of my time working on dies without the proper machinery. You go into a good shop on the outside and you don't even know how to turn the machine on and off." Shoving his baseball cap back on his forehead, the welder shrugged. "Hell," he said, "working out here is just a job assignment, just a way to impress the parole board. It's not going to gain you anything on the street."

Lieutenant Colombo, the officer in charge of work assignments, conceded as much. The parole board gave "good time," a one-third cut in the minimum sentence, to inmates who behaved and had good work records. "Sure, we've created a lot of Mickey Mouse jobs like cleaning the tier. It takes about thirty minutes to do that," Colombo said. "But it's still a job assignment and it looks good to the parole board. The incentive is that these guys don't want to lose their good time."

Colombo assigned inmates to work in the metal plant, furniture shop, kitchen, hospital, laundry, plumbing and carpentry shop, library, control room, engineering shop, clothing room, property room, and recreation areas. The nearly three hundred inmates who were registered for school were counted as having been assigned, as were inmates who participated in self-help programs, who were active in inmate clubs, or who were in segregation or protective custody. Even an unemployed inmate who regularly submitted a "kite" requesting work, was counted as assigned. "It's not his fault if he hasn't got a job," Colombo reasoned. "We just don't have enough jobs."

Adding up all these "assigned" inmates, Colombo was able to say that only three hundred of the fourteen hundred maximum-security inmates lacked work assignments. But it was obvious to all that there was a big difference between having a work assignment and actually working.

While Kim chose a metal-plant job for its higher pay, other inmates sought work assignments that gave them access to food, clothing, or situations that might make life inside the walls more comfortable. For example, George Walks-on-top, a thirty-nine-year-old Assiniboine–Sioux Indian, had a coveted job in the inmate property room, a converted meat locker where inmates' belongings and street clothes were stored. A steady, resourceful, soft-spoken convict respected by both inmates and guards, Walks-on-top arrived punctually at the property-room door every weekday morning at 7:30.

He and his two co-workers waited for the sergeant who unlocked the door and then plopped down into a comfy chair to pass the day watching television. Walks-on-top reached into the "goodie box," a large orange footlocker packed with foodstuffs foraged from the prison kitchen, and poured himself a Styrofoam cup of grapefruit juice. The property room was well provisioned, often with items on loan from some inmate's stored belongings. Aside from the television set, there was a radio, a coffeepot, a hot plate, a cooler, a dart board, a stack of girlie magazines, and a toll-free phone available when the sergeant stepped out for lunch.

Sipping his grapefruit juice, Walks-on-top studied the list of inmates being transferred to other institutions. He took special note of those who "sniveled their way out to the minimum-security building." His job was to inventory and to transfer the belongings of inmates who were arriving or leaving the maximum-security compound. He hand-trucked their possessions to the property room where he rummaged through the boxes, confiscating contraband, and reclaiming state-issue clothing.

The three property-room workers also "dressed out" inmates leaving on court appearances or on parole. They took clothing sizes over the phone, then thumbed through the three racks of defective shirts and trousers purchased by the state from a major sportswear manufacturer. If necessary, they made alterations on an old Singer sewing machine. "We usually try to pick out clothes that match," Walks-on-top said. "But if we don't like a guy, we can send him out of here looking pretty shitty."

Their access to regular shipments of new sportswear allowed the property-room workers to make far more than their thirty-dollar-a-month salaries. Walks-on-top charged five dollars for a shirt, five dollars for a pair of pants, and seven or eight dollars for every jacket that he smuggled to eager customers on the other side of the 9-tower gate. Usually, he took his pay in nickel bags of marijuana. "I'm swamped with orders," he said. "If I had to get everybody what they wanted, there wouldn't be no clothes out here."

To get his merchandise past the guards, Walks-on-top packed the

clothes in a cardboard box, sealed the box with tape, and wrote some inmate's number on the top. That way it looked like a routine inmate-property transfer. He handtrucked the box to the 9-tower gate, gave the guards a phony inventory slip, and turned the box over to an accomplice who pretended that the "belongings" were his personal property.

"Everybody's department has something that somebody else wants," Walks-on-top said. "We scratch their back and they scratch ours." Walks-on-top traded clothes for cheese, soup, sugar, peanut butter, steak, and other foodstuffs peddled by the kitchen workers. He traded clothes to the hospital workers for milk, coffee, and fruit drinks. The twenty-pound tins of hospital coffee came through gate security addressed to the sergeant to avoid suspicious questions.

Guards were often willing partners in the prison's informal barter economy. Although prison rules prohibited taking food out of the kitchen, Walks-on-top's co-worker ordered glazed doughnuts from the bakery, picked up a tray, and paved his way back to the property room by giving a doughnut or two to all the guards en route. The property-room sergeant, who sometimes lunched in his comfy chair in front of the television set, padded the goodie box by bringing unclaimed canned goods from the mail room. In return, Walks-on-top and his co-workers made sure that the sergeant's grilled cheese sandwiches were "done just so."

Guards frequently traded prison provisions like soap, towels, tobacco, and coffee to alleviate temporary shortages as well as to make their jobs more comfortable. "The stuff is already here that people are trading," shrugged a cellblock officer. "You just move it around from place to place without going through the bullshit and the red tape."

While some inmates had job assignments and some were able to buy or finagle their way into comfortable prison jobs, others carved out their own "comfort zones" by becoming club leaders or by joining one of the three inmate self-help groups. These groups—Social Therapy Program (STP), Social Adjustment for Minorities (SAM), and the Awareness Movement, Inc. (AMI)—occupied adjacent twenty-four-cell tiers in the admissions wing, a four-tiered cellblock that had once contained the "fish tank," the cells where new inmates lived.

Prison counselors and guards generally described the self-help groups as "milk and cookie programs." They were convinced that most inmates joined the groups primarily to live in the comparative comfort of a one-man cell. Inmates in the programs, however, argued that the admissions wing was the only place in the penitentiary where criminals were

genuinely being rehabilitated. They called it the prison's "treatment center."

All three programs claimed high success rates. Their leaders insisted that only 5 to 10 percent of their graduates released from the penitentiary had been returned to prison.

The most innovative of the three self-help groups was the Awareness Movement, Inc. Its philosophy was based on the belief that only criminals really understood crime and prisons. An Awareness brochure pointed out that "most of the literature about the criminal mind is as worthless as a used Kleenex" because convicts tell psychologists and sociologists what they want to hear. Consequently, the three inmates who founded Awareness originated a whole new field of study called "conology," the study of convicts by convicts. The founders theorized that once convicts understood why they committed crimes, they could redirect their energy in useful and socially acceptable ways. Those who mastered this understanding were awarded the doctor of conology degree, the "Phd.C.," and became "conologists."

The resident conologist and the executive director of Awareness in 1978–1979 was John Bateman, the only founder of the movement still inside the walls. A habitual criminal and an ex–drug addict, Bateman had spent more than half of his forty years behind bars. He was a squat, solidly built man, an ex-boxer whose barrel chest had slipped down into an ample paunch. Seated, his thinning brown hair dangling over his collar, he looked a bit like a department-store Santa. His expression was open and good-natured, and his soft yet decisive voice made him an ideal convict spokesman.

Befitting his position, Bateman occupied a secluded cell at the end of the admissions wing's B deck, the "Awareness tier." B deck was lined with handpainted posters, slogans, and charts illustrating Awareness concepts. One prominent poster spelled out the Conologist's Creed: "I am a person who evolved from a system of evil. I am now dedicated, heart and spirit, to the elimination of that system and the freeing of those spirits trapped within."

Bateman's cell adjoined the group's office, a partially enclosed area crowded with file cabinets, a card table for playing dominoes, and a mimeograph machine for churning out Awareness literature. Bateman and the Awareness board of directors met in the office to decide who would be admitted to the program and, hence, who would be allowed to live on the tier.

If applicants passed muster with the board, they were asked to sign

a contract that prohibited narcotics, drinking, gambling, "objectionable behavior," "hostile actions," and late-night radio playing on the tier. The contract insisted that "this is not a social club" but a "living and learning experience."

While easy living may have been a motivation for some, Bateman was convinced that the Awareness combination of psychology and dialogue could transform criminals. "A guy can do all kinds of good things in prison, but unless he changes the way he thinks, he's still going to go out with a criminal mind," Bateman insisted.

Awareness began in 1974 as a "leadership training school." With the prison administration's blessing, a group of inmates retired to B tier to develop a program that would, as Bateman put it, "get prisoners on a positive trip." They copied sales-motivation courses, wrote away for leadership manuals, and pored through psychology and sociology texts. Finally, they concluded that, since much of what the professionals had to say was bunk, they ought to develop their own program. Combining their own ideas with an amalgam of tapes and booklets from self-motivation institutes (texts like *Success through a Positive Mental Attitude, The Success System That Never Fails,* and *The Think and Grow Rich Action Pack*), they created Awareness. Members announced their new discipline by wearing buttons that declared: "I AM AWARE."

In early 1976, Awareness incorporated as a nonprofit organization with hopes of setting up branches "within every prison in the nation." The incorporation papers contained the Awareness Creed: "The Awareness Movement is a 'prisoner-helping-prisoner' movement dedicated to the complete revision of the corrections system. After 200 years of injustice and failure, WE, the prisoners doing the time now, offer our total commitment to attainment of that goal."

By the fall of 1978, Bateman and the other Awareness officers had set up an initial twelve-week study period for new members. Awareness beginners studied self-image psychology, success motivation, communication techniques, and the history of corrections. The classes were taught on the tier with Awareness members seated at portable desks ranged in a circle around the instructor, usually Bateman or an "associate conologist." Sometimes the speaker was a guest—the chaplain, the warden, a professor from the local community college. Instructors relied heavily on tapes, visual aids, and other learning materials supplied by sales-motivation and self-help institutes. "We are eclectic and use whatever seems to work," an Awareness pamphlet explained.

The course outline for the self-image psychology class, for instance, included study of the conscious mind, the subconscious mind, the creative subconscious mind, self-esteem, "scotomas" (blind spots), the "G.I.–G.O. syndrome" ("Garbage In–Garbage Out"), the reticular activating system, cognitive dissonance, motivation, self-talk, objective truth, the eight steps of psychological growth, rules for goal setting, and mental health.

One of the most important Awareness activities was called "conceptual semantics." Three evenings a week, Awareness members sat in a circle at their desks and took turns defining one of the concepts on the "disc of consciousness." Propped against a nearby blackboard, the cardboard disc looked like a roulette wheel. But instead of numbers, there were twelve words embodying the ideals that Awareness judged essential for happiness: love, friendship, values, motives, roles, confidence, respect, abilities, fellowship, goals, success, and loyalties. Those were the concepts; the semantics came from talking about them.

The concept that Awareness members discussed at one evening session in early October 1978 was friendship. Bateman opened the discussion with a low-key homily on the necessity of having friends. "Convicts are human," he said. "They hurt, they feel joy, they get depressed."

When he had finished speaking, the pint-sized Chicano to his right admitted, "I used to want to manipulate guys. I was always scheming how to use people."

The little Chicano continued talking for a few minutes and then gave the floor to the next inmate, an earnest fellow who raised his voice to drive home his points. "Friendship is just being able to communicate with someone," he concluded. "Don't look up at me. Don't look down at me. Look right at me and you'll see."

A few turns later, a bookish fellow read Epicurus's thoughts on friendship, then added his own. "I find it hard to make lasting friendships because I've got stung a couple times by friends," he said.

As the discussion continued around the circle, some of the men told stories, some told how their ideas had changed, and others simply offered dictionary definitions. The mood was quiet, thoughtful, almost reverent. No one challenged anyone else. When it was Bateman's turn again, he observed that friendship meant trust and loyalty. Conceptual semantics was over for that evening.

Bateman explained afterward that discussing the concepts helped members to develop "identification and Awareness muscles" by gaining insights from others' observations. Members purposely kept the tone

light and congenial, he said, to avoid the haggling that typified most inmate discussion groups.

The sporadically published Awareness newsletter reflected the high-minded tone of the evening circles. It often contained theoretical discourses written by the conologists. One early discourse, titled "The Outer Disc of Universal Consciousness," began: "Be there a multitude of ways for consciousness to communicate, through material bodies to other flickering specks of human consciousness; and be meaning the singular choice for these communications; then meaning becomes our first hurdle. What has meaning?" The discourse continued by discussing energy with reference to Einstein, perception, intuition, emotion, logic, and two models of behavior: the confusion model and the harmonic model. In the harmonic model, when boy meets girl, he generates harmony "through mutual interest" rather than through "conquest over girl with lies and deceit."

Reversing its earlier thinking, Awareness tried to extend the harmonic model to the rest of the penitentiary. At one time, fearful that the prison's negative environment would impede their rehabilitation, members had isolated themselves from the rest of the population. They had their own tables in the dining hall and had their own seats in the auditorium. But in 1978, Bateman initiated a program called Operation Movin' and Groovin' in which Awareness members purposely mingled with nonmembers in hopes of transmitting "good vibes." That way, Bateman asserted, Awareness benefited the whole prison.

Bateman recalled how the last time that he was free, seven years earlier, he had had a good job, a straight job laying epoxy flooring for ten dollars an hour. But he did not have the right mentality; he quit and soon reverted to his old career as a drugstore-stickup man. "I was still in a culture of convicts," he said. "There was something about doing all that time that made it impossible for me to work. Work had no meaning. I had this alienated type of feeling that I didn't fit in. I'd be there but I was always bored."

The point, he said, was that the clubs, the school, the jobs in the prison industries, and all the other programs that people claimed would rehabilitate convicts, did not make a bit of difference unless the convict "changed his criminal mind."

Despite his job in the license-plate factory, Kim has plenty of time to relax with his cellmate Leomy, a queen, or to go shopping at Bob's "Breezeway Bon Marche."

Many inmates hang out on the breezeways where they watch the day go by or make deals. Other idle men play cards in the Big Yard.

The steadiest and best-paid prison jobs are in the license-plate factory. Because there is not enough real work, the prison invents work; make-work includes sorting screws, mixing them up, and re-sorting them. Even in the license-plate factory, there are hours and hours of idleness.

Some inmates create their own programs to have something constructive to do. John Bateman is the executive director of the Awareness Movement, Inc., and "Stretch" says that the Social Adjustment Program for Minorities saved him from "all that madness out there."

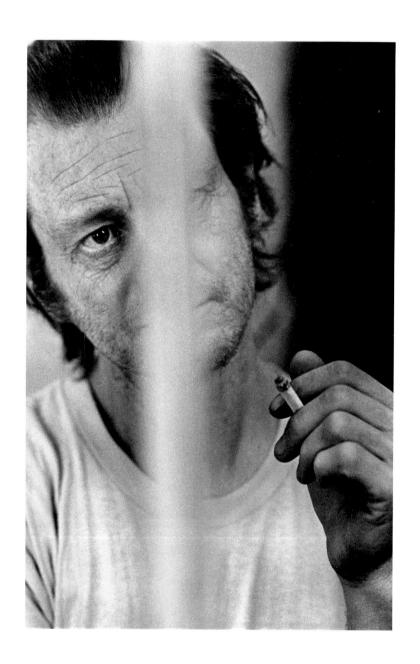

8

Wino: Snitch

Labeled a "rat," a "rapo," and a "ding," Jimmy "Wino" Butterfield came back to prison with three strikes against him.

What made him angry, he said, was that he should not have been in prison at all. He had been framed, he said, arrested for a "bum beef," a trumped-up rape charge. He maintained that his victim, a fifty-year-old woman, had hollered rape to avoid paying bills that she owed him.

But Wino's version did not muster much support. His lawyer advised him to plead guilty to second-degree rape, and the judge gave him twenty years. Sentenced in 1974, Wino spent his first five months in the sex offenders' program at Western State Hospital, a mental institution near Tacoma. He contended that the program was useless because he didn't have a sex problem.

"What caused a lot of my problems," he said, "was being married to whores. My mind was always going like a spring on a shithouse door. I was always worrying about some guy fucking my wife." Wino figured that he had inherited his troubled marital life from his mother, "a pretty little thing" who went through husbands like he went through wives—he had been married five times.

His mother hadn't liked Shirley, his first wife, but he had married her anyway. That marriage soured when Shirley ran off and got pregnant by another man. Then there was a fleeting two-month marriage to a young woman whose name Wino couldn't or wouldn't remember. After her came Birdie, who "tried to catch me in a bigamy rap," Wino said. Birdie was followed by Flo, "a Mexican gal," by whom Wino had two children. But one day, drunk and wired on pills, he walked out on her. Finally, there was Barbara, who had complained to penitentiary authorities that he was writing her threatening letters. "But how can I blame 'em," Wino said. "I was fucking anything I could find. Plus I was an alcoholic who didn't want to stop drinking. My life was all fucked up."

Between bouts in bars and bedrooms, Wino spent his free years hustling anything that would bring a price. He dealt in apples, watermelons, televisions, washing machines, guns, cars, and even food stamps.

In the bars, people knew him as "Lucky." "I had a pickup truck with four on the floor and plenty of fucking money up in the attic," Wino said, recalling his better days as a small-town wheeler-dealer in eastern Washington and northeastern Oregon.

The better days, however, were few. "Drinking a steady diet of beer and vodka," Wino put himself into some dire straits. The army tried to discharge him for "mental problems." Then, after Shirley left him in 1958, he started taking barbiturates to calm his nerves. The combination of pills and alcohol was disastrous.

One afternoon, he drew a knife on a shoe-store salesman in Milton-Freewater, Oregon. The police carted him off to jail, where he set fire to his cell. After the fire had been put out, he crammed his clothes into the cell toilet and kept flushing. Police charged through the flood, bound Wino in a straitjacket, and hauled him off to Eastern Oregon State Hospital, an insane asylum. The episode resulted in arson, theft, and assault convictions and a two-year stint at the Oregon State Penitentiary.

He said that it was the only hard time he had ever done before being convicted of rape and sent to Walla Walla.

A tip that Wino had given to a county jailer eventually forced him to seek protective custody, he said. Wino hated to admit it, but the tip, which had led to a drug arrest, had cost him his prison reputation. The inmate whom he had told on in the county jail wound up as a biker at Walla Walla. "I picked up a snitch jacket," Wino confessed.

Wino's move from the general prison population to asylum in protective custody did not come easily. Now, he would be marked forever as a "rat." "I'd be dead if I went back out there now," he said, peering through the bars of his tiny one-man cell three years after he had "checked in." "I'd be deader than a motherfucker."

The reputation that had followed him from the county jail only compounded Wino's problems at the penitentiary. He had others: He was too little, too sickly, and had too few friends.

Although he was once known as a scrapper, Wino's 132 pounds scarcely covered his five foot five inch frame. Years of drinking, pill popping, and womanizing had worn him down. A chronic stomach ailment forced him to vomit after every meal. The eleven teeth left in

his head, all lowers, were too rotten to chew meat. His nerves were shot, he said, and his bones were bent from "more damn car wrecks than you can take a piss at."

His gray, slicked-back hair and his furrowed face made him look older than his forty-two years. Because of his looks, his messy cell, and his affection for liquor, other inmates had nicknamed him "Wino," although wine was one of the few alcoholic beverages that he did not like. He had always been partial to whiskey, vodka, and beer.

Frightened and friendless, Wino arrived at the penitentiary in late 1974. For five months, he tried to live in the "jungle."

"I was here about fifteen days when two bikers came up and asked for ten dollars," Wino recalled. "I gave it to them. I didn't argue." Wino figured that the bikers probably knew about the incident in the county jail. He was afraid that he had already acquired a reputation as a snitch. Later, another biker dunned him for thirty-five dollars. "Then they started coming up again and again, saying they wanted to borrow ten dollars or twenty dollars. But you'd never get it back," Wino said. "It was no use telling them you didn't have any money because they knew. They knew what you were here for and they knew how much money you had on your books. They probably paid a guy for the information."

Other inmates who saw the bikers harassing Wino offered to back him. "But then you got to pay the backers," Wino objected, recalling how he had coughed up several hundred dollars in protection money. "There's no such thing as friendship."

The bikers not only ripped him off, they also taunted him. "They liked to show me their authority," Wino said. "I'd be at a table in the chow hall and they'd come up and tell me to move. Or one of them would come up and say, 'Buy me a Coke, brother.' Then pretty soon there'd be a whole line of them. What can you do?" Wino even forked over his medication. "I'd get pills on the pill line, put them under my tongue, or keep them in my hand and pretend to swallow them," he said. "Then, I'd go and give 'em up."

Gradually, Wino began to fear for his life. He avoided the weekend movies in the darkened auditorium. He stopped going out at night. During the day, he stuck close to his cell. Still, he felt like a hunted man. "I'd be in bed at night and I couldn't sleep. I was so nervous," he said. "I went through hate and fear trips, mind trips."

The breaking point came soon after. "One day I walked out of A.A. [Alcoholics Anonymous], and two of them come up. One slapped me around and the other pulled a shiv [knife]. They took my watch and said they wanted my tape deck the next day." The next day, Wino signed over his tape deck by transferring its ownership to another convict. "I was paying the bikers to stay alive," he sighed, shaking his head in disgust. "If I didn't, they would have stuck me. I wasn't big enough to take care of myself."

Desperate, Wino decided that he had to do the inevitable. He went to Lieutenant Colombo, gave up the names of the thieves who had robbed him, and thus was forced to check in to "PC," protective custody. There, in the isolation of 5-wing, a bare, clean block of 128 cells, Wino found a measure of safety.

When he moved there in 1975, there were plenty of vacant cells. In fact, the prison could afford the luxury of having a second PC unit within protective custody—a barred row of six cells for housing men who were so despised that even PC inmates were likely to harm them. But now, the overcrowding that characterized the entire prison was especially acute in protective custody.

In the fall and winter of 1978–1979, the penitentiary's PC population fluctuated between 150 and 175 inmates. Since 5-wing was full, new PC cases were put into cells in the segregation unit where they passed an idle, wretched existence, their daily recreation limited to two hours of pacing the tier. Some waited six months in segregation before a cell opened in 5-wing.

Inmates in PC complained that the system punished them for being victims while those who victimized them ran free in the general population. "We're persecuted for being here," griped a biker who had checked in over "some shit that came down in the bike shop."

The guards agreed. "The guys we used to keep locked up, that 10 percent prone to rob, extort, assault, and murder, have driven a lot of people into PC," observed the counselor who worked in 5-wing. "Up until 1971, we never had more than five or ten guys in PC." They blamed the increase in protective-custody cases on the advent of due-process hearings and other legal procedures designed to protect an inmate's rights. In the old days, they simply locked the bad guys in the hole. Now they had to convince a hearing committee that the guy deserved segregation.

In an attempt to reduce the PC population, prison officials periodically culled through the unit asking inmates if they really needed protection. Because inmates who went to "snitch row" acquired reputations as "rats," bringing them back out was difficult. "Once a fellow is here for any length of time, it's not safe to come out," one guard remarked. "Why check out and be dead?"

Usually, the officers checked with the Resident Council to see if an

inmate could come out of PC without any hassles. Occasionally, Lieutenant Colombo told a man that he could not come out because he was too "hot." Sometimes, it was hard to know. In June 1978, an inmate who thought that he had no problems voluntarily signed out and was stabbed to death in a prison lavatory a few days later. His assailant had nursed a grudge for six years.

Kenny Agtuca, Bobby Tsow, and other club leaders were permitted to talk to specific inmates in hopes of allaying their fears and of sponsoring them back into the population. Sometimes, it worked. But other times, it was just another extortion game. "Some of the biggest robbers and backstabbers come over here and say they'll get us out if we slip them some money on the Q.T.," scoffed a black inmate who had shelled out protection money in the past.

After three years in PC, Wino had no intention of checking out. Unlike many of the recent arrivals who spent most of the day locked in their five-by-eight-foot cells, Wino had cadged a job assignment. His job, sweeping a breezeway that connected 5-wing with the prison hospital, allowed him to wander around the tier or to hang out in the dayroom. He could visit with friends and could spare himself the expense of making his own instant coffee. A coffee urn, designated for the workers, sat on the tier.

In the summer, he and some of his co-workers cultivated a patch of earth next to the breezeway. They grew cucumbers, radishes, squash, corn, tomatoes, and, when they could get away with it, marijuana.

"If I'm not working, I'm supposed to be in my cell," Wino admitted. "But I'm pretty good at staying out. After all, the cops are good to the ones that are good to them."

Wino said that he owed his job to his buddy Bud Ferguson, the PC inmate who clerked for the sergeant in charge of 5-wing. A former Hell's Angel and an ex-president of the bikers' club, the forty-three-year-old Ferguson had no use of his right arm. Five years earlier, an inmate had stabbed him in the back, he said. Then, his "old lady" had been told that he would be stabbed again unless she smuggled drugs into the visiting room. He had taken the heat off her, he said, by checking in to PC.

"I can truthfully say that getting stabbed was the best thing that happened to me," reflected Ferguson, sitting shirtless in the sergeant's chair. "When you're one of the weaker people, you change."

But some PC inmates grumbled that Ferguson had not changed. They accused the ex-biker and his clique of stealing scrip, of charging for phone calls, and of selling cells with the more desirable lower bunks. They were resentful that Ferguson, the only PC worker who drew pay (ten dollars a month), spent most of the day out of his cell.

The regimen in PC had improved from the monotonous years of doing nothing but cell time. But still, in contrast to the comparative freedom enjoyed by the general population, PC inmates led a crushingly dull existence. "I read, I listen to the radio, and I beat my meat to death," a PC inmate volunteered. "There's not much we're allowed to do."

The sergeant in charge of the unit explained, "The main difference between here and the general population is that these guys can't do anything for themselves. I or my officers have to do it for them." Guards delivered food, supplies, books, packages, and orders from the inmate store.

Unless they had a job or a school assignment, PC inmates were out of their cells only for "yard time" and for meals in the dayroom. During yard time, an hour and a half in the morning and an hour and a half in the afternoon, they had the choice of playing cards, of lifting weights in the dayroom, or of sunning themselves outside on a patch of lawn just big enough for a volleyball court. On Friday and Saturday evenings, a prison visiting room was reserved for PC inmates and their guests.

Despite the long hours of cell time, Wino figured that he lived as well as could be expected. He was not hassled, and he still enjoyed some of the illegal niceties of prison life. He traded cigarettes for barbiturates hustled off the pill line. He bought pruno when it was available, although, he admitted, "This last batch almost poisoned me to death." He regularly received money and greeting cards from his mother, now a "born again" Christian.

Wino too professed to be a Christian. Blowing the dust off his copy of the *Living Bible*, he said, "My church to me is my Bible. I read it every other day." He opened the cover to reveal the signatures of the four convicts who had owned the holy book before him. "One of them committed suicide," Wino noted. "He hung himself."

Guards said that Wino was a typical PC case, a snitch, a convict who had broken the convict code by tattling on other convicts. Some inmates, like Wino, became snitches by revealing drug schemes. Others had reported weapons caches or had testified in court against other inmates. They had given information in hopes of pleasing the parole board or of being transferred to another prison. Usually, it did not work. Either the information was wrong or the prison staff already knew it. Often, other prisons did not want them.

Snitching was not the only reason that an inmate lived in protective custody. People who committed certain crimes—incest, indecent lib-

erties, child rape, or child murder—were at the bottom of the prison's social register. The "baby raper" was the lowest inmate on the prison pecking order. A killer who had sliced up a little girl with a chain saw never had a choice about where he would live. Guards whisked him into PC as soon as he came through the gate. Child molesters and "rapos" who risked living in the general population often got worked over, extorted, or sodomized. Even the prison staff detested them. A Georgia-born guard who worked in PC conceded that he had to treat all inmates the same. "But," he said, "if a bank robber and a baby raper get in a fight, I hope the bank robber finishes him off."

Other inmates were forced into PC because they could not cover their debts. Some were junkies who owed more than they could ever hope to repay. "I'm a dope fiend, man," explained a sallow-faced inmate who lived in a cell down the tier from Wino's. "For me, it's easier doing time in here. I don't get into debt." But some of the debtors were small-timers who could not come up with a "nickel bag," a mere five dollars' worth of marijuana. When credit turned sour, life turned cheap. Blood was spilled for as little as fifty cents.

Some inmates came to PC because they were easy marks for extortion, for robbery, or for sexual assault. Too young, too old, too weak, or too pretty, they were afraid of living with the other prisoners. One old fellow claimed that he checked in when he heard that there was a hundred-dollar price on his head. "It's hard to know whether it was a murder contract or an extortion plot," he said. "But I don't gamble with my life."

On occasion, the fears of PC inmates were justified, but often, they were not. PC acquired more than its share of whiners, moaners, and chronic complainers who had decided that the bleak security of protective custody was more appealing than living with twelve hundred criminals. "They're a bunch of little sniveling snitches who can't handle their problems," groused one guard. "What we should do is throw them out in the population with a knife and let them settle it."

PC also collected "dings," inmates who were too crazy to adapt to a four-man cell but not crazy enough to be treated on the "third floor," the euphemism for the prison hospital's psychiatric unit. Most of them would not have been in protective custody if the state had had a facility for mentally disturbed criminals. "Nobody wants the crazies," shrugged the PC counselor who dealt with them, "so we put them in with the snitches and the rats."

Not all mentally ill inmates went to PC, however. Sane inmates claimed that as many as one hundred dings still wandered around the maximum-security compound.

Some were obvious. A porky, redheaded fellow who wore a stocking cap whether it was January or July paced the yard quoting the Bible. He called himself "God's avenging angel." A spooky guy with a shaved head haunted the breezeways with a large model airplane. He propelled the plane around tight corners by whispering into the cockpit. A middle-aged cowboy who dreamed of hooking up with a "China doll" removed his clothes and attempted to bathe in a prison urinal. Sometimes he took long walks barefoot in the snow. A ragged inmate, after drinking pruno, crawled around the dining-hall floor eating scraps of food. He smeared his face, hair, and clothes with butter. Inmates called him "The Butterman."

Most of the prison's dings, however, were less visible. Many appeared to be normal until them gave themselves away by going berserk or by asking paranoid questions. Joe Allen, president of the Resident Council, recalled how an inmate pulled him aside one afternoon and told him in dead seriousness, "They're fucking with the cottage cheese."

"What?" Allen responded.

"They're putting fruit in it," the inmate warned.

Most inmates gave dings a wide berth, avoiding them in the dining hall and keeping a wary eye on them on the breezeways. They complained that dings belonged in a mental hospital, not a prison. But the penitentiary hospital's psychiatric unit could not accommodate the growing numbers of mentally disturbed inmates. "Ding wing" had only twenty-eight beds, which were reserved for the most insane of the state's forty-one hundred adult male prisoners.

In early 1979, third-floor patients were under the care of Dr. Joseph Corvino, a thirty-four-year-old psychiatrist whom the prison had hired to work sixteen hours a week at forty dollars an hour. Except for two registered nurses, Corvino was the only health-care professional among the twenty-two employees who staffed the psychiatric unit. He was responsible for evaluating mental patients and for prescribing their treatment.

Corvino, who was just beginning his career, was an exception to the usual prison standard of medical mediocrity. He was a careful, conscientious man whose approach still reflected the thoroughness of a recent medical-school graduate. In 1977, he and his wife had moved from Cleveland, where he finished his psychiatric training, to Walla Walla where he hoped to find enough outpatients for a private practice. While

he built up his practice, he worked at the penitentiary. At work on the third floor, Corvino struck a casual appearance. Slightly pudgy, he wore a mustache, beard, round wire-rimmed glasses, sleeveless sweaters, corduroy pants, and soft leather shoes. His passion for detail and accuracy sometimes irritated his co-workers. He resented inmates, corrections officials, and parole-board members who used psychiatry in unprofessional ways. He complained that "very few are asking me to provide psychiatric care which is what I want to do."

Corvino's limited schedule allowed him only enough time to treat those inmates who were admitted to the mental-health unit. The overwhelming number of requests from the general population for psychiatric help went unanswered. The prison had tried to deal with those by hiring a psychologist and another part-time psychiatrist. But budget cuts did away with the psycholgist's position, and the psychiatrist suddenly disappeared. Prison officials admitted that they had known that the man was a chronic alcoholic, but they had hoped that he would work out. Inmates said that the case of the disappearing psychiatrist was typical. "Most doctors aren't here because they're humanitarians," Allen argued. "They're either at the tail end of their careers, or they're not very good to begin with."

Corvino conceded that he had mixed feelings about his prison job. "You're dealing with a population that will use whatever they can to get whatever they want," he said. "You can't trust what they tell you. That sounds paranoid, I know. But as a psychiatrist, it makes you very uncomfortable." Yet, he added, the job presented real challenges. "I've seen sicker guys here than I have in any other setting. Just terribly, terribly psychotic guys. People who really don't know what's going on."

Corvino's job was complicated by inmates who faked craziness. Some acted like "stone dings" as a way of protecting themselves from inmates who might beat, rob, or molest them. The fakers kept the prison predators at bay by giving the impression that they might strike back insanely.

Others behaved like dings to manipulate prison staff. They wanted pills, a sympathetic letter to the parole board, or a transfer to a state mental hospital where they could make an easier escape. They attracted staff attention by threatening to kill themselves, by scratching their wrists, or by tying a bed sheet around their necks. Corvino called the fakers "malingerers."

"I'm describing a guy who's in prison for violent crimes and been in fights in prison," he explained. "I can see from his record he's been given amphetamines and sleeping pills. He comes to me and tells me he needs his Dexedrine renewed. He says that when he has his Dex, he's just a calm, pleasant guy but when he doesn't get it, he's going to go and beat the hell out of some guards. I think the legitimate response is to say, 'Look, my friend, you're feeding me a line of shit and I don't buy it. There's no way I'm going to write you Dexedrine.' So he gets up and tells me he's going to beat me over the head with a chair. Now in the past that guy would have been given Dexedrine, and I think that's very improper."

During 1978, six hundred inmates received psychotropic drugs, the bulk of them prescribed by the psychiatric consultants who preceded Corvino. "It was easier to say 'yes' than argue for twenty minutes to say 'no,' " observed one physician's assistant.

Corvino's efforts to maintain an adequate mental-health facility were also taxed by the guards' tendency to want to house disruptive inmates on the third floor. Inmates who started fight after fight or who flew into mad rages were carried raving and shrieking into the two hospital holding cells owned by custody. Corvino then decided whether he would admit custody's charges to the unit. Usually, he did not. "Some people raise hell and are constantly fighting and causing trouble no matter where they are, no matter how they're dealt with, because that's the kind of people they are," Corvino insisted. "It's part of their personality to always be raising hell. There's nothing to do to change that type of behavior."

Thus, much to the guards' dismay, the hell-raising inmates were returned to the population or were lodged in segregation. Isolated in the hole, they received neither treatment nor attention. Those thought to be suicidal were stripped of their clothes and locked in bare cells. Guards reasoned that inmates with nothing to use but their hands were less likely to take their own lives.

While fakers and hell-raisers wasted Corvino's time, many inmates who really needed psychiatric care went untreated. They ended up ignored and forgotten, stuck away in 4-wing with the old folks or in PC with the snitches. "If they're not hitting somebody over the head and they're not making a request, nobody cares about them," Corvino said.

The few inmates who received psychiatric treatment on the third floor lived, for the most part, in three- or four-man rooms that were painted blue, orange, or peach rather than drab, institutional green. Some of the men decorated their rooms, accenting the cheerful colors with posters, drawings, and knickknacks.

Mike, a gangly youth trying "to get away from these obsessions I have," had painted his wall with terrified, leaping stallions, fanged vampire bats, and portraits of Norman Bates, the disturbed character played by Anthony Perkins in Alfred Hitchcock's movie *Psycho*. Mike had once identified with Clint Eastwood. In his Eastwood phase, he had killed a restaurant customer who had talked back to him.

A few third-floor residents lived in double-doored, padded cells where, if necessary, they could be locked out of sight and sound. The padded cells were reserved for the scrappers and the "screamers."

The staff kept its patients marginally active by encouraging chores and conversation and by sponsoring tournaments for chess, foosball, checkers, and spades. Tournament winners received candy bars, cigarettes, toothpaste, and deodorant. The principal activity, however, was the therapy group. Staff and residents met on weekdays to discuss, as one practical nurse put it, "emotions and feelings about themselves and others."

One discussion group, which was held in mid-January 1979, started slowly, got a bit of prompting, then focused on the topic of cleanliness. A practical nurse chaired the group of eleven inmates who sat around a mosaic coffee table in the third-floor dayroom.

A black inmate wearing a white turban got the conversation going. "I flushed some guy's big old turd this morning," he complained. "Now what kind of shit is that to wipe your butt but not flush the turd?"

"It's no secret that some people up here lack elementary toilet training," the nurse volunteered.

Mike, the artist who played Norman Bates, pointed out that messiness was an old problem. "This has been brought up and brought up and brought up and brought up over and over and over and over again like a broken record," he said.

Two other inmates carried the conversation until a slovenly dressed fellow named Rick interjected, "I'm sort of guilty about my cleanliness. I haven't been keeping myself clean." Staring at the floor, Rick rubbed his hands together as if he were scouring away years of accumulated dirt.

"Let's talk about Rick's problems," the nurse suggested. "He cleans himself only when he's told. What can he do to remind himself to clean up, bathe, and shave?"

Instead of advice, Rick got criticism. A Mexican inmate who slept in a bed next to Rick's chewed him out for throwing matches and blankets on the floor. The black wearing the turban told how Rick stood in the shower "with no soap or nothing" and refused to come out. Rick bowed his head and rubbed his hands faster. "I think these guys want to help me," he said, his voice cracking with grief. "I want to get on top of things. I want to keep myself clean."

The black wearing the turban pounced again. "Why don't you get up in the morning?" he demanded.

But Rick had had enough. "I got nothing to say about that," he blurted out.

The group fell silent. Finally, the Mexican said, "I don't know how Rick stands it. At Eastern State Hospital, I was put on a hot chair [made the subject of a group-therapy session] and I blew my mind."

Meanwhile, in a dull green office down the corridor, Dr. Corvino was interviewing a skinny Chicano who sat slumped forward, fumbling with his hands. Corvino's makeshift office was equipped with two prison-made desks, a couch that he rarely used, and a large wall calendar that someone had altered to read: "It's great to live in Washington State . . . Penitentiary."

"How are you doing?" Corvino asked the Chicano inmate. "How come you didn't come to the last patient interview?"

"Blessed Jesus was out here scratching himself like he had poison ivy," the Chicano replied, his voice trailing off into more nonsense.

Corvino asked the Chicano why he went to one of the state hospitals. The Chicano answered that he was a Texan and wanted to be paroled to Oklahoma City. Corvino sighed, and the interview was over.

"The guy is obviously schizophrenic," he said afterward. "He's got delusions about Christ, blood, movies. He's typical. You see a lot of guys with that illness in here. Usually, you see them when they're acutely psychotic. They're hearing voices; they're delusional; the television is talking to them. We've got a guy who thinks his left side is possessed by the devil so he cut his left testicle off."

But according to Corvino, the major psychiatric problem among prisoners was what he called an "antisocial personality." People who suffer from antisocial personality, he explained "are continually coming into conflict with other people, with society, and with certain aspects of their own lives. They don't control their impulses. They deal with people by attacking them and mistreating them. They don't feel guilty about robbing or doing violence because their consciences are different than ours. So naturally you're going to find an overwhelming selection for that personality in prison." He added that antisocial personalities emerged in early adolescence from chaotic, violent homes.

Corvino noted that there was a great deal of psychiatric speculation that criminals acted the way they did because it was part of their personality to steal, hurt, and manipulate people. "Even when it's to their disadvantage to manipulate people, they've still got to do it," he said. Unfortunately, the psychiatrist continued, there was no successful treatment for such a personality disorder. "A precondition you've got to have to change someone's personality is that the person himself has some interest in changing," Corvino said. "That doesn't apply to very many people in prison. There have been all kinds of treatments tried with prisoners over the years and none of them demonstrate anything. They've had everything from behavior modification to psychoanalysis where they see an analyst an hour a day, five days a week, for years, and nobody gets results,"

Not all convicts have antisocial personalities, Corvino emphasized. "There are some prisoners for whom you can make interventions and it will help them change. But they tend to look different than the majority of guys I've seen." In addition, he cautioned, they tended to deteriorate in a society in which people with antisocial personalities made the rules. "You spend enough time in any institution and you show a lot of effects of that institution," Corvino said.

The penitentiary psychiatrist conceded that his pessimistic view ran counter to the idea that prisoners could be rehabilitated. He argued that most people who came to prison had a long history of antisocial behavior that would continue after their release. "I can't see anything in prison that's going to be terribly potent in changing that pattern," he said.

Stressing that he was speaking as a citizen and not as a psychiatrist, Corvino said that he would be very reluctant to release a repeat offender "who all his life has demonstrated that he's dangerous and antisocial. Just because you feel guilty or the prison's crowded or whatever reason, you shouldn't try to pretend that all of a sudden the guy's going to change and be an upright citizen. With most of the guys I see, you know they're going to come back. If we know they're going to go out and hurt somebody else, why not keep them here?

"People are bothered by that," Corvino acknowledged, "because they say you're condemning them to prison. They say, 'Why not put them in a place where they can change?' Well, I don't know of any place. If there isn't any place you can put them where they're going to change, then the two alternatives are keeping them where they can't hurt people or letting them out so they can do it again. It's a hard thing. It's a very unpopular opinion, and it's not a psychiatric opinion. Psychiatrists don't have any more expertise to address that question than anybody else has. But it seems so obvious to me."

Being kept behind bars did not mean that inmates with antisocial personalities stopped breaking the law. They were no longer able to freely pick their prey, but plenty of new victims like Wino were locked in prison with them.

Jimmy "Wino" Butterfield prefers his cluttered cell in
protective custody to living in the general population.
"I'd be dead if I went back out there now," he says.

126

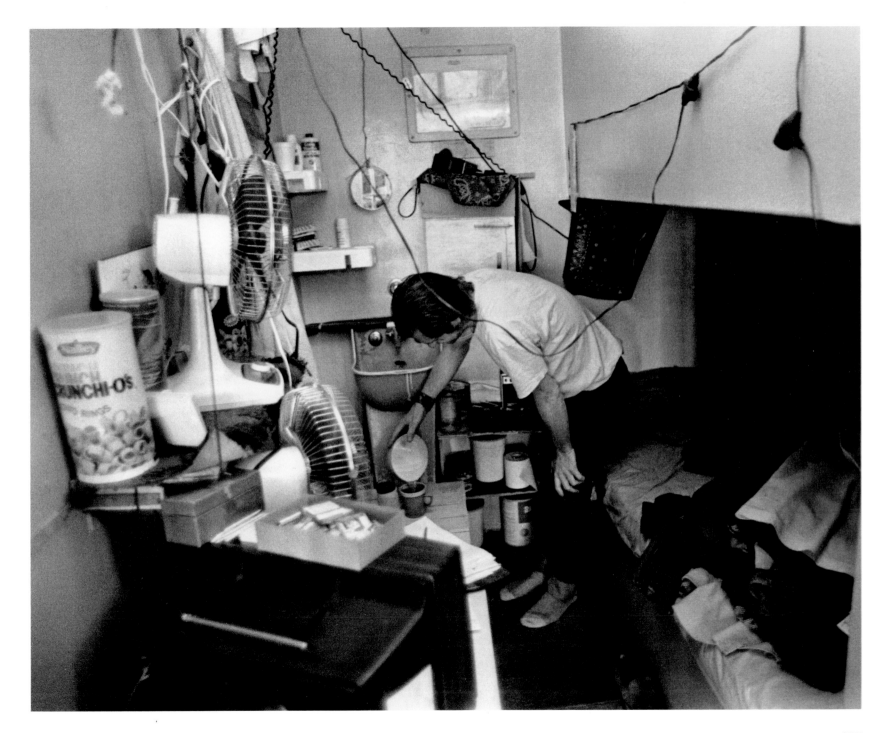

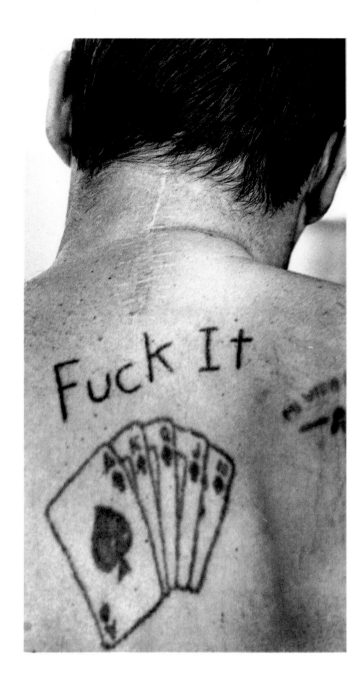

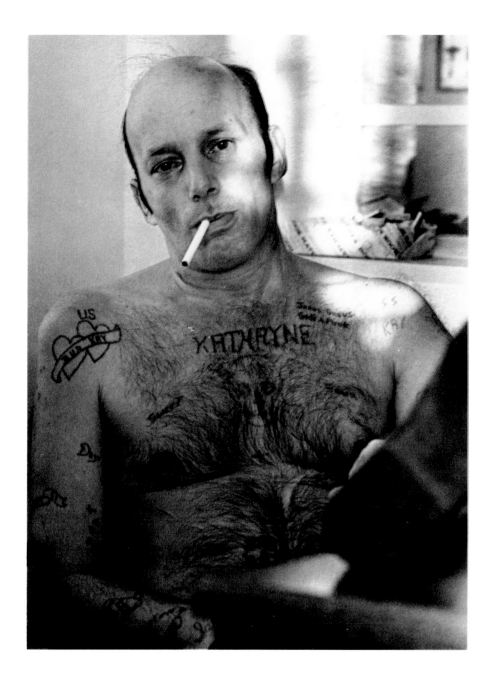

PC tends to collect inmates who are too old, too young, too weak, or too talkative to survive in the general population. Bud Ferguson, former Hell's Angel and past president of the bikers' club, "checked in" after he lost the use of his right arm in a stabbing.

PC inmates, who spend as many as twenty-two hours a day in their cells, are sensitive to the slightest change in routine. "Snitch mirrors" are used to watch activity on the tier.

PC also collects "dings." The older man believes that "convicts are created on Saturn by Satan and angels wing them down to earth." Mike, a convicted murderer, deals with his obsessions by drawing pictures of vampire bats, mad stallions, and tense, crazed men.

133

9

Ed: Revolutionary in "Big Red"

One day in 1969, in the midst of the political fallout from the Vietnam War, Ed Mead had a realization. At the time, he was a prisoner at the McNeil Island Federal Penitentiary near Tacoma. He had been a prisoner most of his adult life, but this time around, he had returned to prison with "a real sense that I'd been messed over in the courts." Rather than pay an inmate "jailhouse lawyer" to work on his appeal, Ed decided to learn the law himself. After two years of study, he became one of the best writ-writers at the prison; he was so good that real attorneys sometimes copied his legal briefs.

In the process of working on prisoners' cases, Ed bagan to notice that "the only people who were doing anything for prisoners were these political activists. I got to thinking about it until one day I didn't identify as a criminal anymore. I identified as a radical. I knew I'd stepped over a line. I didn't know whether I was an anarchist, or a Marxist, or what. But these people out there on the streets stood for what I stood for—whatever that was." Up until that day, Ed said, he had simply been a burglar and a thief.

He had grown up poor in a fatherless home on an Alaskan homestead. "Sometimes it became necessary to help myself," he recalled. "I did burglaries, stole cars, did time in a youth institution." At eighteen, he was caught burglarizing a gas-station cigarette machine for thirty dollars. He got a three-year sentence to the federal prison in Lompoc, California.

"I went in there scared, hearing stories about rape," Ed recalled. "But you get there and the only thing you got in common with everybody is that you've all been convicted of a crime. So you talk about the crimes you've done and the crimes you're going to do. Pretty soon you come to identify criminally."

When he got out eighteen months later, Ed could not fit into straight society. "The people I could relate to hung out at the local crook bar," he said. "They weren't the kinda guys who mowed their lawns."

During the 1960s, Ed was in and out of prison three more times for burglary, larceny, and attempted escape. But when he was imprisoned again in 1969, the situation had changed. He not only learned the law but he also read every piece of radical literature that he could lay his hands on. Then he began to organize. His role in organizing a prisoners'

strike at McNeil got him shipped to Leavenworth, the toughest of all the federal prisons. En route, he was temporarily lodged at the King County Jail in Seattle where he led another inmate strike.

Released again in 1972, Ed helped to establish a prisoner-support house near McNeil and attempted to form a Washington State Prisoners Labor Union. He and his co-workers engineered a work slowdown at the state reformatory. They crashed the American Correction Association convention in Seattle, seizing the stage during a discussion of the psychological effects of long-term incarceration. Ironically, Ed pointed out, the expert witness invited to speak to the convention was an ex–prisoner of war, not a convict.

When the prisoners' union collapsed, Ed went to Buffalo, New York, to raise defense funds for the prisoners who had survived the slaughter at Attica. Then, the Symbionese Liberation Army (SLA) hit the headlines.

"I read their Revolutionary War Declaration in the newspaper, and I cried," Ed remembered. "How they talked about the old people eating out of garbage cans and how they said we've got to share and cooperate. It sparked something in me."

Ed headed for San Francisco. Though he had no contact with the SLA, he put posters in buses and laundromats that showed the seven-headed SLA cobra and the message: "Give THEM shelter." Yet, he was critical of the underground group's tactics. "I saw that they went out too far and too fast," he said. "You have to go slower and develop a support network as you go."

In December 1974, Ed read about a group of Walla Walla inmates who had seized the prison hospital and had taken hostages. The rebellion was crushed, but the act stirred his imagination. Inspired by the Walla Walla rebels and the SLA, Ed decided that it was time "to stand up and take a step against the state." He and a small group of radical friends set out to bomb the Washington State Department of Corrections in support of prisoner demands at Walla Walla.

The explosion that caused a hundred thousand dollars damage to the Olympia office of adult corrections on 1 June 1975 announced the birth of the George Jackson Brigade (GJB), a revolutionary underground group named for the radical black convict who had been killed in a 1971 escape attempt from San Quentin. A brigade communiqué left at

a Seattle phone booth called for prison reform and for the overthrow of capitalism.

"It was the brigade's first public act," Ed said. In the months that followed, the brigade would claim credit for four more bombings—two at a Seattle Safeway store, one at a Safeway office, and another at a Seattle power plant. The brigade hailed the bombing campaign as a "successful attack against property." It picked its targets for their political significance: the giant grocery chain represented capitalist exploitation, and the power plant supplied electricity to one of Seattle's wealthiest neighborhoods. The only casualty was a brigade supporter whose bomb exploded too soon and blew him to smithereens.

On 23 January 1976, brigade members attempted, as Ed put it, "to expropriate forty-four thousand dollars from the Pacific National Bank." Armed, they hit a small suburban branch south of Seattle. In the ensuing gun battle with police, one brigade member was killed, and Ed and another member were captured. Ed was convicted of two counts of armed assault. He received stiff punishment—two consecutive life sentences.

In most prisons, it has always been known as "the hole." At Walla Walla, prison officials called it "segregation," or, if they were inclined toward fancier names, they called it the ISU, "intensive security unit." But inmates simply called it "Big Red," a squat, ugly, red-brick cellblock where guards housed the meanest, most disruptive, and most violent of the penitentiary's fourteen hundred maximum-security inmates. It was a place of punishment with no pretense of rehabilitation.

When Ed arrived at Walla Walla in August 1976, he was led straight to Big Red. Although he had not yet broken any prison rules, officials placed him in segregation on the assumption that he would. They called that practice "administrative segregation," or "ad-seg," a neat convention that allowed them to isolate any inmates believed to be threats to themselves, to others, or to the security of the institution. Warden Bobby J. Rhay had read Ed's dossier—brigade member, strike organizer, Marxist revolutionary—and had decided that he was a troublemaker. "Any GJB member is going to be ad-segged right off the git-go," remarked one of the sergeants who ran Big Red.

Ed sued the prison's administration, arguing that he had been denied due process by being placed directly in segregation. He won his suit and in spring 1977 was transferred from Big Red to the general prison population.

Free to circulate among the other prisoners, Ed began organizing. He formed a Prisoners' Justice Committee whose purpose was to get more inmates out of Big Red, to mobilize "progressive people in the outside community," and to put responsibility "for treatment in inmate hands." He served as legal adviser in the Indians' battle to erect a sweat lodge and to practice their "native spiritual ways." He set up Men against Sexism (MAS) as a gay-rights group that sought to protect gay and weak inmates from prison bullies.

But on 1 July 1978, Ed and four other inmates attempted to use an MAS party in the visiting room as a cover for an escape. Aided by armed guards, they planned to knock out one guard tower, to cut through the visiting yard's cyclone fence, and to scurry into two waiting vehicles.

On the eve of the party, however, guards searched Ed's cell in 8-wing. They found knives, pipe bombs, a compass, wire cutters, files, timing devices, and a loaded .22 caliber pistol with additional rounds of ammunition. They also found a three-page communiqué hailing the "freeing of Walla Walla's political prisoners" as a "judicious application of revolutionary violence." The communiqué was signed: "Red Dragon Unit, George Jackson Brigade." One of the escape vehicles was rumored to be a high-powered van decorated with a red dragon.

The captured contraband and the foiled escape attempt gave prison officials ample cause to hustle Ed back to Big Red, where he was "ad-segged" indefinitely.

At thirty-seven, Ed was thin, about 155 pounds, and anemic-looking from the many years he had spent indoors. He was five feet ten inches tall and not especially muscular. His blonde hair reached down below his shoulders. A scar ran across the bridge of his nose, and his right eye was artificial. He said that he had shot out his real eye while cleaning a gun that he did not believe was loaded.

Ed spoke slowly and deliberately, punctuating his sentences with long "ahhs," as if his mind was racing too far ahead of his mouth. His intelligence and his dedication to a cause gave him a powerful influence over other inmates. In a group, he was a cool and articulate spokesman. When he failed to convince with his logic, he was prepared to use his fists, but he conceded that he was often afraid "of having to fight to raise somebody's consciousness."

For the most part, guards detested Ed. They ridiculed his blatant homosexuality and called him a "queen" behind his back. But they were cautious with him. They were intimidated by his knowledge of the law and were fearful of the hold that he exercised over some of the other inmates in Big Red.

Ed usually dressed in blue jeans; black-and-white, high-topped tennis shoes; and sometimes a green T-shirt stenciled with white letters reading "P.O.W." The prison allowed him and the other segregation inmates only two sets of clothes. His one-man, six-by-nine-foot cell on B tier, where most of the ad-seg cases were housed, was packed with books, papers, and political propaganda. Segregation cells had no sockets for radio or television, so inmates usually depended on the mail and on the prison library to keep them in touch with the outside world. Above his door, Ed had a sticker that read: "Free Political Prisoners."

During his daily hour of exercise, the only time when he was allowed outside his cell, Ed paced the dreary, narrow confines of B tier with Danny Atteberry, his lover, who lived in the next cell. Atteberry, also a brigade member, led the 1974 attack on the prison hospital.

Although Ed had lived with women when he was out of prison, he said that he was now giving expression to his love for men. "We all have our yin and yang, our masculine and feminine sides. We should give expression to each," he said. Ed's homosexuality was well suited to his politics of championing the oppressed. Gays were undoubtedly the penitentiary's most oppressed inmates. "Prisoners will never get themselves together unless they develop a consciousness that gays are people, that gays have rights," Ed said. "The masculine thing is so oppressive in here. These guys drive themselves to the wall trying to live up to this fucking tough-guy image."

In the fastness of Big Red, however, Ed could do little to protect the prison's vulnerable gay inmates. In his absence, MAS had reverted to a social club run by queens, void of political consciousness.

But Ed had a new war on his hands now, a continuing battle, as he saw it, to correct the dire conditions and abuses that inmates suffered in segregation. "You're in a constant state of helplessness," Ed said, explaining life in Big Red. "You're dependent on your captors for every little need."

Among other things, guards controlled the food, heat, light, mail, phone calls, visits, showers, clothing, and toilet supplies. They decided when and with whom segregation inmates would exercise. At all hours of the day, at least one guard was constantly watching, peering down the tier from behind electronically controlled double gates. If the guard saw something suspicious, he could order an inmate to submit to a strip search and to a "finger wave," a rubber-gloved probe of the anus. If the guard feared bigger trouble, he could call the tactical squad, a group of gung-ho officers who would arrive on the tier equipped with helmets, Mace, and riot batons.

Guards admitted that they sometimes took care of troublemakers by working them over with lead-lined gloves or by drenching them with the spray from the fire hose. But, they insisted, those were only occasional, unprofessional excesses that occurred in the heat of the moment. "When you go into a fight situation," explained one member of the tactical squad, "you want to end it real quick. You want to choke the guy out or put him out before he can stick you or somebody else. Then you've got the situation controlled."

The guards assigned to Big Red conceded that it was difficult to remain cool in the face of repeated inmate attacks. Sometimes when guards walked down the tier, inmates hurled debris from their cells or bombarded them with cups of urine and feces. They also harassed guards by throwing burning garbage out on the tier or by jamming the toilets and then flushing them until they overflowed, spilling water out of the cells and onto the tier. On occasion, the angry, frustrated inhabitants of Big Red punched, stabbed, and even captured their keepers.

Guards who lasted out their segregation assignments tended to be philosophical about the abuse. "When a convict throws piss and shit on you, he's throwing it on your uniform, your symbol of authority," figured one veteran officer. "As much as I hate the smell, I'd rather have shit thrown on me than have a shank stuck in my side."

Ed said that the harassment of guards, the arson, the violent attacks, and the property destruction were a natural response to "the indifferent and sometimes criminal treatment" in Big Red. The treatment, he said, included "3:00 A.M. raids and unprovoked assaults"; indefinite confinement "on evidence that would not pass constitutional muster"; being locked in a cage twenty-three hours a day without rehabilitation programs or release standards; less than the minimum lighting, air flow, and space requirements established by law; no access to the law library, chapel, educational, recreational, and vocational facilities; being forced to eat all meals next to the cells' open toilets while the segregation building's dining room went unused; and occasionally being served food that guards had tainted with bleach, soap flakes, or urine. "Seg makes people angry," Ed concluded.

Ed spent much of his cell time reading, writing, and preparing civil-rights lawsuits. He filed suit seeking access to the prison's law library. He filed another suit in hopes of halting the "arbitrary way" in which guards strip-searched inmates. He asked the federal court to outlaw the use of isolation cells—the double-doored concrete boxes that the penitentiary used to punish inmates who committed major infractions of the prison's rules. Isolation time, legally limited to ten days at a

stretch, was the prison's most severe punishment. In isolation, all an inmate had were the clothes on his back, a blanket, a book, and silence.

Ed corresponded with prisoners across the nation including radicals like Bill and Emily Harris, the SLA members who had been Patty Hearst's comrades-in-arms. He and other imprisoned brigade sympathizers, writing under the name "The Walla Walla Brothers," printed a sixteen-page paper called *The Belly of the Beast*. A collection of prison critiques, leftist news clips, and inmate commentary, the paper prominently quoted Ho Chi Minh on its masthead: "When the prison doors are opened, the real dragon will fly out." The "dragon," the paper suggested, would destroy prisons, "the state's control apparatus," and would topple the ruling classes that had used them to contain the impending revolution.

While Ed worked to create the consciousness that would lead to a revolutionary, classless society without prisons, others endured Big Red in more mundane ways. They read pornographic books, looked at girlie magazines, dawdled over their food, fantasized, and slept.

The short-timers, those who were being punished for infractions like punching an officer or carrying a knife, did their ten days of isolation and their twenty days of segregation and got out. They tended to get less involved in the hell-raising esprit de corps that characterized Big Red's long-term tenants. Those inmates who spent months, even years, in Big Red were generally organizers, escape artists, hostage takers, or assault and murder suspects awaiting trial. According to the guards, they were the prison's most desperate and dangerous men.

It was the long-term residents who learned and used the pig-Latin-type languages that had been invented in the hole years ago. One language, called Agana, was simple to learn but difficult to understand if the speaker talked quickly. Agana speakers inserted the expressions "agana," "bagana," "cagana," or some other variation between the syllables of English words. For example, "cigarette" became "cigagana-arbagana-rette."

Ellafa, another prison language, worked in a similar manner. "Ella" was attached behind the first letter of the English word, while "fa" was placed before the remainder of the word. For instance, "car" became "cella-far."

Carny, a language developed by carnival barkers, substituted rhyming expressions for the intended word. For example, "mince pies" meant "eyes," "chip 'n' chase" meant "face," "hunks of lead" meant "head," "moan 'n' groan" meant "phone," and so on. Skillful prison linguists could plot openly within earshot of their captors.

Ed's battle to win fair and legal treatment for segregation inmates was aggravated by the guards' reluctance to accept the growing number of due-process safeguards written into prison disciplinary procedures. Many of the older guards longed for the "good old days" when they could throw an inmate into the hole at the drop of a hat. In those days, the hole really was a hole—a clammy, unlit, empty cell with a drainage hole in the floor.

Browny, a convict who had done a good bit of "hole time" decades ago, remembered it well. "Once a day the door would open and they'd throw in a hunk of bread and a cup of water. On the tenth day, you got a little pan of whatever they had in the mess hall that day. You'd be so hungry you'd eat the whole pan and then you'd have to vomit it all out. All you had to wear was a pair of overalls and once a week they'd cut your hair off with clippers."

In the early 1970s, a series of federal court decisions forced the state to establish procedures and fair hearings for inmates charged with prison infractions. The early hearings, however, were often little more than mock justice. Warden Spalding remembered prison officials who walked into disciplinary hearings with blank infraction reports, made up the charges, then locked up the inmate for months. But Spalding insisted that his staff follow the letter of the law. "If they want to bag somebody, they're going to do it according to the law or it's not going to happen," he said.

A guard who "tagged" an inmate for breaking a prison rule was required to complete an infraction report noting time, place, witnesses, the specific rule that had been violated, and the circumstances. If the infraction was especially serious, for example, attempted escape, as in Ed's case, the guard could put the suspect on "awaiting action" status and could immediately lodge him in Big Red. Otherwise, the report was filed, and the inmate could expect to appear within five days before a disciplinary-hearing committee composed of three prison staff members, usually two guards and a counselor.

At the hearing, the inmate had the rights to remain silent, to call witnesses, to present evidence, to examine the disciplinary report, and to be accompanied by a "lay adviser," usually another inmate. If the inmate was displeased with the committee's judgment, he had twenty-four hours in which to file an appeal with the warden. The warden had five days in which to uphold, reduce, vacate, or remand the committee's decision.

Spalding estimated that he spent two hours a day writing responses to inmates who had appealed disciplinary decisions. He was convinced

that following the letter of the law rather than making backroom deals would ultimately curb the lawlessness inside the penitentiary. "If there's some bad ass who is creating problems, then he should reasonably surface through the normal process of disciplinary procedures," Spalding said. "If he can't function in population lawfully, we're going to put him in a place where we control what he does, what he eats, when his lights are on, when they're off, what he watches on TV, what he listens to on the radio, and so on." That place, of course, was Big Red.

The legal provision that guards most resented was the one that allowed inmates who were accused of prison infractions to consult with inmate lay advisers in preparing a defense. Ostensibly, the lay adviser helped to investigate the charges, to line up witnesses, and to do other legal legwork. But the harried guards who patrolled Big Red regarded lay advisers as the main source of the drugs, weapons, and other contraband that were smuggled into segregation. Consequently, guards strip-searched lay advisers at the door, then forced them to change from their own clothes into special, pocketless, blue overalls. The guards also inspected paper, pens, and pencils, the only objects that the advisers were allowed to bring in. Nevertheless, things slipped through. "I've picked up heroin right on the tier," groaned one sergeant. "They could get it in with a keister stash [hide it in their anuses], grunt it down their pant leg, and then kick it into the cell." Jimmy Joe Lucero, often a lay adviser to Big Red's Chicanos, candidly admitted that "taking in weed and all that shit" was the whole point of going in.

When it came to the actual disciplinary hearings, however, lay advisers tended to be shrewd jailhouse lawyers whose counsel might genuinely help the accused inmate to beat the charge. One of the shrewdest lay advisers was Roger Braithwaite, a gravel-voiced, gray-haired, forty-nine-year-old armed robber who looked and spoke like a college professor. Braithwaite had an enviable record of acquittals. If his case was weak, he tried to plea bargain ahead of time with the lieutenant who chaired the disciplinary committee. If he went to court and the committee chairman denied his request to speak in his client's behalf, Braithwaite had other ways of communicating. He stroked his beard to tell a client to say "yes," tugged his ear for "no," and drummed his fingers on the table for "I don't remember."

"One reason I'm successful," Braithwaite said, "is because I will not lie. My clients lie to me all the time, but I've been around long enough that I'm not going to be taken on many trips." Although he did not charge for his services, he expected to receive a "gratuity," such as a pack of cigarettes.

His most common cases, Braithwaite said, were representing inmates tagged on "603s," possession or use of drugs or intoxicants, and "558s," interfering with a staff member in the performance of his duties.

In a typical 603 case that came before the disciplinary committee in December 1978, Braithwaite represented three cellmates accused of drinking pruno. The fourth man in the cell had pleaded guilty. "Usually the guy with the fewest tags cops to the beef," Braithwaite explained, since inmates with fewer infractions generally received light or suspended sentences.

The first inmate called before the committee was Buddy, a short, thick-shouldered convict with a guilty grin. Before the hearing, Braithwaite had suggested that Buddy confess to taking a sip since the infraction report said that the guards had smelled pruno on his breath.

In the hearing room, the lieutenant advised Buddy of his rights, informed him of the charges, and read the infraction report. The report noted that a half-gallon of pruno had been found in the cell.

"Do you understand the charge against you?" the lieutenant asked.

"We plead not guilty," responded Braithwaite.

Buddy replied that he had taken a sip of the jug to see what was in it. He said that one of his cellmates, the one who had pleaded guilty, had been acting drunk and crazy. "I tried to get him into the cell to calm him down," Buddy added.

"It seems apparent to me that the cell partner made a substantial dent in the jug," Braithwaite volunteered.

The committee looked skeptical, so Buddy pursued another tack. "Look," he said, "I been trying to get out of this place. This is my first tag in a year."

"He's been doing a devil of a lot better," Braithwaite said. "I'd ask the committee to take into consideration whether a sip makes a 603."

The committee excused Buddy and Braithwaite from the room and deliberated. Five minutes later, a buzzer summoned the two inmates.

"We've thought it over," the lieutenant told Buddy. "We find you guilty, but I don't believe you were drunk. Your last tag was in July. You've been working and going to college. So we're recommending a reprimand and a warning."

"I appreciate that, sir," Braithwaite answered.

Ed's appearances in the hearing room were not so propitious. Every thirty days, Ed represented himself before the "ad-seg committee," a three-member body chaired by the associate warden. Rather than deciding guilt or innocence, the ad-seg committee determined whether

Ed was a threat to the security of the institution. Ever since the July escape attempt, the committee had decided that Ed was indeed a threat. Consequently, he remained in Big Red.

His dreary confinement on B deck only served to strengthen Ed's revolutionary resolve. "Just look at prisons," he said, his voice edged with anger. "The last four presidents and the last two Supreme Court [chief] justices have condemned the corrections system as a total failure. These places contribute to the problems they purport to solve. This place is a factory and it turns out a product. The product is angry people bent on revenge. They either internalize that anger and take drugs or they externalize it and lash out.

"Prisoners have a high consciousness of the fact that they're being messed over. They know this place is destroying them. But they don't have any understanding of the source of that oppression." The oppression, Ed argued, was the inevitable result of a capitalist society that enriched the wealthy, robbed the working class, and imprisoned those who threatened the system.

"The state has ways to communicate with us. They've got lead gloves, clubs, and Mace. Violence and the threat of violence is a constant part of our day-to-day reality." Consequently, Ed said, "The time comes when we need to meet the state with the violence it can understand. If the state can't protect itself from our attack, we undermine its legitimacy." If the state's legitimacy is challenged, Ed went on, people would begin to understand that its power had limits and that revolution was possible. The understanding will come when working people, particularly prisoners, realize whom their real enemies are, he said. "They have to develop a certain consciousness."

Ed figured that the prison could be organized if he and other "progressive prisoners" could win over the "intermediate element" in the population and could "neutralize the backward element." He saw the bikers as the most backward, as the prison "toughoisie," and as "out-and-out fascists" who collaborated with prison administrators. The rival lifers, however, had "progressive potential," Ed said, despite "their escapist, doper ideology."

Ed conceded that organizing efforts were impeded by the fact that the average inmate viewed the prison radicals with a mixture of awe, dislike, and incomprehension. "We're not regarded as tough because we don't murder people. We don't use or deal narcotics, which makes us squares. And some of us are gay, which, in some eyes, makes us punks," Ed said.

There were three possible scenarios for the penitentiary, he predicted. It would become increasingly racist and divided with "reactionary prisoners maintaining the status quo for the pigs." It would blow up in an unplanned and unexpected explosion, just like Attica did. Or it would be radically changed by prisoners who took responsibility for their lives and who bargained with their captors.

In hopes of bringing about the third scenario, Ed and the other Walla Walla Brothers had drafted a program for a state prisoners' union whose purpose was "to create revolutionary alternatives to the failing criminal justice system." The postrevolutionary goal, Ed said, was to abolish prisons altogether, replacing them with radical therapy, peer reinforcement, self-criticism, and reeducation. "We might have to smash people up to reeducate them," he said.

Meanwhile, the proposed union had several short-range reformist goals. Its program called for the immediate release of one thousand nonviolent offenders from the state's overcrowded prisons; visiting facilities allowing privacy and sexual expression; the minimum wage for prisoners who worked; the right to vote in local, state, and national elections; and control of treatment funds so that prisoners could run their own rehabilitation programs.

"I'm reasonably confident that we'll win in the end because right is on our side," Ed said. Yet he admitted that he sometimes had doubts. Cooped up day after day in the clammy belly of Big Red, he sometimes felt that the new classless society was an impossible dream, a utopia that he would never see.

"I feel a lot of interior conflicts," Ed said. "One side of me feels the need to stay here and build programs; the other side of me feels I'd rather get the fuck out or be dead. I'm in prison because I tried to help prisoners. But goddamn, they're so backward. They've been fucked over so bad."

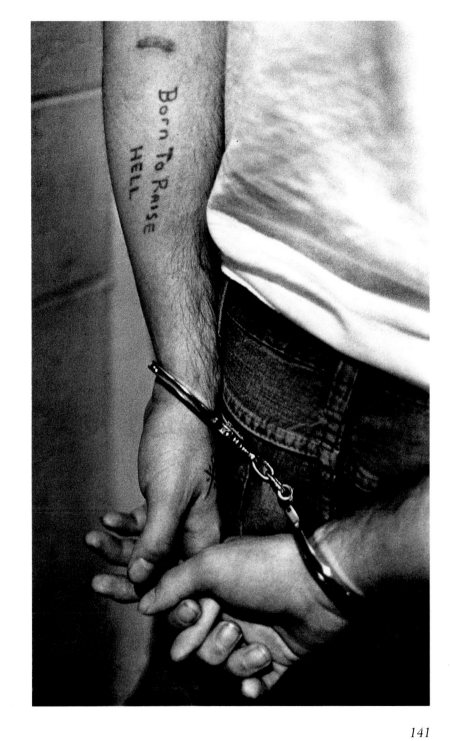

Segregation inmates are handcuffed whenever they leave the tier.

Ed and his lover, also an inmate revolutionary, walk together on the tier during the one hour a day they are allowed out of their cells. Danny is in segregation for assaulting a guard.

"Oso," a suspected murderer, was given an indefinite stay in Big Red, while these four imates received the usual punishment for a major prison infraction—ten days' isolation and twenty days' segregation.

Inmates in isolation are locked out of sight and sound in double-doored cells on A tier. B tier, the most hostile place in the penitentiary, houses the long-term segregation cases. "We Will Win" is a souvenir of a recent disturbance.

10

Don: Murderer on Death Row

Donald Snook, Jr., came to prison as a twenty-year-old kid convicted of joyriding in his aunt's car. He had broken into her home, had grabbed her keys, had taken the car, and had roared off down the freeway at 115 miles per hour, lights flashing, horn blaring, with no destination in mind until he slammed into a blockade of police cars and shotguns. His father, then a deputy sheriff, was one of the arresting officers.

When Don arrived at Walla Walla in 1974, he was so afraid that he briefly checked in to protective custody. But by the fall of 1978, he had a reputation as one of the meanest men in the penitentiary. During those four years, he had murdered two inmates with his bare hands. For the first murder, he was sentenced to life imprisonment. For the second, he was sentenced to die. Now he lived on Death Row, waiting to hang.

Don said that he was in kindergarten when he was first told that he was crazy. All through elementary school, he harassed his teachers and picked fights with other students. At twelve, he was sent to juvenile hall for turning in false fire alarms. He said that he loved the sirens and the red lights. He remembered his father, purple with rage, hollering at him, "You son of a bitch, get the hell out of here." Don said that his parents, who were never around, really weren't parents, just "associates."

When he was fifteen, his parents had him declared "incorrigible" and packed him off to a children's treatment center. The center sent him to a forestry camp, which transferred him to Green Hill, a detention home for juveniles. Don spent eleven months at Green Hill; for the last thirty days he was kept chained to a bed in an isolation cell. The day that he turned seventeen, he was persuaded to join the marines.

"After a while I decided the marines wasn't my trip," Don said, "so I filled my nut hand." He swallowed hallucinogens like candy and wound up in the neuropsychiatric ward at Balboa Naval Hospital in California where doctors sedated him with tranquilizers and anti-psychotic drugs. With obvious relish, Don recited the hospital's final report: "Balboa Naval Hospital has far too short a staff to handle this extremely difficult patient, therefore we are discharging him and recommend further hospitalization."

Committed by his parents, Don endured three more years of hospitalization, alternating between the psychiatric wards of two public hospitals in the Tacoma area. He claimed that he set hospital records for both the number of shock treatments and the time spent in bed restraints. But one day, he said, he asked the doctor to discharge him "AMA," against medical advice.

" 'Well, Don,' " he said, mimicking the doctor, " 'you never have been crazy. So yes, you can go.' This really struck me," Don recalled, his voice rising in anger, "because this fool had given me seventy shock treatments and had me so doped up on tranquilizers, and then he says he has no grounds to commit me."

The doctor, like the prison and the judge, had apparently concluded that Don was a sane man who acted insane.

Don's few months of freedom following his release from the hospital were full of troubles. He ripped up two police cars, wrecked a hospital ward, then asked the female judge who tried him on the property-damage case if she would "like to suck on my lollipop."

The flabbergasted judge told him, "Young man, you've got to be crazy or stupid or just plain both," Don recalled, chuckling. She sentenced him to sixty days in the county jail, but after the episode with his aunt's car, another judge sent him to Walla Walla.

On 29 August 1975, only a few hours before he was to see the parole board, which probably would have given him a release date, Don choked another inmate to death. Several days earlier, when Don had been chained to a bed in the prison hospital, his victim had wrung a mop full of urine into his face. Don had bided his time until he had an opportunity to get even.

Don had no regrets about that slaying, but he would not admit to the strangling that took place in the segregation unit in January 1977. The jury in that case heard how Don had raped his victim, had choked him to death, had tied a sheet around his neck to simulate a suicidal hanging, and then had left to play Ping-Pong. Don was again convicted of murder. Since he was already serving a life sentence for the previous killing, the judge sentenced him to "hang by the neck until dead."

Four iron gates, one cyclone fence, five metal doors, and two concrete walls separated Don from the free world outside the penitentiary. Alone,

out of sight, he spent twenty-three hours a day in a dark, seven-by-eight-foot concrete box on Death Row.

The other hour was "yard-out," a time when Don's double cell doors were unlocked so that he could pace back and forth, up and down the 150-foot concrete corridor that passed in front of the other twenty isolation cells on A tier of "Big Red," the prison's segregation unit. Don, like the other three prisoners on Death Row, yarded alone.

While on yard-out, he could yell through the bars to other caged prisoners or to the two officers who, constantly on watch, were separated from the condemned man by two steel gates. He could shower in an open stall where the water always dripped. He could do chin-ups at an exercise bar. With permission, he could reach between the steel gates and use the telephone to make a legal or personal call. He was entitled to six calls per week.

When he had a visitor, which was rare, Don was handcuffed at his cell door and was led by officers through two metal doors onto an outside breezeway. A tower guard, notified that Don was coming, was out on the catwalk, his rifle in hand. Just outside the view of his visitor, Don was unshackled and was escorted into a small visiting room where his visit was observed and timed. When time was up, he was stripped and examined, reshackled, and returned to his concrete box.

Inside the box was a poured cement slab for use as a writing table, a steel sheet bolted to the wall that served as a bed frame, and a small sink that drained into a lidless toilet. Don used the steel sheet to hold his law books, stereo, records, television set, and other possessions. His mattress lay on the floor. The walls were decorated with posters and personal paintings, one a childlike crayon drawing of a huge butterfly. Above and to the right of the sink were clothes hooks. The hooks were hinged to the wall so that they would collapse if a prisoner tried to use them to hang himself.

Like the other isolation cells on A tier, Don's cell had two doors. The inner door was made of parallel steel bars a finger's width apart. About waist level, the bars were interrupted by a small opening so that the U-shaped food trays could be maneuvered into the cell. Except for a sliding peephole, the outer door was a sheet of solid metal. To the right of the door was a screened window that could be closed with a metal flap. When the door and the flap were both closed, no natural light could enter the cell. There was an overhead lamp inside the cell, but the switch was in the corridor.

The prison's rationale for all this security was that the inmates on Death Row were desperate men. "If you knew you only had a few months left, you'd go around killing people," figured the sergeant in charge of guarding the men who were waiting to die.

Although Don had lived on Death Row for less than a year, he had spent most of his four years at Walla Walla in isolation. By his own admission, he was a suspect in one prison bombing and in eight stabbings. The stabbings did not include the three or four times that he had cut and stabbed himself. "I don't have a pretty track record," Don conceded, peering through his cell bars.

He was twenty-five years old. He wore blue jeans, a handmade leather belt, and a T-shirt stenciled with the trademark for Zig-Zag rolling papers. He secured his long brown hair with a blue bandanna. Since being confined to Death Row, he had become less concerned with his physique. His beard was spotty and a few days old. His waistline sagged. Overall, he had the grubby appearance of the sort of hippie hitchhiker that all but the most sympathetic motorist would pass by.

Don spoke evenly, self-confidently, and even boastfully at times. After all, he was an important figure at Walla Walla. Because he had been condemned to death, his name and his picture had been in the newspapers. There were people out there telling his story and organizing a committee to prevent his execution. Like all Death Row inmates, Don had become a bit of a celebrity. He had acquired a certain charisma.

He thrived on his notoriety, boasting that he had managed to compile one of the prison's thickest "jackets," or dossiers. He said that he had threatened the life of the president, the governor, several judges, a sheriff or two, and a commandant of the marine corps. "The Secret Service has me on a potential assassin list and considers me a threat to the national security," Don said, smirking.

He claimed that he had superhuman strength when he got angry. "When I get kind of cuckoo, my adrenalin gets going." He said that he had broken out of fifteen pairs of handcuffs and five sets of leg irons. Guards said that he was a prison-wise convict who knew how to pick locks and crack cuffs.

But when he was feeling peaceful, Don spent days at a time mothering mice, sparrows, and black widow spiders. When he spoke about his pets, he became enthusiastic and animated. "I dig on birds," he said. "Birds to me are the only true sign of freedom."

Earlier in the year, when the segregation unit still had a small, walled, outside yard, Don had rescued two featherless sparrow chicks. He had built an incubator in his cell and had used a pin to poke sugar water

down the birds' throats. He named his first two sparrows Chance and Cato. Chance, his favorite, perched on his shoulder like a parrot. When she died, Don gave her a proper funeral and asked the inmate arts club to fashion a gravemarker.

His most recent pet was Constance, a female black widow spider that he had tracked for days before trapping her between two Styrofoam cups. He built her a house and walked her on a pencil. "The guards never seen a black widow as big and fast as she is," said Don, exuding delight. "I'd put a cockroach in there and she would hit that cockroach. We timed her one time and in twenty-eight seconds she hit that cockroach thirty-four times." When Constance wove an egg sack and prepared to give birth, guards got edgy, and Don either hid or smuggled the spider out. He would not tell where she was, but he said, "She is alive and well and having a very good time."

Recently, Don realized that he was gay, or, at least, "more gay than bi," he said. He wrote and told his parents. "The next letter I got wasn't a letter," he said. "It was my birth certificate and all the pictures they had of me."

Don's homosexual identification came about after a middle-aged gay minister from Seattle began visiting him. Although the two of them got "married," Don said, "it's hard to say" whether he loved the minister. At any rate, they were collaborating on Don's autobiography, which was titled *They Make Us and Destroy Us*. Don expected the book to become a blockbuster movie.

Assuming that he avoided the gallows, Don was resigned to a life in prison. He crossed the days off on his calendar one by one, but, nevertheless, he said that he lost track of time.

Only the meals at seven, eleven, and five and the yard-outs punctuated the timeless monotony of Death Row. The meals, like the yard-outs, could be refused. The four condemned men who lived behind the final green door woke, slept, and ate when they chose. One of them, who had murdered a child and who had become increasingly withdrawn, slept twenty hours a day. Another watched TV until the test pattern came on, then read until dawn, and dozed until dinner. Night and day seemed the same in the forever indoor light of A tier.

Sometimes, Don stayed up all night. He did legal work, talked to the other Death Row inmates, or played chess with them by calling out his moves and waiting to hear theirs. The chessmen were moved on separate boards in separate cells.

Don also had other ways of whiling away the long hours. He bickered with guards. He fermented pruno. He read textbooks delivered by one of the prison teachers. He said that he was within a quarter of completing a two-year college degree, had a 3.58 grade-point average, and planned to earn a Ph.D.

When he was angry, he sometimes yelled and screamed for hours, taunting guards with the vilest insults. Since Don was already confined to an isolation cell, guards had no way to restrain him further. But their sentiments were obvious. Scrawled on the wall of the elevator that guards used to go between segregation tiers was a solitary message: "Fuck Snook. Hang the Bastard."

Other inmates who briefly shared A tier with the men on Death Row said that some guards delighted in nettling Don. They told him that they could hardly wait to see him hang, that they would eat popcorn and drink Coke while the hangman strung him up, that Don's pet bird would fly circles around his head as he strangled to death.

But Don did not expect to hang. At least not in the near future.

When the U.S. Supreme Court struck down Washington's 1975 mandatory death penalty, it reserved its opinion in one situation: the case of a prisoner already sentenced to life for a previous murder. Don was the only Washington inmate in that situation. But his case was further clouded by subsequent court decisions. Three times during the 1970s the state legislature had drawn up death-penalty statutes and each time the courts found them unconstitutional. But with the prevailing mood in favor of capital punishment, lawmakers were determined to come up with a hanging law that would pass any court test.

Washington remained one of only three states (Montana and Delaware were the others) that prescribed hanging as the death penalty. Since 1904, when the penitentiary received responsibility for executions, seventy-four men and one woman had gone to the gallows. The last hanging had been on 20 June 1963 when Joseph Self was executed for the murder of a Seattle cabdriver.

Don figured that the dubious constitutionality of the law and the slowness of the appeals process would drag his case out for ten to fifteen years. "Hopefully, in that time, society will come to their senses," he said. "Hey, the death penalty ain't where it's at."

By the end of 1978, Don had had four state-appointed attorneys and had "fired every single one of them." He was now acting as his own attorney because "if I hang, I want to hang myself. I don't want no incompetent fools hanging me."

Don could understand how some people could be outraged at his

conduct and would want to see him hang. He realized that he was responsible for what he had done. "But I believe that none of the acts would have ever happened if they hadn't said I was crazy," he insisted. "I went to the nuthouse and got all these shock treatments and all this. Well, now they're saying shock treatments destroy the brain cells. So then I go to the third floor [the prison's psychiatric unit] and they destroy a whole bunch more brain cells."

During his first year at the penitentiary, Don spent much of his time on the mental ward, then under the direction of Dr. William Hunter, an outspoken psychologist who practiced his own unconventional methods of behavior modification. Hunter ran the third floor for ten years until lawsuits and a public outcry hounded him into early retirement.

Noting that many convicts had come from fatherless homes, Hunter argued that they had developed a female orientation that they masked with impulsive, violent, and macho behavior. He maintained, for instance, that many bikers were "out-and-out homosexuals." Hunter told all his new patients that he would teach them what a father should have taught them: "You don't do as you damn please."

He began by reteaching inmates the formative lessons of childhood. He forced some of them to wear diapers and to crawl around carrying baby bottles. Rather than sedating violent behavior with drugs, he relied heavily on peer pressure and on enforced discipline. Don recalled how he was shackled to his bed, drenched with buckets of water, and locked naked for days in a padded cell. He remembered how Hunter had come to his cell one day and said, "Snook, I've been breaking horses for thirty years. If I can break a horse, I can break any man."

"Well," Don said, taking an exaggerated drag on his Camel cigarette, "he didn't break me."

Don inhaled again deeply, exhaled, then crushed the butt of the cigarette against the dirty green wall of his isolation cell. "I'm not a murderer," he said. "I'm not an animal. Maybe at one time when I was getting shock treatments and behavior modification, maybe then I was an animal."

But it was society that did that, Don said. "It's kinda like I was an experimental guinea pig all these years, ya know. They made what they call a monster out of me. And so, after so long, after I start becoming hip to them, they decide to kill me instead. That's how society takes care of its problems, it offs them."

If the courts decided that his death sentence was constitutional, Don said that he was prepared to go the gallows. If he were executed, he predicted that society would remember him much longer than even George Jackson, the radical black prisoner who died in a California prison shootout in 1971. "If they murder me, they'll know it's murder," Don said. "No matter what name you give capital punishment, it's murder."

If the day of Don's execution did come, he would be led from Death Row in the evening, after the other inmates were locked in their cells. They would know, however, that the appointed time had come for one of them to die. They would protest mightily, threatening, hollering, clanging their food trays against their cell bars.

Guards would escort Don out of the segregation unit, along the empty breezeway, around the back of the auditorium to the rear of 6-wing, near the 8-tower gate. Through that seldom-used gate would come the witnesses and the hearse.

But Don's attention would be focused on an inconspicuous metal door at the back of 6-wing. The door led to what inmates called "the fourth floor," the death chamber.

In 1978–1979, the death chamber showed the effects of years of disuse. The prison's chief engineer, the plain-spoken, crew-cut fellow responsible for maintaining the gallows, had readied the hanging machinery a half-dozen times in the previous fifteen years only to have reprieves nullify his preparations. Now he rarely entered the building. When he did, it was usually to give tours to legislators or newsmen.

Unlocking the rusty metal door, the engineer pulled it open with a sharp, scraping sound. Way up above in the rafters blew a low, mean wind, hollow and forlorn. The engineer said that the gallows was the only place in the penitentiary where the wind always blew.

Three flights of stairs, the dust disturbed here and there by footprints, led to the witnesses' entrance to the hanging room. The room itself was stuccoed, painted blue and white like the sanctuary of a Mediterranean church. Halfway across the room, three Moorish arches supported the hanging balcony—the fourth floor.

From the balcony hung a large white sheet that rippled faintly in the low wind. It draped all the way to the floor, preventing the few select spectators from seeing the condemned man's final agony. Instead, two light bulbs flanking the body would project a silhouette onto the sheet.

Years ago, the engineer explained, a warden had let out too much

rope, botching the hanging so badly that the man's head was all but torn off his body. Though he was dead, his body kept twitching, his heart furiously pumping blood over the spectators. Since then, the sheet had been up.

Back underneath the arches was the morgue room where, on a bare wooden table, the prison doctor would make a final examination of the corpse. It was the doctor's duty to make sure that the man was dead, a task that he accomplished by climbing a short wooden ladder and inspecting the body while it still hung suspended on the rope. In the morgue room, the doctor signed the death certificate, listing the cause of death as strangulation.

If Don was ordered to hang, he would not enter the hanging room through the witnesses' entrance. He would be led through a separate metal door, up an enclosed staircase, through another metal door into a small skylit room behind the death chamber. The room contained two steel holding cells, each equipped with an iron bed frame, a mattress, a toilet, and a sink. The cells, numbered "1" and "2," could be locked three times, once with a key, once with a lever, and once with a huge brass padlock. In one of those cells, Don would pass the last eight hours of his life.

Two guards would sit outside his cell, making sure that Don did not take his life prematurely. They would try to make his final hours comfortable. If he wished, they would summon the chaplain. They would also serve him his last meal, which would be anything he wanted. Self, the last man who had been executed at Walla Walla, had had fried chicken and a pint of whiskey.

If a last-minute reprieve should come, Don would hear the ring of the phone on the wall behind the guards. If there was no ring, the final preparations for the hanging would begin shortly before midnight.

If Don should resist the state's plans, the guards would bind him to one of two heavy wooden skids that sat near the holding cells. They would use the thick leather belts attached to the skid to strap down Don's torso. If he persisted in struggling, he would be hung with the skid bound to him. Most of those who had been executed, however, had chosen to die unbound.

Meanwhile, the engineer would have already prepared the rope. He would have soaked it for a week, then tied it to the ceiling weighted with two sandbags to remove the stretch. The rope was carefully measured so that the condemned man would drop the length of his body and not the full twelve feet to the hanging-room floor.

In a closet adjoining the morgue room, several nooses still hung waiting for executions that never happened. Each was tied with seven to nine turns, just enough to create the bulky knot that went behind the condemned man's neck. On a shelf above the nooses was an old brown can of "Pasha Egyptian Rare Talc." The talc would be sprinkled on the rope so that the noose would slip more easily. That way, when the rope went taut, the noose would close quickly, and the bulky knot would break the neck, cutting off the blood supply and snapping the windpipe.

Beyond the noose closet was a tiny, narrow room, bare except for four old-fashioned, push-button-style light switches fixed side by side beneath a naked red light bulb. The switches were numbered "1" to "4," a switch for each of the four guards who had volunteered to push them. One of the switches would trigger the trapdoor that would send Don plunging to the end of the rope; only the engineer would know which one.

At the appointed time, Don would be led out of the holding cell and through a metal door at the top of the enclosed stairs. He would emerge on the hanging balcony. Below, on the far side of the hanging room, would be the doctor, the coroner, and the witnesses. With Don on the balcony would be the guards, the chaplain, the engineer, the warden, and the hangman.

In the middle of the wooden balcony, Don would see two trapdoors, both levered shut. Years ago, both doors had been used when two brothers were hanged within minutes of each other. In Don's case, however, only one trapdoor would be wired and ready.

Above the trapdoor, a heavy steel eyelet was fixed in the ceiling. The hanging rope would be tied to the balcony railing, run through the eyelet, and looped around a frail wire that protruded from the wall. That way the slack would run out without snagging.

On the wall between the two trapdoors was the switch that lit the red bulb in the hidden room. On the warden's command, the engineer would flick the switch to let the four guards know that it was time to push the buttons. If, for some reason, the electrical mechanism failed, the engineer would step on a large metal bolt that, when depressed, sprung the latch on the trapdoor.

Once, in an earlier execution, the commanding officer was afraid that the guards in the hidden room might get jumpy and press the buttons too soon. So he removed the fuses and forgot to put them back. When the red light came on, the guards pushed the buttons but nothing

happened. The condemned man stood waiting, the noose around his neck, until the engineer hit the bolt release and the man went down.

As Don stood with his feet planted on the black square of the trapdoor, the warden would ask him if he had any last words. Most condemned men had nothing to say, but the law required that the warden give them a last opportunity to speak.

As the final moment approached, the hangman would bind Don's feet, tie his hands behind his back, and slip the hood over his head. Next, he would take the noose down from the frail wire and slip it around Don's neck. Carefully, he would tighten the knot behind Don's left ear.

At a second past midnight, the hangman would nod to the warden. The warden would nod to the engineer. The engineer would push the switch. The red bulb would go on. The four guards would push the buttons. The trap door would fall open, and Don Snook, a man deemed too evil to live, would die, dangling at the end of a rope.

Nooses prepared for men who got last-minute reprieves hang in a closet next to the morgue room; a new rope is readied for each hanging.

The condemned man passes his last hours in one of these holding cells, which are reached by climbing a hidden staircase. The "skid" is used to drag reluctant inmates to the gallows. The trapdoor on the hanging balcony opens at the warden's signal.

11

Yvonne: Visitor

Yvonne Auday was married to a man whom she had never lived with and had never seen outside prison.

She and her seven-year-old daughter Gracia came to the penitentiary visiting room sixteen times a month, the maximum number of visits allowed by prison rules, to be with Dean. On visiting days, the newlyweds had three hours to talk and embrace in a room crowded with other inmates, wives, lovers, friends, relatives, and children. Other than those three hours, four days a week, their lives did not touch.

"We figure if we make it through Dean being up here, we'll make it," Yvonne said. Two months earlier, she and Dean had been married in a brief ceremony in a corner of the visiting room. Afterward, the groom returned to his cell and the bridal party went to Joe's Tavern where Yvonne cried and "got smashed."

It was Yvonne's second marriage and Dean's third. They were trying to help it along by talking a lot. "We don't know that much about each other's lives," Yvonne said.

Born in Portland, Oregon, Yvonne had found boys more interesting than books and had barely finished high school. She got married at eighteen, gave birth to Gracia a year later, and left her husband in North Carolina a year after that. She returned to Portland, worked for a while, and then moved to Wenatchee, Washington, to live with a man. Their relationship soured, and her "old man" wound up in the county jail, where he met Dean. Dean and Yvonne wrote to each other, and later she began visiting him. Finally she went to jail herself for smuggling hashish to Dean in a shampoo bottle.

The judge gave her a ninety-day sentence and, inadvertently, an opportunity to get to know Dean better. Dean, a jail trusty, recalled the hours that he spent mopping the floor in front of her cell, spilling the mop bucket, and mopping again. Sometimes, the county jailer, one of the few people on Dean's current penitentiary visiting list, allowed the lovers to meet in the jail storeroom.

The two had planned to marry in the jail, but Dean, who was awaiting sentencing for assault, was transferred to the penitentiary before they could complete the paperwork. In early 1978, Yvonne followed him.

In Walla Walla, Yvonne and Gracia lived in a decaying one-story house divided into three apartments. Their unit came with scuffed, secondhand furniture; fake wood paneling; and a large, gas floor furnace that whooshed when it went on. A worn beige couch faced a black-and-white television set that sat on a trunk. On the wall above the TV was a rug with a picture of a whirling belly dancer. The rug was Yvonne's. In the corner of the living room she had hung an oil painting of Gracia, a work commissioned by Dean and done by an inmate artist.

Yvonne paid $150 a month for the apartment; the lights and the heat were extra. On and off welfare for the past four years, Yvonne received a monthly assistance check of $245 plus $100 worth of food stamps. She said that she would like to find a job. She had worked as a clerk, as a nursing-home aide, as a waitress, and as a weaver. She said that she had been offered a job as a cook on the graveyard shift at a downtown short-order restaurant. But Dean made some inquiries, heard stories about rowdies and drunks, and told her to turn the job down. "I don't understand his reasoning, but I didn't argue," she said, adding that she and Dean still had much to learn about each other.

Yvonne was twenty-six but looked younger. She dressed informally and wore little makeup. Although she joked about gaining weight, her figure was slender, almost petite. She wore her light brown hair cut straight and short. She had a friendly, infectious laugh and a buoyant enthusiasm that seemed to carry her through adversity. She dealt with Gracia lightly and lovingly, as if the two were sisters rather than mother and daughter.

Dean teased Yvonne by calling her "brat." He gave her a piece of ivory that she wore in a necklace. The ivory was engraved with a butterfly and the words "Brat and Dean."

An affable fellow with a toothy grin and a full beard, Dean talked like he knew something about women and marriage. He was thirty-three and his first two wives had left him while he was in prison.

Born to parents who trained animals for the Ringling brothers' circus, Dean claimed that he had traveled around the world twelve times before he was eight years old. When he struck out on his own in his mid-teens, he ran into trouble—vagrancy in Arkansas, heroin possession and armed robbery in California.

He said that he escaped from one California prison by fashioning a dummy out of old clothes, running a surgical tube between the sink and the dummy's midsection, standing the dummy in front of the cell toilet, and turning on a trickle of water. "I figured that if it looked like I was taking a leak, the guard would pass by," he said. It worked: The guard moved past, Dean slipped out of his cell, went under one fence, over another, and on to freedom.

He was living a quiet life near Wenatchee when he hit a man. He claimed that the man was a burglar, but the jury called it assault and the judge sent him back to prison.

Dean and Yvonne had gotten married at the penitentiary in hopes of hurrying his release date. They knew that the parole board looked favorably on inmates who could be paroled to their families. Although Dean's scheduled parole date was nearly two years away, the couple hoped that his good behavior would earn him an early release. Meanwhile, they endured the tedious visiting procedure.

Dean also took advantage of his job in the inmate phone room and called Yvonne whenever he had a free line. Often he would call just to say hello; then he would hang up and call again. She used to wait for his calls at appointed times in a phone booth near her apartment, but now she had her own phone at home.

At work, Dean sat at one of three master phones that served as a switchboard in front of eight battered phone booths. Inmates signed up and then waited for an open booth. Dean's responsibility was to see to it that inmates did not talk too long or charge calls to the prison or to other unsuspecting third parties. He placed all calls collect through the operator. Working four hours a day, seven days a week, Dean's salary was twenty dollars a month. He quadrupled his earnings by accepting bribes from inmates who wanted to talk more than the allotted ten minutes. He got the job so that he could call Yvonne without having to wait in line. Otherwise, he said, the job wasn't worth it. Inmates were always complaining about getting cut off or about having to wait too long for the phone. Sometimes fights erupted.

Besides their numerous phone conversations, Yvonne and Dean also wrote to each other. Dean, like most prisoners, listed his return address simply as "Box 520, Walla Walla." Yvonne's letters, delivered to Dean's cell during the 4:00 P.M. count, arrived open. Three civilians checking for contraband inspected every first-class letter, poked through newspapers and magazines, and unpacked all gift packages. A big hit in the mail room were the candid snapshots that inmates received from wives and girl friends. "One woman sent her husband a picture of a guy screwing her," one mail-room worker swore.

Besides money, weapons, drugs, and liquor, "contraband" included items like homemade cakes and cookies, aerosol sprays, health foods, leather jackets, and women's clothing. The prison's rationale was that baked goods could be spiced with marijuana, aerosol sprays could be made into bombs, health foods contained yeast for pruno, coveted leather jackets disrupted the inmate economy, and women's clothing encouraged kinky sex. Dean laughed, recalling how he had sold a pair of Yvonne's $1.29 panties to a prison queen for $5.00.

Restrictions on reading material were less severe. Inmates received everything from the raunchiest sex magazines to the most militant tabloids. Books on drugs, guns, bombs, ammunition, and medicine were not allowed, nor was *Soldier of Fortune* magazine, presumably because of articles like "How to Kill Silently."

All but a few inmates were permitted to write to anyone they wished as often as they pleased as long as they had postage. The state provided each prisoner with three fifteen-cent postage stamps a week. When the prison received complaints about an inmate's sending obscene or threatening letters, the inmate's name landed on the mail room's "hot list." Henceforth, all his incoming and outgoing correspondence was examined and read. "Hot" letters were returned.

Despite the letters, the phone calls, and the visits, Yvonne still felt estranged from the husband whom she was permitted to see for only twelve hours a week. "Loneliness," she said, "is the hardest thing about being a prisoner's wife." Sometimes, sitting up after Gracia had gone to bed, she realized, "I'm all alone." Other times, she said, "I'll see couples together and it will get to me."

Yvonne came to the prison on Wednesday mornings and on Monday, Thursday, and Saturday evenings. Gracia usually came with her in the evenings. Yvonne preferred the evening visits because the two guards in the visiting area were more lenient. During the day, she said, some guards "get smart-mouthed" and "act like you helped commit the crime."

Like other prison wives and girl friends who lived in the Walla Walla area, Yvonne had signed a contract agreeing to visit only on weekday mornings and evenings. That way, the visiting room was less congested when out-of-town visitors arrived on afternoons and weekends. Morning visits were from 8:00 to 10:30, afternoon visits from noon to 3:30, and evening visits from 5:00 to 8:30. Saturday evenings were for "family

visits," an extra visiting time that was not covered in the contract.

Because Yvonne did not have a car, she usually rode to the penitentiary with another prison wife. On most evenings, she, Gracia, and the other woman arrived early and ended up waiting with the other visitors in a narrow lobby crammed with vending machines, a couple of sofas, and a few torn chairs. The lobby, actually the foyer of the administration building, provided the only access to the front gate. Consequently, a steady stream of guards, counselors, maintenance men, and minimum-security inmates snaked their way through the growing crowd of visitors waiting to see their loved ones.

Yvonne used to be friendlier toward the other visitors. Most of them had also moved to Walla Walla from other cities and shared her feelings of being unwelcome in a town where local politicians blamed the families of prison inmates for increasing crime rates. The prison wives commiserated with each other by gossiping about what they heard from their menfolk inside. "I used to associate with quite a few of them," Yvonne said. "But so many of them can't wait to tell their husbands what each other's business is. That causes a lot of problems among inmates."

Dean said that what inmates feared most was losing their women. Cooped up in their cells while their women were free, they often got insanely jealous. "You're not out there with your woman," Dean explained. "You're in here with people who've lost their women or you remember how you messed around when you were on the street and you think your woman's doing the same." He told a story about a prisoner whose wife faithfully visited him at every opportunity. One evening, she told him that she was planning to take the kids to the drive-in movie. Her husband didn't like it, got to brooding, and called the police. He told the cops that his wife was at the drive-in, rapping on car windows, and offering to screw all comers.

Dean said that Yvonne incurred the disfavor of the other prison women because he let her "run a little looser." He either felt secure about their marriage or was far less possessive than most husbands. "If she wants to go out and get laid, that's her decision," Dean said, shrugging as if there was nothing that he could do about it.

Forty-five minutes after Yvonne and Gracia arrived in the lobby, an officer appeared at the information desk. Because he recognized Yvonne and Gracia he did not bother to pull Dean's visiting card to make sure that they were listed.

To visit an inmate, a guest first had to complete and return a notarized questionnaire that went to the inmate's counselor. The counselor checked the inmate's visiting card, examined his file, and sometimes ran a police check on the prospective visitor. Counselors could approve up to ten visitors per inmate. Since members of the same family counted as one visitor, few inmates used up their full allotment.

New visitors were told to read a list of visiting rules. The rules read: "No tank tops, tube tops, extremely low-cut, transparent or midriff blouses. No purses, billfolds, combs, brushes, lipsticks, jacknives [sic]. No MEDICATION. No cigarettes, cigarette lighters, candy, food, gum or drinks. No folding money. No hats, scarves or wigs." A final rule informed visitors with children that they were allowed "one diaper bag with not more than four diapers and two bottles" and "one quiet toy." Yvonne said that the rules were flexible. She had brought Dean home-made avocado sandwiches, and she said that she had seen other visitors bring in chocolate-fudge brownies seasoned with marijuana.

At the information desk, Yvonne filled out a slip of paper, listing her name, Dean's name and prison number, and their relationship. The paper included a written warning: "ANY VISITOR ENTERING THE VISITING AREA MAY BE SUBJECT TO A THOROUGH SEARCH OF HIS/HER PERSON."

A female guard called Yvonne's name and ushered her into a closet-sized room across from the information desk. Inside the room, the guard frisked Yvonne by running her hands over and under Yvonne's out-stretched arms, along her torso, around her buttocks, and up and down her legs. If officers found nothing but still believed that someone looked suspicious, they could ask the visitor to disrobe and submit to a "skin search." Yvonne had never been skin-searched. She figured that she had been skipped because she did not wear a bra, presumed to be a popular hiding place by some prison staff. Once in a while, she smuggled Dean a little marijuana or money, but she was wary; a second drug conviction would probably send her to prison. If she wanted to bring in some marijuana, she packed it in her shoe or put it in Gracia's pocket. They never searched Gracia, she said.

Some female visitors packed a balloon full of marijuana, cocaine, or heroin and hid the balloon in their vaginas. After entering the visiting room, the women slipped into the bathroom, removed the balloon, transferred it to their mouths, and went back out to kiss their men. The inmates swallowed the balloon in mid-kiss, then later, back in their cells, vomited or passed it. Sometimes, an inmate would mouth it for a while, wait until he could retire unobserved to the bathroom, and

"keister" the drug-filled balloon by poking it up his anus.

After being frisked, Yvonne and Gracia were conducted through the sallyport, a secured passageway that joined the lobby with the walled prison compound, and into the upper visiting room. An outside staircase screened with cyclone fencing and barbed wire connected the upper and lower visiting rooms.

Inside the walls, inmates who had guests gathered in front of the control room. Those who were unaware that they had visitors were summoned by loudspeaker. Guards searched the inmates for drugs, money, weapons, and other contraband, collected their ID cards, and led them through the sallyport to the visiting area.

Recently refurbished, painted, and carpeted, the visiting area was one place that prisoners said did not feel like a prison. The atmosphere was convivial, like a church social. Children played tag and pickup sticks. In the lower room, an inmate-operated snack bar sold ham, cheese, barbecued beef, and supersubmarine sandwiches as well as hamburgers, pizza, doughnuts, coffee, soft drinks, and cigarettes. Inmates and guests ordered at a long white counter, paid with prison-issue scrip, and ate at prison-made tables. A sign near the menu board reminded inmates: "This Is Your Area—Please Keep It Clean."

If things ran smoothly, Yvonne and Dean met in the visiting room at about the same time. But it there was trouble inside the prison or if the count had come up wrong, Yvonne and the other visitors sometimes had a long wait. "We sat until 7:30 one night, singing and raising Cain, waiting for men to come in," Yvonne recalled. If the prison was on lockdown, all visits were canceled.

Once they were united in the visiting room, Yvonne and Dean had figured out ways to make love. Sexual intercourse was a major infraction of prison rules, but usually, if the passion was polite, guards looked the other way. "If we have a chance to fool around, we'll plan it ahead of time," Dean explained.

Planning meant that Yvonne wore a dress, although not necessarily one of the long gowns fancied by some of the women who sneaked a little draped sex in quiet corners. Couples used the gowns like tents, pitching them over their private parts. They sat rump to crotch on the carpeted floor, or they faced each other through open-backed chairs.

Yvonne and Dean were more discreet: They retired to the men's or women's restroom. As long as they were not too obvious, did not tie up the restroom, and did not flaunt themselves in front of the lone officer who patrolled the area, they had no problems.

The snack-bar storeroom also served as an impromptu love nest. One inmate stood guard, another inmate distracted the officer's attention, and couples slipped quietly in and out.

Some inmates said that they discouraged their families from visiting because they did not want their children to see a sex show. How can you talk, they complained, when people around you are petting, sucking, and screwing? Officers assigned to the visiting room joked about taking cold showers when they got home. "A lot of us don't like it either," Dean said, adding that inmates sometimes would ask a guy to cool it. "But we don't want anybody in our face telling us what to do."

Inmates did recognize that they could go only so far. The Resident Council paid two inmate monitors fifty dollars a month to assist guards by warning prisoners who became too sexually indiscreet. Although the monitors did issue warnings, they also helped to shield the bathroom rendezvous by occupying the officer's attention with idle chatter.

Dean argued that visiting-room sex would be less obvious and more natural if the penitentiary permitted conjugal visits. He recalled how the California prisons parked house trailers inside the walls and allowed families to live together for seventy-two-hour periods. "That would save a lot of families," he said.

However, the fact was that most prisoners did not even have visitors. Penitentiary records indicated that only 125 of the prison's 1,400 maximum-security inmates had regular visitors. Some inmates had committed such horrible crimes or had served so much time that they had lost their family and friends. Others said that their families could not afford the day-long trek from Seattle, Tacoma, and the other coastal towns where most of them lived. For most inmate families, traveling to Walla Walla was at least a five-hour trip.

Still other inmates said that they discouraged visitors. They were ashamed to be in prison. They were afraid that the three-hour visit might prove too long, become awkward, or erupt into an embarrassing scene or a fight. "Just the other day, we had an inmate swing a chair and knock his wife's teeth out," an officer said.

Guarding the visiting room was "almost like watching a soap opera," said a female officer who generally drew visiting-room duty. There were welfare mothers who came diligently week after week "only to be dumped when the guy gets out." There were women dressed in furs and slinky dresses, honor-bound to visit their former pimps. And there were wives and girl friends who sat nervously, hoping that the three hours would pass quickly without incident.

The female guard said that there were two types of women visitors: women who had known the inmates before they went to prison, and those who had met them afterward. She said that she felt sorry for the second type. They often came to the penitentiary in response to inmate advertisements in newspapers, religious newsletters, or lonely-hearts magazines. They included unattractive, overweight women looking for companionship; "religious fanatics" looking for converts; and women who, for whatever reason, liked to love convicts, she said. "We've got one lady who married a guy in here," the officer said. "He got out and deserted her. She turned him in for violating his parole, and now she's back visiting him again." A few women even became "professional visitors," bouncing from one inmate's visiting list to another's, looking for their captive dream man.

Dean conceded that sometimes women were used by inmates who wanted money, drugs, or sex. But other times, he said, a guy just wanted a visitor. Some men cultivated relationships with two women and carefully juggled their visits so that they did not coincide. Dean said that several inmates had asked him to "have your old lady get some chick from downtown to come up and visit me." But Yvonne wasn't inclined to play matchmaker.

Dean and Yvonne's evening visit ended abruptly at 8:30 when a crew of five officers marched in. "C'mon ladies, let's go," one of them ordered.

Yvonne and the other women lingered for a final hug or kiss, then filed out of the visiting room. The men stayed behind. Each officer selected one inmate and ordered him to strip. The others were patted down and allowed to leave.

Dean was ordered to strip. As he undressed, he handed each article of clothing to the officer, who bunched the material, feeling for hidden items. Once naked, Dean extended his arms, shook his hair, slapped his ears, opened his mouth, lifted his scrotum, spread his buttocks and coughed, then showed the soles of his feet. The officer found nothing. Dean dressed while guards combed the visiting area for any money, drugs, liquor, or bombs that might have been left behind.

Finally, Dean and the remaining inmates were led out into the sallyport. Yvonne and Gracia were there on the other side of the gate, waving.

"Bye, bye, baby," Dean shouted as he turned to go back inside the prison compound.

"I love you," Yvonne shouted back.

Lovers share an affectionate moment at an annual club "banquet." Though lovemaking is forbidden, couples learn to hide beneath long dresses or retire discreetly to the restrooms. But some visits are painful; this mother is unable to reach her depressed, mentally disturbed son.

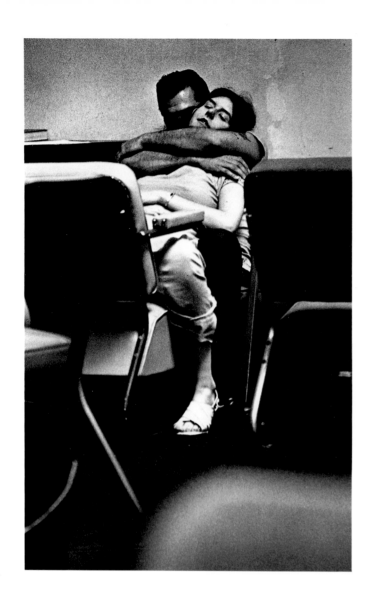

Inmates can meet their wives, lovers, families, and friends as many as four times a week in the crowded visiting room. Most couples manage to overcome their inhibitions about public displays of affection.

Newlyweds Yvonne and Dean visit as often as the penitentiary allows. Evening visits end abruptly at 8:30. Guards tolerate a final embrace, then usher the visitors out.

Once the visitors are out of the room, guards single out a half-dozen inmates, including Dean, and order them to strip. As Dean goes back inside the prison compound, Yvonne and Gracia wave a last good-bye.

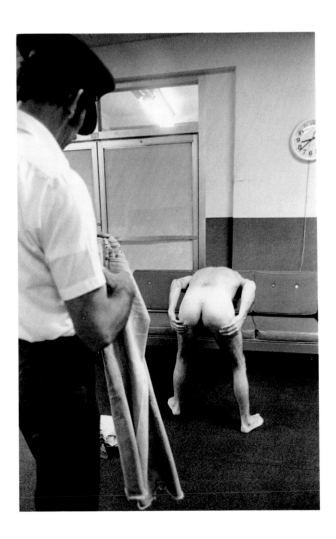

12

Officer Edwards: The Man

Though he had been born and raised in Walla Walla, Parley Edwards never intended to be a penitentiary guard. After graduating from Walla Walla High School, he moved to the coast, where he worked in a Longview lumber mill, married, and joined the army. The army sent him to radar school in Texas and then stationed him in New York City.

When Parley returned to his hometown three years later, he found work in a sawmill. But the work was seasonal, and in the winter of 1958, unemployed and needing money, Parley applied for a job at the prison. He was twenty-four years old. He got the job immediately. "They handed me a bunch of keys and sent me to 7-wing," Parley recalled. "If it wasn't for the convict desk man, I wouldn't have known what to do."

Despite the lack of staff training, the penitentiary was run like a marine boot camp, Parley said. "You could tag insolent looks in those days. Convicts talked to you when you talked to them. We had a real seg [segregation wing] and we had strip cells [isolation cells where inmates were confined naked]." But actually, he said, the rules were too tight. He said that the associate warden had once chewed him out for buying an ex-con a beer in a local tavern.

"Turnover was real slow. Take-home pay was $385 a month. That was damn good money back then, so a lot of guys born in this area went where the higher money was and that was the pen."

But Parley really wanted to be a farmer. In 1962, he quit his prison job and bought a ranch. Over the next nine years, he farmed and logged on ranches in Washington and Idaho, but then his wife contracted a rare vascular disease. The uninsured medical bills wiped him out; he lost his farm and his livelihood. In 1971, his wife died, and he returned to the penitentiary. "When I quit in '62, if somebody had told me I'd be back in ten years, I would have told them they was full of shit," Parley said. "But I needed a job."

A rugged, handsome man of forty-four, Parley looked like an extra in a western movie, the quiet, resourceful type who was dependable in a tight situation. Calm and earnest, he spoke in a flat, monotonous voice that was so unexpressive that he seemed continually depressed. But his cool, impassive manner hid a fiery determination. Named after a Mormon composer of religious music, Parley harbored a strong sense of right and wrong. He was convinced that much of what had happened at the penitentiary during the 1970s was wrong.

"The change came in 1971 when the cons started gaining control with the leniency and all," Parley said. "An officer quit being an 'officer' and a 'sir' and became a 'motherfucker' and a 'pig.' "

Parley's quiet outspokenness led to his election in early 1978 as president of the penitentiary local of the state employees' union. Although the union also represented prison counselors, clerical workers, and civilian work supervisors, it was commonly called the guards' union because guards were its most vocal members. Dissatisfied with prison policies that they felt had eroded their control over the prison's inmates, the guards adopted an increasingly militant stance toward the penitentiary administration.

They took advantage of the August–September 1978 lockdown that marked the transition between the Vinzant and Spalding administrations to press their case for more security, for tighter restrictions, and for tougher control. "When you lock down," one guard observed, "you throw a whole new psychology into the joint. A lockdown disorients convicts completely, and they begin to expect new rules."

As union president, Parley warned that guards would walk out unless the Spalding administration moved the bike shop to Prison Industries, intensified surveillance, increased contraband checks, and searched the entire prison compound with dogs trained to sniff out drugs and explosives. The administration complied. The lockdown ended, and the guards stayed on the job.

But Parley believed that Spalding had to do a great deal more to wrest control from the inmates and return it to the officers. "We're still living in the same jungle," he sighed, "but now, at least, there's a little hope."

The Tuesday before Christmas 1978 was a typical day. Parley went to work feeling apprehensive.

The prison was restless and tense as it often was before a holiday. A snitch, whose information was usually good, had told a guard that a group of convicts was planning to seize 8-wing. The snitch said that the group was prepared to go beyond the taking of hostages; they would

kill anyone who tried to stop them.

But when Parley mustered with the five dozen other officers on the afternoon shift, there was little talk of trouble. After all, he had heard plenty of rumors before. He saw no point in talking about them and getting a lot of people nervous.

Parley smoked a cigarette as he waited for the sergeant to call roll and to make the assignments. He was already dressed in his well-worn uniform: white shirt, narrow tie, blue wool pants and jacket, blue cap, and blue parka with the shoulder patch that read "Washington State Penitentiary."

Thanks to his seniority, Parley could expect to get the assignment that he had bid for. He knew that he would draw "utility," an all-purpose assignment that sent him wherever he was needed. He worked on a cellblock for two days a week and did utility duty for the other three.

As usual, a couple of men waiting for the roll call were unfamiliar to Parley. He said that new guards came and went so fast that he scarcely learned to recognize their faces, much less remember their names. There had been instances where convicts had taken advantage of this situation by dressing in an officer's uniform and walking right out the gate.

More than half of the officers hired in 1978–1979 quit before a year was out. Turnover was so high that the penitentiary was usually ten to twenty guards short of the 291 budgeted positions. Officer's pay, which started at $932 a month and peaked at $1,189 after five years, attracted applicants but failed to keep them. "We can be fully staffed and then have a major blood-and-guts problem and they're gone," Parley said.

Moreover, Parley complained, many of those who got the job were unqualified. "The state of Washington has scraped the bottom of the barrel for these young officers," he groaned, shaking his head in disgust. "We had a black that came from Seattle that never had a job in his whole damn life. So he got off of welfare and came to the penitentiary. We got officers now that are worse than the people we're keeping, guys who ain't worth the powder to blow them to hell. We got officers with sick, warped minds. God, I hate to admit it because I'm proud of the officers."

Officers who took pride in their work resented the public's perception of them as turnkeys and low-level cops. They insisted on being called "correctional officers," not "guards." They pointed out that it was correctional officers, the people who had the most contact with inmates, who did the most "correcting." "Every officer knows convicts whose

criminal thinking he has helped change," Parley said.

New officers were supposed to receive two weeks of training. But when manpower was down, as it often was, they patrolled the cellblocks two days after their employment interview. In conjunction with Walla Walla Community College, Vinzant had set up a "Correctional Officers Academy," an eighty-hour training program, but Spalding canceled it. "I can't justify sending an officer downtown for sensitivity training, social awareness, and those types of things when he comes back up here, goes up in a tower, and shoots his hat off when he's checking his rifle," the new warden said. "I had four rounds fired through the tower the first month I was here just from people not knowing how to work their weapons."

Most officers, however, had little recourse to weapons. Aside from the tower guards who were armed with both a rifle and a shotgun, officers went about their duties unarmed. Unlike their charges, who had knives, clubs, and pipe bombs to fall back on, the guards had only their wits. Unfortunately, Parley sighed, too many guards did not have their wits about them. "In front of convicts, I've had to personally go up to a fish officer [rookie guard] and tell him to shut his goddamn mouth. The confrontation this officer was creating because of ignorance was a bum beef on the convict and was going to cause a big scene."

A young sergeant who was determined to make a career of corrections said that the situation was further aggravated by the lack of communication between the new guards and the veterans. The new guards drew the tough assignments in the cellblocks or in the yard, he said, while the old-timers waited out their pensions at desk or tower jobs removed from hostile inmates. "An 'old school' lieutenant sits at his desk and tells a fish cop to go down there and tell some convicts to do something," the young sergeant grumbled, "and the convicts laugh at him."

At 1:45 P.M., the roll call was over. Parley stubbed out a second cigarette, adjusted his cap, and walked with the rest of the afternoon shift through the sallyport gates into the maximum-security compound. Despite the rumors of a riot, he did not look nervous. At the control room, he picked up a walkie-talkie and checked in with the shift lieutenant who sent him to relieve an officer at the 9-tower gate.

At the gate, Parley and another officer watched inmates walk through a metal detector and then patted them down. Parley began at the fingertips, running his hands under the inmate's arms, down his torso,

around his midsection, and down both legs. If he found nothing suspicious, he let the inmate pass. "You aren't going to have them strip unless you got a hot suspect," Parley explained, conceding that drugs were going to come inside one way or another. He pointed to a garbage truck that had just lumbered through the gate to the back of the prison kitchen. Driven by a minimum-security inmate, the truck had been searched superficially by two guards. Inmates were now dumping garbage into it at the kitchen dock. "If a guy had a stash underneath that hood," Parley said, "it'd be gone by now."

When the regular guard returned from his break, Parley chatted for a while, had a cigarette and a cup of coffee in the gate guard station, then returned to the control room. The lieutenant sent him to the kitchen where the electricity had suddenly gone off an hour and a half before supper.

Inmate cooks stood waiting in the dark in front of their cold grills, and a crew-cut kitchen guard, his belt jangling with keys, fretted about supper being late. "The kitchen is the heart of the institution," he said. "If it goes down, then everything goes down." Parley was inclined to agree. He had worked in the kitchen until the administration had cut back on the number of officers assigned to the detail. The situation then became unmanageable. "The pruno started flowing real heavy and pretty soon the place was a shambles," he said.

Poking around with a long-barreled flashlight, Parley found the inmate electrician and discussed the wiring problem. The electrician thought that he could restore power in a few minutes.

As Parley waited in the half-dark, an inmate approached and handed him a diplomalike roll of paper. "Mr. Edwards," the inmate said, "this is a certificate of commendation for your role in riding the fence during the lockdown."

Puzzled, Parley unrolled the scroll. His name was printed on a line beneath large letters that spelled Calvary Faith College. He thanked the inmate, who nodded and left, disappearing into the dark.

Moments later, the lights came on, and everyone seemed to breathe a sigh of relief. An inmate dishwasher spotted Parley and asked, "Are you putting in a parole recommendation for me?"

"Have your counselor send me a form," Parley replied. Pleased, the dishwasher said that he would. Inmates knew that Parley was a good guard to have in their corner. In turn, guards like Parley knew that they had to depend on inmates to maintain control.

"Look," explained Sgt. Harold Lee, who worked in the segregation unit, "the only goddamn way we run the institution is because the inmates let us. We've got to keep enough rapport going so things don't go tilt." Lee, formerly a guard at California's Soledad Prison, argued that guards had to use "backyard psychology" and "discretionary decisionmaking." "You've got to be able to deduce fairness in unorthodox situations," he said. "You've got to be compassionate yet have the backbone to say 'no' a lot of times when it would be easier to say 'yes.' Convicts may be sons of bitches, thieves, rapists, and murderers, but they have a high sense of fair play and integrity. The thing that will get you a lot of respect from a convict is: Don't promise anything you can't deliver. Explain your position. And, first and foremost, be the same every day."

Sgt. Dick Morgan, a young, conscientious officer in charge of the two lowest tiers in volatile 8-wing, tried to strike up friendships with his charges. "Except for some of the older cons and the youngsters, I could go down there and park my butt in any cell and have a cup of coffee," he said. "If you get them in a position where they're vulnerable, they'll work a deal."

Yet guards who became too friendly opened themselves up to their superiors' suspicions and to inmate bribes. "Yeah, they've tried to bribe me," Morgan said. "They'll say, 'Morgan, my wife's going to send you five hundred dollars. You bring four hundred in to me.'"

Some guards, like Lee, figured that the only difference between them and the inmates was that inmates were convicted felons. "We're both human beings," Lee observed. But other guards, like Morgan and Parley, thought differently. "Personally, I'm not like any of these guys," Morgan said, and Parley was well aware that "here you got your sex offenders, your child molesters, your baby rapers, your murderers, actually all the scum of society."

After the lights came back on in the kitchen, Parley returned to the control room where he was pulled aside by an angry officer. The guard was upset because he had taken a convict who had thrown coffee at him over to "Big Red" (the segregation unit), and the convict was already out. The warden had "squashed" the tag. Parley listened sympathetically but offered little advice. "It's actions like that that tear down the authority of the officers. It just demoralizes them," Parley complained afterward. "When officers' tags aren't honored, it ain't doing the convicts any damn good either. They got to go out and live in a society with rules."

Many guards longed for the return of swift and sure punishment in

a hole where no convict would want to go. They felt that the reports, the legal processes, and the hearing committees worked too much to the inmates' advantage. "It works like this," griped one disgruntled officer. "The convict says, 'Get off my case, pig, or I'll cut your head off.' So you tag him for disobeying a direct order and for threatening a staff member. He goes to the hearing committee and they give him a warning. They say, 'Gee, you shouldn't have done that.' So the next day, the convict's already got away with threatening you, so he hits you. He goes back to the committee, and they'll give him a whole ten days of seg where he watches TV and listens to the radio. Then he goes back on the breezeway. You stop him for a shakedown and what's he think? He got away with threatening and assaulting you, so now he's going to stick you. He's a hero among the other convicts, but you're dead. You're dead because the hearing committee is a big joke. It happens all the time."

Nevertheless, Warden Spalding insisted that allowing inmates due process was a better way to govern the prison than imposing arbitrary punishment. Punishment accomplished little or nothing, he said. "We're not going to teach these kids a lesson," Spalding argued. "For example, I don't think strip cells make any difference to people. I've seen people do thirty days in a strip cell under extreme conditions—freezing cold, all the lights out. They had the hole in the floor that they missed because it was dark in there. So you went in once a week with the fire hose and cleaned the thing out. The first action I've seen out of a lot of people when they walk out of the strip cell is to take a swing at the first officer they see, and they end up right back in there."

Parley lingered in the control room through the count and the evening meal. When inmates finished eating dinner, the shift lieutenant sent him and another officer out to patrol the yard. It was a cold night with snow underfoot. Few inmates ventured outdoors.

Parley and his partner watched as three inmates conducted a group of college students through People's Park and into the admissions wing where the students and inmate members of the Social Therapy Program would conduct a "rap session." The students huddled together, staring at their surroundings. Their smiling inmate escorts gabbed cheerfully, trying to dispel the students' fears.

"It's always the same with these student groups," Parley grumbled. "When they first come down, they're scared and it's 'Officer this and Officer that.' But in a month's time, I'm a 'pig.' These convicts are telling them, 'Society's been on my ass ever since I was twelve years old,' and pretty soon these kids believe that every convict on that tier was there because an unjust society put him there. Because the cop down the street picked on him or because he didn't like his folks or some goddamn thing like that. And they converted those kids. This is breeding trouble in the future and disrespect for authority. Makes you wonder who should be getting the college credits, the students or the convicts?"

Parley and his partner walked past the admissions wing and on to the auditorium where about a hundred inmates were gathered to listen to an impromptu rock concert. The two officers watched for a while, then moved on. They retraced their steps and wandered through the recreation area, past the crowded card tables, the empty television rooms, and into the inmate phone room. "I tell you," Parley said to his partner, "if these guys are uptight, they sure don't act like it."

He began to discount the riot rumors, but he still kept his guard up. "You got to have a suspicious mind," Parley explained. "If something's out of the routine, you better know. You gotta be asking yourself questions like: Why is this guy coming in early? Why is that guy hanging around there? How come, all of a sudden, there's a different group in the recreation area? If you know something's wrong but you don't know why, then it makes the hair creep up your back."

After all, Parley's partner observed, "These guys got twenty-four hours a day to figure out how to beat you. You only got eight hours to catch 'em."

On tense days, officers steeled themselves for a good bit of abuse. "I've racked cells [simultaneously closed all the cell doors on a tier] and had twenty guys say, 'I'm going to cut your head off, motherfucker, and roll it down the tier,'" Sergeant Morgan said. "You've got to have a pretty discriminating ear to tell the difference between the guy who's just shooting off his mouth and the guy who's saying something dangerous."

Officers tried to prepare for dangerous situations by cultivating inmate snitches who secretly passed them information by phone, by tape recording, or by messages written on matchbook covers. To avoid suspicion, snitches and guards developed elaborate ruses. One officer would stand his snitch against the wall for a shakedown, would pretend to bust him for drugs, would haul him off to Big Red, and there, in the secrecy of a holding cell, would collect his information. Guards paid off their snitches with prison-issue clothes, better work assignments, and letters of recommendation.

At 8:00 P.M., Parley and his partner were sent to Big Red where they helped to search four inmate lay advisers who had permission to enter the unit. Twenty minutes later, they were back outside again, walking through People's Park.

"Hey, Edwards," an inmate yelled at Parley. "I just saw someone throw a half-pound of heroin down there. Why don't you go get it?" Parley ignored the taunt.

Despite the abuse, the frustration, and the danger, Parley enjoyed his job. "I'm dealing with the most dangerous thing in the world, a human mind," he said. "It's a personal challenge if I can go in and come out on top and hold my head high."

Parley had faced some tough situations. He had been pelted with urine and feces, beaten with broom handles, cracked over the skull with a pipe, and bruised and fractured in fistfights. "I've had shanks [knives] drawn on me, too, but so far I've been able to talk myself out," he said.

At 9:00 P.M., inmates were locked in their cells, and Parley returned to the control room. If the count cleared, he could go home. But if the number of convicts came up short, he would have to wait.

While the count went on, the utility detail got an emergency call from the "third floor," the prison hospital's psychiatric unit. "We got a ding [a mentally disturbed prisoner] up there who won't go in his cell," the shift lieutenant explained.

Parley and three other officers trudged outside again, walking the short distance to the hospital. They climbed the stairs to the third floor where a big black inmate, sweaty and naked to the waist, greeted them at the door. He demanded to know who the sergeant was, demanded to call his mother, and demanded to be let out of this "fucking prison." Calmly, professionally, the utility detail ushered him back down the corridor toward his cell. He glared at them but retreated, stepping backward until he was inside his cell. The guards slammed the cell door shut. "We never lay a hand on 'em unless we have to," Parley said afterward as he prepared to go home. "You go up there with power and numbers and 99 percent of the time you can handle it."

In sudden, unexpected situations, however, unarmed officers can expect to have neither power nor numbers. "And you can't put your faith in convicts," Parley said. "If one of those convicts comes up in your defense, that man is putting his life on the line because he's living with his own kind. You cannot trust a convict. You cannot expect a man to come up and die with you if you're going to die. We officers have to be brothers. In a riot situation, you might be in the middle of hell. In your mind you're wondering what am I going to do? Am I going to stoop over and ask for the grease to be raped? Am I going to fight and die? Am I going to fight and kill? This is the personal challenge of any officer up here."

Many guards complained that the system they protected with their lives rarely sought their advice. Their only effective way of shaping prison policy was threatening to walk out. As for influencing an inmate's fate, they were virtually unconsulted, although, as they argued, they knew better than anyone else which inmates were likely to go straight and which were likely to return to prison. "We know them better than the administration; we know them better than the parole board who sees them once a year; we know them better than the counselor who sees them once a month. Yet we have no input," Parley objected.

One person who valued the guards' opinion was Mrs. Helen Ratcliff, one of the seven members of the State Board of Prison Terms and Paroles. "You get your best information from the guards," said the silver-haired, fifty-three-year-old social worker.

A warm, gregarious woman whose round bifocals magnified her florid complexion, Ratcliff was the parole board's senior member. In the fall of 1978, nearing the end of her second five-year term, she was a leftover from the heyday of prison reform, a liberal holdout on an otherwise largely conservative board named by Gov. Dixy Lee Ray. Ratcliff believed that only those who committed the "most heinous and violent crimes" should be sent to prison.

Parole-board jobs were coveted, well paid, and powerful. Subject to no authority but its own, the parole board decided how long a convicted criminal would actually be imprisoned. Although the sentencing judge set a felon's maximum term, the board had broad discretion in adjusting the minimum term. Under its 1976 guidelines, the board set minimum terms ranging from one to thirty years for assault, six months to fifteen years for property offenses, and one to ten years for drug offenses. Certain minimum terms were set by law, but a two-thirds vote of the board could waive all the mandatory sentences except two: those for first-degree murder and for selling heroin.

Working in rotating two-member panels, the parole board set an in-

mate's minimum term at an initial meeting that usually took place within his first six weeks of imprisonment. After that, board members saw the inmate once every one or two years. At the yearly "progress hearings," the board shortened or lengthened the minimum sentence and awarded "good time," time off for good behavior.

When an inmate neared the end of his term, the board summoned him to a "parole hearing" at which it decided when and under what conditions he would be released from the penitentiary. Conditions for parole could include prohibitions against associating with ex-felons, against entering places that served liquor, against getting married, against buying a car, and against changing addresses or jobs without permission. If a parolee broke the law or violated his parole conditions, the board could return him to prison and could set a new minimum term. "It can play God," grumbled a convict returned to prison for "having a few beers."

The board also acted as a disciplinary court, deciding the guilt or innocence of inmates charged with prison infractions that were also capital crimes. It punished the guilty by extending the minimum sentence.

By controlling the rate at which parolees left prison and the conditions under which they could remain free, the parole board determined the penitentiary's population. In 1978–1979, the decisions of the board's conservative majority aggravated prison overcrowding by keeping inmates in prison longer. The parole-board chairman insisted that public safety, not overcrowded prisons, was the board's first responsibility.

The situation angered Ratcliff. She argued that the board should help to relieve the overcrowding by "paroling every person possible." She criticized her fellow board members for being "hell-bent on punishment for punishment's sake. They don't believe in rehabilitation," she charged. "They really don't believe in people because they don't believe people can change." She said that she was so "contemptuous" of the new, punitive policies written by the board's conservative majority that she had refused to learn them. "I'm ashamed of what we're doing," she said.

A former parole officer in the juvenile division, Ratcliff believed that most offenders could be treated in the community. "It costs about two hundred dollars a year to keep a man on parole," she said. "But it costs about sixteen thousand dollars a year to keep someone in an institution. If we can keep people in society working, paying their debts, making restitution, paying their taxes, we're all a hell of a lot better off."

Every three weeks, a panel of two parole-board members came to the penitentiary to conduct parole hearings. Supplied with prison records, parole-board files, recording equipment, and a burly correctional officer who silently stood guard, they saw as many as one hundred inmates in three or four days. They met in the old administration building, in a bare, blue room lit by harsh fluorescent lights. Outside the door, in a narrow, L-shaped corridor, up to a dozen inmates waited, nervous and subdued, chatting about their chances of getting "good action." Each of them would have no more than twenty minutes to advance his cause.

Ratcliff and the Reverend Matthew Naumes, the two board members who conducted the week of hearings held in September 1978, had a reputation for giving good action—cuts in minimum sentences and unexpected paroles. Most of the inmates scheduled for hearings felt fortunate: They could have ended up with a very different panel, like the one composed of the retired FBI agent and the former police lieutenant.

Since they generally agreed, Ratcliff and Naumes worked quickly and harmoniously. Although Naumes was a Ray appointee, he was a moderate. A Benedictine priest and a former liberal-arts-college president, he wore a Roman collar, glasses, short hair, and a ready smile.

He and Ratcliff took turns leading the hearing. While one of them questioned the inmate, the other thumbed through the inmate's prison file. The file contained the prosecuting attorney's summary of the crime; a "rap sheet" listing past convictions; psychological evaluations; test scores; counselors' reports; letters from attorneys, employers, and friends; and a record of prison infractions. The inmate had no access to his file, although its contents were often used against him.

A prison counselor usually attended the hearings to read a one-page report reviewing the inmate's progress. But sometimes the counselor scarcely knew the man and could do little more than ad-lib. Some inmates said that they saw their counselors as often as they saw the parole board—once a year.

The first inmate whom Ratcliff and Naumes saw on the second day of hearings was Browny. His hair neatly combed as always, his blue denim jeans pressed to a sharp crease, Browny entered the hearing room with his head slightly bowed. He seemed submissive and penitent. He waited for Naumes to invite him to sit.

Browsing through Browny's voluminous, dog-eared file, the priest asked him, "Why did you get involved in all this stuff?" Browny's rap sheet started in 1924 and was three pages long.

Sitting cross-legged in the examination chair, Browny squirmed. "I

had no trade, no education," he replied. "I was sixteen when I first went to the penitentiary. I was just a kid. I didn't know any better."

The board members listened and then excused Browny from the room. Naumes flicked on the recording machine and spoke into the microphone: "The cause of his latest crime spree is his emotional involvement with a thirty-five-year-old woman. The woman seems to have gone on to other things and there's hope that Brown might not reoffend."

When Browny was summoned back, Naumes announced that the board had decided to cut his sentence by two years and would see him again in two years. "We're voting with you that all this stuff is in the past," the priest said. Ending the hearing, he warned, "You're going to be out there again someday in a cold, cold world at a very difficult time for you."

Browny nodded and silently left the room.

Within the month, Browny would receive a statement of the board's "Decisions and Reasons." Many inmates complained that the statements contained evidence of being punished for "silent beefs," unsubstantiated allegations that appeared in their files. They said that the parole board was more apt to penalize them if their conviction came as a result of plea bargaining. Often, they objected, the board ignored the bargain struck between the prosecutor and the defendant and bombarded them with questions about the original charge. For instance, an inmate who pleaded guilty to robbery was grilled about pimping.

Ratcliff and Naumes moved on to the case of Richard, a wiry, twenty-two-year-old black convicted of armed robbery and burglary. While Richard waited in the corridor, his prison counselor told the board, "I've seen quite a change in this fellow since he's been at the institution. I'd like the board to consider his parolability at this meeting."

The board members looked unconvinced. Richard was called in. Ratcliff led the questioning. She asked about a tag that he had gotten for having a knife.

Richard replied that two of his friends were fighting and that one of them had a shank. He said that he rushed in and grabbed the shank so that neither of them would get hurt. When the guards arrived, he said, he got caught holding it. "Look," he said, pointing to a scar on the palm of his hand. "I got cut trying to take the knife away."

Neither Ratcliff nor Naumes gave any indication that they believed or disbelieved Richard's story.

Ratcliff explained later that she tried to elicit truth by making eye contact and by establishing rapport. "About 5 percent of them really try to be con artists," she said, "but I think I'm pretty good at picking them out. I usually say to them, 'I don't believe you and this is why I don't.' "

At the hearing, Ratcliff asked Richard what he did in prison. He handed her a manila folder. Inside he had fastened patches and citations certifying that he had completed an auto-body and fender course, passed a safety exam, and received a general educational development (GED) degree. Inmates believed that if they participated in work, in school, in Alcoholics Anonymous, or in other self-help programs, the board would reward them with an earlier parole. Some prisoners collected citations like Boy Scouts collected merit badges.

"What about drugs?" Naumes asked Richard. "You were a heroin addict, Richard. You were dangerous. You robbed someone who was in a wheelchair."

Richard responded that he had not used drugs since 1975.

"What about marijuana?" the priest rejoined.

Richard paused, then confessed. "I use marijuana all the time. I can't lie, Father."

Ratcliff told Richard that she and Naumes would ask the full board to consider reducing his mandatory seven-and-a-half-year sentence. Then she excused him.

The mandatory sentences, especially the stiffer ones, rankled Ratcliff. "I don't believe in them," she said. "I can imagine a first-degree murderer on probation or doing a year in prison but not thirteen years and four months. Instead of spending money on concrete and steel, I'd spend it on hospitals and therapists."

Richard was followed by Hubert, a seventy-two-year-old retiree serving a four-year term for sexually molesting some children whom he was baby-sitting. Clad in prison denims, Hubert entered, walking slowly and unsurely. Cautiously, he lowered himself into the examination chair. He appeared to be hard of hearing, but Naumes suspected that his "deafness" was strictly a play for the board's sympathy.

After a little prompting, Hubert told the board that he was taking literature and psychology in school. He said that he preferred psychology.

"What would you say about your psychology?" Naumes inquired, twice repeating the question.

"I committed a crime and it just got to me," Hubert answered. "But," he added, "psychology and the Bible have turned me around."

Both board members asked about Hubert's home life, his wife's work, how often she came to visit him in prison, whether she would be around

if he went home. He said that his family had accepted his crime and had "stuck by me."

Hubert was excused from the room while Naumes and Ratcliff conferred. They studied the prison psychiatrist's report that noted that Hubert collected pornographic magazines in his cell. The report warned that Hubert was likely to reoffend.

"I wouldn't parole him until his wife stays home to look after him," Ratcliff told Naumes. The priest suggested that Hubert could be paroled to a nursing home or to some other facility for full-time care.

"Let's ask the parole officer to interview his wife," Ratcliff volunteered. "If she's willing to stay home, we could parole him. If not, he'd better do the maximum term."

Hubert was called back and informed of the decision. "What happens if she can't quit her job?" he asked.

"Then we move to another plan," Naumes responded, without being specific.

Hubert asked no more questions. "I'll tell you one thing," he said, rising to leave. "I've learned an awful bitter lesson."

After Hubert's hearing, the board took a coffee break. Mulling over Hubert's case, Ratcliff conceded that she had a reputation for being hard on sex offenders. "We all have hang-ups," she said. "I still feel that there are some sex offenses which are very difficult to modify. Like a person who exposes himself, gets paroled fifteen times, and reoffends exactly the same way. That's one of the ones you give up on and keep in prison."

Other parole-board members also had reputations for being tough on certain types of offenders. A black board member was said to be tough on blacks. Another member was said to be tough on drug offenders, especially educated ones.

Naumes did not think that he was tough or easy on any particular type, not even the Bible-quoting inmates who figured that he was a sucker for religion. Laughing, he recalled parole hearings at the state women's prison. "Some of the girls show up wearing more medals than a field marshal—medals of St. Francis, the Virgin Mary, the Sacred Heart. They trade them outside the door," he said. "You see the same medals over and over again."

Ratcliff and Naumes resumed the hearings with Robert, a swaggering, middle-aged convict who told them that he was suing because he had been falsely imprisoned beyond his release date. Quoting sections of state law from memory, Robert protested that his parole revocation violated a court order. Moreover, he complained, "The parole board doesn't answer my letters."

"You're better informed than us," Ratcliff interjected. "Why don't you write this all out, and we'll submit it to the attorney general."

Robert replied that he had $5.2 million in lawsuits pending against the state. He said that he had no parole plans and did not want to be paroled. "As long as they're making mistakes and I'm going to profit by their mistakes, why should I correct them?" he asked the board. "Every day is the same, as long as I get the money."

When Robert left the room, Ratcliff conceded that he might have a case. She said that the state attorney general's office had erred in tallying his time.

As noon approached, the board whipped through three quick hearings. They paroled an elderly convict with a broken jaw, deferred a decision on a Chicano convicted of a sex slaying, and told a biker that they would take his drug-offense case before the full board.

They puzzled, however, over George, a round-faced, closely shorn youth serving five years for attempting to burn down a federal office building. As he entered the hearing room, the inmates behind him muttered, "Ding, ding, ding." They thought that George was crazy. In a report that his counselor submitted to the board, George had declared: "I have varicose veins in my nuts, which has rendered me impotent."

Ratcliff asked George why he had burned the building. He replied that it was a "second-rate suicide" because he did not have the guts to kill himself. "I thought if I came to prison I'd get killed here," he explained. "That would be my suicide."

George told the board that he had been disgusted with his life. "I used a lot of speed, smoked dope, took acid," he said. "I thought everybody in the world was some sort of policeman following me."

"If you could live in an ideal society where there were no police, what would you do?" Naumes asked.

"I'd kind of like to be an explorer like Lewis and Clark and be out in nature a lot," George replied. He added that he was interested in Zen Buddhism and in the writings of Alan Watts. From his pocket he produced a round silver container that looked like a snuffbox. He opened it and inside, encased in red leather, was a little rock mounted on a shiny piece of wood. He said that it was a "Zen pocket shrine."

"If your parole plan called for mental treatment, would you resent it?" Ratcliff asked.

"I wouldn't resent it, but I don't need it," George answered.

He was excused from the room. Conferring with Ratcliff, Naumes argued that keeping George in prison was doing him no good. "Anyway," he added, chuckling, "anybody who carries a Zen pocket shrine can't be all bad."

George was summoned a second time. "We're going to take a chance with you," Ratcliff told him. "We're going to parole you to an acceptable mental-health plan."

In making parole decisions, Ratcliff said later, she tried to weigh the man's problems against his assets. She asked herself questions like: "Does he have normal good sense? Has he had psychotic or neurotic problems? Is he using excessive denial and rationalization? Does he have a supportive family? Does he have a way to make a legitimate living? What is his cultural outlook?" She wished that more corrections officials would ask those questions. "It's absolute goddamn nonsense," she groaned, "to bring a pimp to prison after he made a thousand dollars a day on the street and teach him to milk cows."

After George, the board breezed through a few more hearings and then astonished a sixty-nine-year-old veteran convict named Joe. A skinny man with sunken cheeks and dull brown eyes, Joe had been in prison off and on since 1935. His speciality was writing bad checks.

Shuffling slowly to the chair, Joe complained that his heart had been "acting up." He said that he had no family or friends in Washington but had a son in San Francisco.

Naumes asked him how long he had lived in prison. "I don't know," Joe replied. "It's frightening."

"Yes, it is," the priest agreed, "to live in the blind alleys of these correctional institutions."

Ratcliff asked Joe how he had passed his time since their last meeting. Joe said that he went through the Awareness program, worked in the metal plant, and did some serious writing.

"Joe," Ratcliff snapped, "you've done some serious writing, all right, and most of it's been on checks."

Joe bowed his head. "I've sweated blood and tears over my record," he whispered. "I can't see why I should be punished more for it."

Ratcliff excused Joe from the room. "He'll be right back writing checks," she shrugged, "but hopefully in California."

Naumes nodded, thought a moment, proposed a plan to Ratcliff, and then called Joe back.

"Okay, Joe," the priest said, "we're authorizing you a 'sundown parole.' You know what that is? It means the sun shall not set on you in this state. If you ever come back here again, the thunderbolts will be striking on the right and on the left of you."

"Joe," Ratcliff interrupted, "We're cutting you loose."

Joe sat, stunned, lost for words. Gradually, a thin smile broke his tight lips. "I can't believe this," he mumbled. "I really can't."

As he rose to leave, Ratcliff issued a final warning. "Joe," she said firmly, "don't write a check at the airport for your ticket out."

Joe walked out the door and down the corridor where more inmates still waited to see the board. "They cut me loose," he exclaimed, shaking a few outstretched hands. "They cut me loose."

Back in the blue room, Ratcliff was grinning. "That old guy isn't going to benefit from institutionalization," she said, "so you give him a chance."

This officer is wearing a belt buckle made by an inmate. Sgt. Harold Lee, a veteran corrections officer, supervises the segregation unit. The least experienced officers often draw the most dangerous assignments; the unarmed cellblock guards are outnumbered one hundred to one.

Parley returns to the "control room" between assignments, but the tower guards work uninterrupted eight-hour shifts. Strict rules prohibit them from having newspapers, books, radios, and artificial lights in the towers.

Warden James Spalding is determined to reassert control over the inmates and to prevent incidents like the pipe-bomb explosion that killed Lt. Roger Sanders.

187

Parole-board members Helen Ratcliff and the Reverend Matthew Naumes conduct parole
hearings. Sgt. Bill Brewer, the officer assigned to the hearings, listens without comment.

Epilogue

Warden Spalding's tool for taking charge of the prison was "the WAC rules," the often-ignored sections of the Washington Administrative Code that outlined procedures for dealing with prison inmates. The WAC rules became Spalding's Bible. "They govern most situations and I intend to follow them," he vowed.

Invoking the WAC rules, he ended Warden Vinzant's practice of allowing escorted inmate leaves. That meant no more "business leaves," the excursions that selected inmates had used to sell club products or to further club programs. As a result, convict-run businesses failed, aggravating the penitentiary's acute unemployment problem.

The bikers, who had the equipment and skill to customize motorcycles and to manufacture speciality cycle seats, watched their business shrink to an occasional paint job on a guard's car. For a while, the Felons Unification for Self-Endeavor (FUSE) continued to operate a concession stand that sold hot dogs, slurpees, and girlie magazines. But a more ambitious proposal that had had Vinzant's blessing—a "mobile labor force" of carefully screened, nonviolent offenders to help local orchardists to prune trees and pick fruit—collapsed.

The lifers' club, which was reroofing and weatherizing low-income homes in Walla Walla; the Black Prisoners Forum Unlimited (BPFU), which had set up counseling sessions to scare crime out of juvenile offenders; and the Awareness Movement, whose speakers were telling high-school assemblies about the horrors of prison life all saw their outside programs end when Spalding elected to follow the letter of the law.

"Inmate-run businesses create situations which are not controllable," he argued. They increase custody costs, contribute to escapes, and provide avenues for drugs and weapons to slip behind the walls, he said. Moreover, he added, he didn't think excursions outside the walls did convicts any good. "I don't see how putting a roof on a house or going to a basketball game is going to improve their situation," Spalding said.

Inmates knew what prison officials wanted: a more regimented prison that they could control without having to consult with convicts, one that would reflect a growing public desire for punishment.

Inmate leaders, however, contended that closing the door on outside contact deprived them of opportunities to earn some money, to learn new skills, and to readjust to "straight society." "Why should we behave," one club president asked, "when Spalding isn't showing us any light at the end of the tunnel?"

The week that we left the penitentiary, its population reached an all-time modern high—1,440 men were crammed inside the walls. As prison officials talked of bedding down new arrivals in the gymnasium, the inmates talked of rioting. They were determined to retain the privileges that they had won under previous wardens. On 8 February 1979, three weeks after we left, a suspected snitch was stabbed to death in Lifers' Park. His slaying was followed by several nonfatal stabbings and by a 9 May incident in which three armed inmates protesting the prison's "inhumane" conditions held ten staff members hostage for ten hours.

On 12 June, an Indian inmate was stabbed to death in the prison phone room, and three days later, Sgt. William Cross, a quiet, well-liked officer, was killed by two inmates as he came to the aid of another guard in a fight at the dining-hall door. Cross was stabbed four times and died within minutes. Warden Spalding candidly declared that the penitentiary was more explosive than ever and locked all inmates in their cells.

The riot came on the night of 7 July 1979. Convicts in 8-wing, tired of the lockdown and provoked by a destructive search of their cells, set fires, hurled debris, and ripped out sinks and toilets. Helmeted guards herded the rioters to the Big Yard where they lived for seven weeks under a hot summer sun in shelters made of blankets and aluminum trays. In the aftermath of the riot and of a similar disturbance in segregation, guards were charged with urinating on prone inmates, with beating them with lead-lined gloves, and even with sodomizing one man with a riot baton. Five guards were fired, eight others were suspended, and forty-two more quit their jobs in disgust. Pandemonium reigned. The FBI investigated, the ACLU called for a special prosecutor, and a national panel of corrections experts visited the prison and labeled conditions there "intolerable."

The four-member panel from the American Correctional Association

blamed the penitentiary's troubles on overcrowding, idleness, inmate gangs, poorly trained staff, and shifting philosophies of how a prison should be run. The panel, composed of four wardens, said that the prison "seemed to be caught" between a progressive policy of sharing decisionmaking with inmates and a traditional policy "in which the staff run the institution and the inmates play a passive role." The clash between the two policies—in effect, between the Vinzant policy and the Spalding policy—had created a situation in which guards were "beleaguered, besieged and confused about their role," and inmates were convinced that "a new approach to modern correctional practices had been constantly thwarted."

When the penitentiary's longest lockdown finally ended in mid-October, inmates reemerged to find that Spalding had taken advantage of the 146-day ordeal to re-create a traditional, authoritarian prison. He had erased the reform experiment once and for all. There were metal detectors at cellblock doors. Concrete covered People's Park. Loitering was forbidden. Guards frisked inmates as many as thirty times a day and what were once exclusive club areas had become closely watched dayrooms. Spalding further destroyed the clubs by shipping their leaders off to other prisons.

Cells were to be clean and free of clutter. An inmate's belongings were limited to the contents of a footlocker. Pinups, posters, and other decorations were no longer permitted on cell walls. The Resident Council, which had once governed in partnership with the prison administration, became a "Resident Advisory Council." Its new charter stated that the council was not to "usurp and interfere with the authority of the superintendent." Eventually, Spalding did away with inmate government altogether.

In the wake of the July riot and the summer lockdown, inmates sued in federal court, seeking redress for the guards' brutality, the overcrowding, the lack of medical care, the pervasive racism, and the inhumane treatment. They won their suit. On 23 May 1980, Federal District Court Judge Jack Tanner ruled that confinement at the state penitentiary in Walla Walla violated the constitutional ban against "cruel and inhuman punishment." Tanner held that conditions at the penitentiary violated the Constitution in several areas: overcrowding, idleness, lack of health care, inhumane conditions in isolation cells, and inadequate classification of violent and nonviolent prisoners.

At the brief trial that preceded his ruling, Tanner heard stories of beatings, stabbings, and murders by inmates and of brutality by guards.

He heard testimony from an inmate who had been held naked in a darkened isolation cell for days, from an inmate whose ingrown toenail had gone untreated until gangrene had set in and his leg had to be amputated, and from the inmate who had been sodomized by a guard. "No judge, no jury sentenced them to that," Tanner said.

The inmates' evidence was shocking enough, but the candid and damaging testimony of prison officials lost the case for the state. On the stand, under oath, Warden Spalding was asked if the prison should be closed. Though he later tried to explain away his answer, Spalding told the court, "Yes, it should."

After ruling in the inmates' favor, Judge Tanner ordered the state to improve conditions and named a special master to oversee state efforts. Many of the improvements ordered by the judge helped to reduce the chaos and overcrowding and further consolidated Spalding's hold on the prison.

By early 1981, the inmate population had been reduced from the record 1,440 of 1979 to 850. Reducing Walla Walla's population, however, aggravated the overcrowding at state institutions that were not under court order to improve conditions. During late 1980, the state reformatory at Monroe and the state corrections center at Shelton both erupted in fiery riots that resulted in one inmate dead, more than two dozen inmates injured, and $2 million in property damage.

Despite the reduced numbers and the court-ordered improvements, the "new" penitentiary failed to impress some people. Charles W. Colson, the convicted Watergate conspirator who had become a "born again" Christian and a prison reformer, toured the penitentiary, then told legislators in Olympia the next day, "Walla Walla is the worst prison I've seen in the United States."

Inmates ended 1980 by looting and burning a prison office building and began 1981 with an eight-day work strike whose sole demand was Spalding's dismissal. Less than five hours after the strike ended, Spalding locked down the prison to foil what he said was a well-planned riot and mass escape attempt.

Spalding's efforts to re-create a traditional, regimented institution meant drastic changes for some of the people in this book. Kenny Agtuca, prison boss and president of the lifers' club, was toppled overnight and transferred to the federal penitentiary in Atlanta, where he wound up in the hole, a suspect in a prison murder. Angry and frus-

trated by the mismanaged attempt to regain control of the chaotic prison, Officer Parley Edwards quit his job and resigned the presidency of the guards' union. In a parting blast, he accused Spalding of being "a cheap politician who passes the buck."

But for others, who experienced Walla Walla as just another prison where life was cruel, time was hard, and days were long, things had not changed much. Browny, who turned seventy during the long 1979 lockdown, did not miss the club areas that he never frequented. Don Snook still whiled away twenty-three hours a day in his concrete box on Death Row waiting for his date with the hangman.

The end of prison reform at Walla Walla did not return the penitentiary to the striped-uniform days of the 1950s. Muslim inmates still ate and worshiped as they pleased; Indian inmates still purified themselves in their sweat lodge; and the bikers kept their motorcycles, although they were no longer allowed to run them in the Big Yard.

Conjugal visits, a long-overdue reform that nervous corrections officials kept delaying in the 1970s, were finally introduced in 1981. However, with space limited to three refurbished house trailers, each of the penitentiary's ninety married inmates was unlikely to enjoy more than four conjugal visits a year. In any event, the reform came too late for Yvonne and Dean. Dean was paroled in August 1979.

Despite the retention of some reforms, a whole era of liberal penal thinking had ended not only at Walla Walla but also at most of the nation's prisons. The ideas that a prisoner ought to be able to make decisions behind the walls; that he should have regular contact with family, friends, and the outside community; that he should have the opportunity to exercise initiative, independence, and responsibility have all been dashed by the explosive prison violence of the 1970s.

Hard-line administrators, those who like to see prisons run like boot camps, blame the violence on liberal policies that try to make prisons like the rest of the world. Prisons, like prisoners, they argue, are not like the rest of the world. The more freedom inmates have, the more unsafe prisons will be.

The reformers, however, reply that the history of American corrections proves that men warehoused in regimented, authoritarian prisons return to society ill-equipped to lead constructive lives. They maintain that prisons reinforce antisocial behavior by undermining the inmates' maturity, confidence, and self-esteem. As a result, prisons discharge bitter, mangled men bent on revenge.

At Walla Walla, the reformers may not have had a fair chance, but they did have their turn. In the wake of the tumultuous 1970s, the penitentiary has returned to the rule of a simple concept: Prisons are places of punishment where men who have broken the law are deprived of the privileges that the law protects.

Glossary

A

ad-seg: administrative segregation; the automatic confinement of inmates thought to be dangerous to themselves, to others, or to the security of the institution.

B

baby raper: a child molester.
backing: support or protection provided by other inmates.
bag: a large quantity of drugs.
beef: the crime for which a man was convicted, or a new crime, infraction, or problem that the convict faces in prison.
bitch: a conviction received for being a habitual criminal; for example, "I got bitched."
breezeway bum: an inmate whose primary activity is hanging out on the breezeway.
breezeway commando: a tough inmate who stalks the breezeways to rob and extort other inmates.
bro: a brother.
bulldogging: persistently harassing another inmate to get one's way.
bum beef: a conviction for a crime that one is innocent of; also known as a "bum rap."

C

chain: a group of new inmates who arrive at the penitentiary chained to each other.
chipping: having sex with other men when one is pledged to a particular inmate; usually applied to queens.
cold shot: a calculated, heartless action done with no regard for others.
count: a tally, taken three times a day, of all the inmates in the penitentiary.
crank: amphetamine tablets; also known as "speed."

D

ding: a crazy or highly unpredictable inmate; "dingy" behavior may be real or feigned.
drive on: to verbally harass someone in order to get what one wants.
dry snitching: informing within ear- or eyeshot of the person being told on.
dust: to kill.

F

finger wave: the use of a rubber-gloved finger to probe an inmate's anus for contraband.
fish: a new inmate, especially one who has never been in prison before.
fish cop: a new guard.
fix up: to inject heroin or some other drug into the bloodstream.
flip-flop: to take turns playing the male and female roles in a homosexual relationship.

G

gate: release from prison.
get down: to fight with fists or weapons; also, to "mix it up."
get in someone's face: to butt in or to intrude into someone's personal affairs.
git-go: the start, the beginning; also known as "jump street."
go down: to happen, usually refers to an untoward or unexpected event; also, to "come down."
good time: a one-third cut in the minimum sentence given by the parole board to inmates with good records.

H

have a hard-on for: to strongly dislike; for example, "He thinks that the judge had a hard-on for him."
have heart: to be fearless in dangerous situations.
hole: the segregation cells where inmates are sent as punishment; also known as "Big Red."
homeboy: a street-smart and con-wise person with whom one shares a similar background.
hot chair: the position of being the object of discussion in a therapy group; also, the "hot seat."
house: a cell.

J

jacked up: to be harassed, usually by guards, over matters deemed to be inconsequential; also known as "button pushing."
jacket: an inmate's prison file, or his reputation.
jailhouse lawyer: an inmate with no formal legal training who does legal work for other inmates.
jailhouse turnout: a previously heterosexual inmate who takes on an overtly homosexual or female identity in prison.
jam up: to put someone into a tight spot.
jocker: an aggressive, macho inmate who consistently plays the male role in a homosexual relationship; also know as a "wolf."

K

keister stash: drugs or other contraband hidden in the anus, usually inside a rubber balloon.
kite: a form used to request an interview with a counselor or with some other prison staff member.

M

making a play: going through the motions to deceive someone; for example, "I'm making a play for the gate."

Man: an authority figure like the warden, a guard, or a counselor; usually refers to authority in general.

mule: one who smuggles drugs or other contraband into the prison at the behest of an inmate.

N

nickel bag: five dollars' worth of marijuana.

9-wing: the prison cemetery.

nutsack: manliness or courage; scrotum.

O

off: to kill.

out of pocket: to depart from the rules of fair play; for example, "I get what I can as long as I'm not playing out of pocket."

outfit: a syringe and hypodermic needle for injecting drugs; also known as a "horse and carriage."

P

packing: smuggling drugs or other contraband into the prison; carrying a hidden weapon.

pat down: a superficial search technique in which a guard passes his hands lightly over the inmate's clothed body.

PC: protective custody, a separate cellblock for inmates seeking asylum from the general population.

pen punk: a previously heterosexual inmate who is coerced into taking on a homosexual identity in prison.

pink look: a fresh-faced, pure, and immature appearance; also known as "cherry."

point man: an inmate stationed as a lookout to warn others of the approach of guards, rival inmates, or any other potential sources of trouble.

popped: arrested.

program: to participate in work, school, vocational training, or a self-help group.

pruno: prison-made wine concocted from yeast, water, jam, jelly, canned fruit, or fruit juices; known as the "poor man's high."

punk: one who plays the female role in a homosexual relationship; also known as a "kid," "boy," "fruiter," "faggot," or "queer."

put in a cross: to be caught in a situation in which there appears to be no safe way out; to be "jammed up."

Q

queen: a transvestite; also known as a "lady" or a "girl."

R

rack cells: to pull a lever that closes all the cell doors on a tier simultaneously.

rapo: an inmate convicted of rape.

ratpack: to gang up on someone.

real estate: the buying and selling of bunk space in four-man cells.

reefer: a marijuana cigarette; the marijuana itself.

running wild: serving a sentence for which no minimum term has been set.

S

scrip: prison coupons issued in lieu of hard currency.

shank: a prison-made knife; also known as a "shiv."

shine on: to deceive by ignoring or not addressing the issue.

skin search: an intensive search technique in which inmates must remove all their clothes.

sky pilot: a chaplain or minister.

smack: heroin.

snitch: an informer; also known as a "fink," "rat," or "stool pigeon."

snitched off: betrayed by an informer.

snitch jacket: a reputation as an informer.

stash: hidden drugs or other contraband.

stick: to stab.

stone ding: an inmate who is obviously insane.

straight: conventional or law-abiding.

street person: one who has had no experience of prison; also known as a "square john."

streets: the free world outside the prison.

strip cell: a bare isolation cell in which an inmate is stripped of his clothes and confined as punishment.

T

tag: a citation given for a prison infraction; a reputation for liking or disliking certain types of behavior, usually used in reference to prison officials.

third floor: the prison hospital's psychiatric unit; also called "ding wing."

thumpers: inmate-made brass knuckles.

trick bag: a ruse or scheme set up to extort or coerce another inmate by trapping him in a predicament.

tricking: prostitution.

W

weed: marijuana; also known as "pot," "grass," "dope," "smoke," and "reefer."

white money: hard currency.

wolf ticket: a claim to some feat or prowess that greatly exaggerates the reality; for example, "I sold that dude a wolf ticket."

Y

yard-out: the exercise time given to prisoners in segregation.